Luke Rivington

A Plain Reason for Joining the Church of Rome

Sixth Edition

Luke Rivington

A Plain Reason for Joining the Church of Rome
Sixth Edition

ISBN/EAN: 9783744664592

Printed in Europe, USA, Canada, Australia, Japan

Cover: Foto ©Lupo / pixelio.de

More available books at **www.hansebooks.com**

AUTHORITY

OR

A PLAIN REASON FOR JOINING THE CHURCH OF ROME

BY

LUKE RIVINGTON, M.A.

MAGDALEN COLLEGE, OXFORD

'*I speak with the Successor of the Fisherman*'
S. JEROME *ad Damasum*

SIXTH EDITION

LONDON
KEGAN PAUL, TRENCH, TRÜBNER, & CO. Ltd.
1890

A LETTER
TO THE
AUTHOR OF 'ROMAN CATHOLIC CLAIMS

PREFACE

TO

THE SIXTH EDITION

CANON CARTER AND 'IDEAS OF TRUTH.'

SINCE the last edition of this book appeared Canon Carter has avowed the authorship of the 'Roman Question,' which I have noticed on pp. 29-35, 52 and 72. He has withdrawn the quotation from S. Chrysostom which I felt compelled to stigmatise as a *suppressio veri*: and also the supposed document of Convocation which was the solitary foundation for his assumption that the Reformation had a clerical origin.

But he has rather emphasised than otherwise the value of the so-called 28th Canon of the Council of Chalcedon, and has insisted as strongly as ever on the non-Erastian character of the Royal supremacy under Henry and Elizabeth.

And he has added a passage on the cultus of our Lady, which contains the strangest theology; and he still prides himself and his co-religionists on the possession of superior 'ideas of truth' (the title of one of his chapters), and accuses the Catholic Church of 'disregard for historical truth.'

In view of these serious accusations (to which, indeed, we are accustomed, for it is a note of the Church thus to be abused, but which we none the less deplore, as a grievous thing on the part of those who make them) I propose to point out that Canon Carter has committed himself to statements which are altogether without foundation.

He imagines that he stands on the sure foundation of Catholic consent; but, in the exercise of his own judgment as to what comes under that head, he has fallen into most serious mis-statements.

In endeavouring to account for the separation between East and West, he relies on two Canons which were not received in the West, and considers them, nevertheless, to have the value of an Ecumenical decision. They are to him the voice of the Church.

He begins with the 3rd Canon of the Council of Constantinople (381).

But this was not an Ecumenical decision. The Council itself was not acknowledged as such until the sixth century; and then *only so far as related to its Creed.* S. Leo tells us that its Canons had not even been sent to Rome; and S. Gregory the Great, writing at the end of the sixth century, says that 'the Roman Church hitherto neither has nor receives the Canons or the acts of that Council, but has received it so far as its definitions against Macedonius.'

How then can Canon Carter quote this as though it were an Ecumenical decision? Canon Carter, moreover, differs *toto cælo* from S. Gregory in his estimate of the 'motif' of this Canon; S. Gregory traces it to carnal pride, Canon Carter to the Holy Ghost.

Preface to the Sixth Edition

Here, then, Canon Carter's argument halts in its beginning. It assumes that to be Catholic which was Erastian in its origin and local in its reception.

He then deals with the so called 28th Canon of the Council of Chalcedon. And here his history halts still more formidably. He speaks of its being urged by us, that 'the then Pope Leo' (we generally speak of him as a Saint) protested against it 'so as to save his prerogative': and says that the Council 'after hearing *this protest*' (the italics are mine) 'persisted in carrying the decree as originally framed.'

He seems to imagine that S. Leo protested whilst the Council were sitting. How else could the Council 'after hearing this protest' carry the decree? Whereas the Council, or rather some of the bishops, about 200 only out of more than 600, who, as Dean Milman says, 'lingered behind,' passed their decree in spite of protest *on the part of the legates*, and *then* sent it for 'confirmation' to S. Leo. S. Leo refused, and the decree was not entered by the Easterns in the list of canons passed at Chalcedon.

What therefore are we to think of Canon Carter's assertion that the Council, after hearing the protest of 'the then Pope Leo,' carried their Canon in spite of 'this protest'? Canon Carter has a chapter on 'ideas of truth' in which he brings terrible accusations against the Catholic Church; what are we to say of his own 'ideas of truth' after this perversion of history? Canon Bright seems fond of saying that the Easterns 'acted' upon this Canon. That may be: but it is clear that they had not the Council's sanction for their action.

The dogmatic definitions *were* accepted by the

Council as a whole, not merely, as was the case with the supposed Canon, by an Erastianising portion of the bishops without the concurrence of a single Western. And therefore, from an Anglican point of view, the dogmatic definitions alone had the stamp of the Catholic Church upon them. This appears to be the judgment of the present Archbishop of Canterbury in his decision as to his authority over the Bishop of Lincoln. Canon Carter, probably, is not prepared to submit to the decision of an Archbishop of Canterbury on such a question; but it is a significant fact that even on such a point as this we can discover no authoritative utterance, no clear and unanimous judgment, in the Church of England.

Canon Carter quotes Canon Bright as giving 'a very full and apparently most impartial account of what passed.' This 'very full' account is comprised, according to Canon Carter, in three pages. And as for the impartiality, Dr. Bright speaks of the 28th Canon being 'enforced throughout the East' in spite of its repudiation by the West. Yet it was not so much as numbered amongst their Canons for centuries. How, then, could it be enforced as a *Canon*? If the Easterns acted upon it, it is clear that they were not acting under the shelter of an Ecumenical decision, but on their own responsibility, and in spite of protest on the part of the West. And then Canon Bright has the hardihood to say that S. Leo 'himself was content to denounce it, not on the ground of S. Peter's prerogatives, but simply in the name of the Council of Nicæa.' It would have been more 'impartial,' because more in accordance with the facts, to have said that S. Leo denounced it as the *guardian* of the Nicene settlement, and that he acted as guardian of that settlement by reason of 'S. Peter's prerogatives,' by whose authority he expressly told the Empress that he annulled the Canon. And he should have added that the bishops expressly said that they left the decision of the matter to their 'head,' namely, S. Leo.

But again, Canon Carter goes so far as to eliminate the Holy See from all active participation in the great struggle by which the doctrine of our Lord's Divinity, and that of the Third Person, were established. His statement is perfectly astounding. He says (p. 49): 'Thus the main articles of the Christian Creed, those 'touching the Divinity of our Lord and of the Holy Spirit, 'were determined without any special reference to Rome, 'indeed, in part without her concurrence. Is not this 'conclusive as to the point that I have undertaken to 'establish?'

Now, first, he quite fails to appreciate the enormous influence which the mere fact of the continuous orthodoxy of the Popes, during those eventful times, must have had on the rest of Christendom. So that it was felt, and there are plain evidences of the feeling, on the part of emperors and patriarchs, that 'the faith of the Romans' was, as S. Cyprian said, something to which 'perfidy cannot have access.' It must be remembered, too, that the situation of the Popes was most perilous, and that the scene and nursery of the heresies that desolated the Church was Canon Carter's favourite East. They were not times in which a Pope could exercise his prerogative with ease over that distant home of rebellion. But what actually happened? The century opens with a Martyr-Pope, and continues, after two short reigns, with S. Melchiades. S. Augustine tells us how the Donatists appealed to the

Emperor, *and the Emperor referred them to this Pope*, and how the Donatist heresy was dealt with by a Council under the presidency of another Pope.

Next comes S. Sylvester, who, to begin with, held the true faith, and whose relation to the Council of Nicæa is not so easily disposed of as Canon Carter seems to imagine. S. Damasus has some claim to be heard on this matter, living as he did in the same century. At a Synod of ninety-eight bishops, in the year 360, he, together with them, writes to the Eastern bishops a letter in which occurs the statement that 'Majores nostri cccxviii Episcopi, atque ex urbe sanctissimi Episcopi urbis Romæ directi, apud Nicæam confecto concilio, hunc murum adversus arma diabolica statuerunt.' This gives us quite a different view from Canon Carter's. Hefele has shown, as have others, that Hosius and the legates represented the Pope, who thus bore as active a part in that supreme settlement of the Christian faith as was possible under the circumstances.

Then we come to S. Julius, who summoned S. Athanasius to the Apostolic See, pronounced him innocent, and helped to reinstate him in his See. Where would S. Athanasius have been without S. Julius? Next comes Liberius. Of him, in a passage which all Anglicans consider genuine, S. Athanasius speaks in altogether different terms, in regard to his services to the faith, from what Canon Carter does. Whatever happened when he was in exile, it is certain that Liberius was, on the whole, a most formidable champion of the true faith, and he won the crown of martyrdom. The saints of that day (for the passages often quoted from S. Hilary certainly cannot be insisted on as genuine) speak of Liberius in terms of enthusiasm. S. Athanasius himself speaks of him with gratitude.

Then comes S. Damasus, whose activity had so much to do with the condemnation of the Macedonians, and their heresy in regard to the Third Person. S. Siricius, after him, combated the Novatians, and assisted Theodosius in repressing the Manicheans. And the century closes with S. Anastasius, whose piety and orthodoxy and activity against the Origenists is so praised by S. Jerome. Is it right, then, that one should come forth and accuse the Apostolic See in the way that Canon Carter does, setting at naught the plain history of the matter? Is Canon Carter in a position to accuse the Holy See of disregard for historical truth, when he has based his own position on such utterly unhistorical statements?

From ancient history, thus misrepresented, we will pass to more modern history. Here, too, Canon Carter is demonstrably at fault. He slurs over the subject of Henry's divorce. One would imagine, from reading his account, that the so-called Reformation was immediately caused by the question of annates. After Father Bridgett's book on Blessed John Fisher, and Friedmann on Anne Boleyn, it argues certainly different 'ideas of truth' to relegate the divorce question to a subordinate place in the determination of the breach with Rome. Anyhow, when he is anxious to convince us that the Church reformed herself in England, he should, at least, produce a jot of evidence to that effect. If, as he contends, the transfer of the annates from the Pope to the King was the first great step in the 'Reformation,' it is certain that the bishops did not concur in the step, for they voted against the Bill. As for the people clamouring for Reformation, one would have thought that their speedy return under Mary would have disposed of that contention.

But there is another point on which Canon Carter makes perfect havoc of history. He is anxious to prove that the rupture in Henry VIII.'s reign did not involve any ecclesiastical breach with the See of Rome, viewed as the 'Chief Patriarchal' See of the West. It is a little difficult to discover what Canon Carter means by the 'Chief' Patriarchal See of the West. But as he maintains that Canterbury was a Patriarchal See, he can only mean that Rome was something beyond. But is it possible, in the face of history, to maintain that the Patriarchal rights of Rome were not invaded by the movement of the sixteenth century? Canon Carter wishes to stand right with the Nicene settlement, and as the Province of England cutting herself off from her Patriarch would be contrary to Nicene rules, he simply denies that England did break, ecclesiastically, with the 'Chief Patriarchal' See of the West. What, then, could a Patriarch do which Elizabeth did not do? She suspended an archbishop in spite of protest on the part of the bishops; she settled the question, put to her by her future archbishop, as to whether there should be any archbishop at all (see Parker's Letter to Lord Burghley); and she decided what ordinal should be used, and all this without consulting the Patriarch.

But Canon Carter has another supposed fact on which he relies for a very important point. He endorses an extraordinary statement of Canon Dixon's, viz. 'that Arch-
' bishop Anselm received from the Pope at the Council of
' Bari the title of Patriarch . . . that is to say, the Primate of
' the English was acknowledged to be a Patriarch, owning

'indeed the Primacy, but not the Supremacy of Rome.' But there does not seem to be any notice of this supposed fact in the Acta of the Council of Bari. And we know that the statement is not true from another source, i.e. from S. Anselm himself. For S. Anselm never signed himself as Patriarch, nor did any Archbishop of Canterbury; he never sat in any Council as Patriarch; nor was he ever in official documents addressed as such. In fact, the idea is a pure dream. Are we to suppose that Henry and Elizabeth would have allowed the title to drop if it had really belonged to the Archbishop of Canterbury? And as for S. Anselm or the Pope talking of a Primacy and not a Supremacy, or of a Primacy less than Divine in its institution, it shocks our sense of truth that such an assertion should be made. No one seriously supposes that the Pope of the day ever spoke thus, or that S. Anselm held such a theory. Why, S. Anselm actually says, 'It is certain that he who does not obey the ordinances of the Roman Pontiff... is disobedient to the Apostle Peter... nor is he of that flock which was given to him by God.' S. Anselm's faith differed *toto cælo* from Canon Carter's, and had he been constituted a Patriarch he would still have rendered obedience to the Roman Pontiff, as the successor of S. Peter.

There remains another statement, extraordinary as coming from one who insists on our 'disregard for historical truth.'

Canon Carter says that King Oswy 'gave' to Rome 'the first ruling authority it ever possessed' in England, and that that gift did not involve 'any spiritual rights.' And yet Oswy decided to submit to Rome on the ground that Rome represented S. Peter, 'that doorkeeper, whom I do not choose to gainsay.' Surely it is an abuse of language to speak of such a gift as not involving spiritual rights, or as one that could be taken back at any time by the hand that gave it. Oswy recognised a Divine institution, a 'doorkeeper' appointed by our Lord, to whom he submitted. To 'give' subjection to a Divinely appointed ruler, as Oswy understood S. Peter and his successors to be, is not to make a present, but to acknowledge a right. And a submission thus given may be withdrawn, it is true, but clearly not without sacrilege. Henry VIII., according to Canon Carter, only took back what Oswy gave. Oswy gave in his submission to a Divine appointment: Henry withdrew it, and forced his bishops, on pain of going to the block, to do the same. They repented of it afterwards as a grievous sin, but it was too late. It is on this sinful act that the Church of England rests to-day.

Once more. There is a chapter in Canon Carter's book which he has enlarged, and which is painful to the last degree, as coming from himself. From those who deny all sacerdotal ministrations, or from a writer like Dr. Littledale, we should expect anything of the kind. But from one who has endeavoured to recall his co-religionists to a recognition of the sacerdotal theory, such statements as are to be found in this chapter sound strange indeed.

Canon Carter thinks that we ascribe Divine attributes to our Blessed Lady, and give her a 'co-ordinate share' with God Himself in the work of Redemption. What does Canon Carter produce in the way of proof?

He quotes passages in which a certain co-operation in the salvation of the world is attributed to our Lady. I

Preface to the Sixth Edition

suppose no one but a pure Calvinist would deny some co-operation. But the passages he quotes to censure are such as might be almost used of any priest in saying Mass. 'She likewise offered Him' (i.e. our Lord) 'as a thing so entirely her own, with profound reverence and burning charity for her salvation' (notice that) 'and that of all men, desiring greatly that all should know, value, and esteem this inestimable benefit.' And on this passage he positively founds the charge, incredible as it seems, that 'authorised popular devotions invest the Blessed Virgin with a *co-ordinate share*' (the italics are mine) 'with God Himself in the merits of the Passion.' S. Jerome on one occasion bursts out with an indignant exclaimer to Vigilantius, saying, 'You dolt, do you suppose we are idolaters?' The simplicity of imagining that the above passage justifies the charge founded on it is not less than that of Vigilantius for supposing that Christians worshipped the martyrs.

But there is another passage which seems to me to argue still greater recklessness of assertion. Canon Carter has recourse to that famous (I had almost said infamous) book of Dr. Littledale's, unequalled, I suppose, for reckless assertions, apparently studied perversions, and inventiveness of calumny. He quotes one of Dr. Littledale's worst passages. I do Canon Carter the justice to suppose that he did not verify the reference. The quotation is: 'At the command of the Virgin all things obey, even God.' This is a quotation from Bernardine of Siena, made by S. Alphonsus. What does it mean? Common sense would naturally reply, to say nothing of Christian charity, that it cannot mean that real and literal omnipotence is ascribed to a creature—that a Divine attribute can be predicated of a created person. And this is what S. Alphonsus says: 'And here we say that although Mary, now in heaven, can no longer command her Son, nevertheless her prayers are always the prayers of a mother, and consequently most powerful to obtain whatever she asks.' Presently he quotes the sentence quoted by Canon Carter, and continues: 'S. Bernardine fears not to utter this sentence; meaning, indeed, to say that God grants the prayers of Mary as if they were commands.' Then he quotes S. Anselm, Canon Carter's imaginary Patriarch, to the same effect. And he adds, 'of course it is always true that where the Son is omnipotent by nature, the Mother is only so by grace. . . . Mary then is called omnipotent in the sense in which it can be understood of a creature who is incapable of a Divine attribute. She is omnipotent, because by her prayers she obtains whatever she wills.' And, of course, we know that what she wills she wills by the inspiration of the Holy Ghost. Thus Canon Carter's charge proves to be unfounded.[1]

But, in this whole matter, Canon Carter is at serious issue with the Photian schism, or, as he would call it, the Eastern Church.

In the seventeenth century the Easterns solemnly anathematised a Patriarch of Constantinople, who had become a Calvinist, for the very same position that Canon Carter holds. Their synodical condemnation on this particular point runs thus: 'To Cyril dogmatising . . . and believing that the Saints are not our mediators and inter-

[1] He also omits the preceding sentence, which gives an entirely different complexion to the one he quotes. It is, 'All things obey the Divine command, even the Virgin.'

cessors with God, saying that Jesus is the only Mediator . . . and rejecting the traditions to be observed by us, of which the invocation of Saints is one, Anathema.'

Painful as it is to have to say it, yet truth demands that it should be said, that Canon Carter's position is that of pure Protestantism with several Catholic truths tacked on—held on private judgment, and not on the authority of the Church ; picked out from writers in the early ages and put together, with more or less, according to the individual taste, the one thing lacking—submission to the supernatural authority of the Holy Ghost, living and speaking in the One, Holy, Catholic and Apostolic Church.

Consequently, his 'ideas of truth' are not those of the Catholic Church. She has her perpetual consciousness of her own past, and her witness is worth all the learning of the student, and all the theories of the ingenious— and infinitely more than all these. She knows she is of God, and speaks from God, and she is therefore what Canon Carter considers 'intolerant,' for she has a treasure to guard, and she guards it with a Divine jealousy. Comprehension, in the way in which the term is used nowadays, is in her judgment a synonym for disregard of truth.

In this edition I have withdrawn one assertion (p. 60), viz. that the translators of the Oxford Library of the Fathers transposed a certain sentence without sufficient authority. I do not know whether the authority is sufficient or no. It was not that which originally concerned me, but the substitution of the word 'James' for the pronoun 'he,' which I think I have proved to have been quite unauthorised in my book called 'Dependence,' to which I would refer my readers for a refutation of another assertion of Canon Carter's. The 'Church Quarterly Review,' bitter as its articles have been, supports me in this. It admits that the word 'James' ought not to have been substituted in the passage in S. Chrysostom alluded to below.

If any one wishes to see to what an extent misquotation can be carried, he will do well to read Father Richardson's article in the 'Dublin Review' for January last, on Mr. Gore's quotation of B. Albertus Magnus in the preface to his last edition of 'Roman Catholic Claims.' I have dealt with other assertions of Mr. Gore's in 'Dependence,' and in the preface to the fifth edition of this book. In his last preface he refers his readers to 'Janus' with approval. It is difficult to suppose that he can have read Hergenrother's crushing reply.

There is one point on which Hergenrother is peculiarly powerful. He literally shatters to atoms the idea that Rome owed anything essential to the False Decretals. It is, however, not so easy to eradicate from the minds of Anglicans such a convenient explanation of the phenomenon, which presents itself in the history of the Church, of Rome's actual possession of Supremacy. How did it come to pass? How did men come to believe it, in such millions? 'It was due to False Decretals,' says the Anglican. Canon Liddon, even in the thirteenth edition of his Bampton Lectures, is possessed of this idea. He compares the Infallibility of the Pope with the Infallibility of our Lord. He calls it, what the Vatican Council does not call it, and what Catholic theology does not call it, a 'personal' Infallibility. He supposes, it would seem that it must reside in the Pope in the same way as in

Preface to the Sixth Edition

our Divine Lord. He ignores the constant teaching of the Church that it is an official infallibility, due to the assistance of the Holy Ghost. And he contends that it must involve, if it means anything, the capacity of distinguishing between genuine and false documents ! S. Nicolas, he maintains, did not so distinguish, but 'cited' the False Decretals on behalf of the 'growing claims' of the Holy See ; therefore S. Nicolas was not infallible.

Now, in the first place, the False Decretals, as I have shown in an appendix to this book, did not initiate anything that belongs to the *de fide* teaching concerning the Holy See. In the second place, there is no instance of S. Nicolas 'citing' the False Decretals. In one letter he lays down the rule that Decretals, which are not contained in a certain code, may yet be of binding authority, but it is not certain that he ever saw the False Decretals. Neither he nor his successor ever quoted from them ; that is certain. The authority to which Canon Liddon refers (Walter) does not bear him out, but asserts the precise contrary. What mountains of prejudice are opposed to the Church's progress when a man like Canon Liddon can misrepresent such an important doctrine as Papal Infallibility, and rely on such oft-refuted statements as in this passage !

P.S.—Since the above words were written, this accomplished, amiable, and eloquent Canon has been taken from us, to my own deep personal regret, and to the great loss of his Communion.

23 Burlington Road, W.
  October 1890.

A PLAIN REASON

FOR

JOINING THE CHURCH OF ROME

My dear Sir,

I have just read a little book called 'Roman Catholic Claims,' originally published in the form of letters to the 'Indian Churchman.' It is recommended by high authority at Oxford to those who are uneasy about their position in the Church of England.

One of my reasons for sending forth a reply to that I find it is given to the world as 'the summing up of the controversy between Bishop Meurin and 'Father Rivington' (see fly-leaf), and in it you draw special attention to my 'apposite references' to S. Chrysostom, apropos of what you call the Bishop's 'inconceivably misleading and perverse quotation of the words "all the multitude held their peace," Acts xv. 12.'

The allusion is to a controversy which took place in India in 1883 between Bishop Meurin, then Roman Catholic Bishop of Bombay, and myself, at that time a member of the Anglican Church.

As, since that time, I have felt called (in the fuller exercise of my judgment on this question), by the mercy of God, to return to my spiritual Mother the Catholic and Roman Church, I feel in duty bound to submit some of the reasons which weighed with me in deciding that

B

I was mistaken in my opposition to the authority of the See of Rome.

And, in doing so, I desire to adopt (with infinitely more reason) the words of S. Francis of Sales in his introduction to a work of his own on this same subject. He says, 'I must protest, for the relief of my conscience, that all these considerations' (which he has previously given) 'would never have made me take the resolution of writing. It is a trade which requires apprenticeship, and belongs to learned and more cultivated minds. To write well, one must know extremely well; mediocre wits must content themselves with speech wherein gesture, voice, play of feature, brighten the word. Mine, which is of the less, or to say the downright truth, of the lowest, mediocrity, is not made to succeed in the exercise, and indeed I should not have thought of it if a grave and judicious gentleman had not invited and encouraged me to do it.'[1]

Dear St. Francis! Student, Saint, and Apostle, all in one! whom I have loved so well, and whose mutilated writings I have enjoyed these many years! aid me with your prayers at the Throne of Grace, that I may say something concerning the Catholic Church to some, whom I have loved and must ever love, which shall breathe something of your own sweetness, combined with your clear, incisive enunciation of Divine truth!

THE QUESTION IS AS TO THE FORM OF UNITY.

The difference between your own position, as set forth in 'Roman Catholic Claims,' and my own present

---

[1] The course of philosophy and theology through which the Saint went was a long one, and his notes are still in existence, showing that he was a much more learned man than most people would imagine. His sanctity has overshadowed his intellectual power.

position, may be summed up in the words of S. Francis of Sales, words which deserve to be written in characters of gold :—

'If, as S. Jerome says, in the time of the Apostles, "one is chosen from amongst all, in order that, a head being established, occasion of schism may be taken away," how much more now, for the same reason, must there be a chief in the Church? The fold of our Lord is to last, till the consummation of the world, in visible unity; the unity, then, of external government must remain in it, and nobody has authority to change the form of administration, save our Lord, Who established it.'

Now it was the question of government, the question as to what S. Francis calls the 'form of administration,' that was the point at issue between Rome and England in the sixteenth century. It was for this that martyrs like the blessed Bishop John Fisher and the blessed Thomas More shed their blood in that century.

'My lords' (says blessed John Fisher, Cardinal and Bishop), 'I am here condemned before you of high treason for denial of the King's supremacy over the Church of England, but by what order of justice I leave to GOD, who is the Searcher both of the King, His Majesty's conscience, and yours; nevertheless, being found guilty, as it is termed, I am and must be contented with all that GOD shall send, to Whose will I wholly refer and submit myself. And now, to tell you more plainly my mind, touching this matter of the King's supremacy, I think, indeed, and always have thought, and do now loudly affirm, that His Grace cannot justly claim any such supremacy over the Church of GOD as he now taketh upon him.'

And in his dying speech he says: 'Christian people, I am come hither to die for the faith of Christ's Holy

Catholic Church.' His last words were: 'In thee, O Lord, have I put my trust.'

'I have' (said blessed Thomas More, Lord Chancellor of England), 'by the Grace of GOD, been always a Catholic, never out of Communion with the Roman Pontiff, but I had heard it said at times that the authority of the Roman Pontiff was certainly lawful and to be respected, but still an authority derived from human law, and not standing on a Divine prescription. Then when I observed that public affairs were so ordered that the sources of the power of the Roman Pontiff would necessarily be examined, I gave myself up to a most diligent examination of that question for the space of seven years, and found that the authority of the Roman Pontiff which you rashly—I will not use stronger language—have set aside, is not only lawful, to be respected, and necessary, but also grounded on the Divine law and prescription. That is my opinion, that is the belief in which by the grace of GOD I shall die.' He ended his life with an appeal to the people to bear witness that he there died in and for the faith of the Holy Catholic Church. And after kneeling down and saying the Miserere, saluting and forgiving his executioner, he won his Martyr's crown.

Now there are no new literary discoveries, of any importance, about the early centuries of the Christian life. You do not cite any authorities that were not well known to Sir Thomas More, and S. Francis de Sales, who shows an intimate acquaintance with all the Fathers whom you quote. But S. Francis de Sales and Sir Thomas More drew one conclusion and you draw another.

They understood our Lord to have established in the commission given to S. Peter a 'guardianship of the Vine,' and to have made S. Peter the 'source of unity,' to use S. Cyprian's expression. You understand that our Lord's solemn declaration to His Apostle was only 'a symbolic act to emphasise His intention of unity' (p. 36).

WHY I HAVE COME TO MY PRESENT CONCLUSION.

Now I have come to the conclusion that S. Francis de Sales and Sir Thomas More were right in their understanding of Holy Scripture, and that the Reformers (as they are called) were wrong in acknowledging the King's supremacy and breaking with the Holy See. In other words, I believe that our Lord in the promise made to Peter—'On this Rock I will build My Church .... and I will give *unto thee* the Keys of the Kingdom of Heaven,' and in the charge given to him, 'Feed My sheep'—constituted His Apostle His own representative as Head of the Church, and so established, as the *form* of its unity, one undivided Episcopate, of equal fellowship and honour in sacerdotal power, bound together under one Head; and did not merely perform 'a symbolic act to emphasise His intention of unity.'

And I have come to this conclusion from nothing else than a careful consideration of the reasons urged on either side, and from a pure desire to obey our Lord's will in this important matter.

And my reasons were these :—

First, I saw that the *plain, obvious* meaning of our Lord's words to S. Peter involved the institution of a visible Head to His visible Church, *besides* the fact that His Church is described as an organised body, and that to talk of a body, without a head *in the same order of life* as the rest of the body, is to use words without meaning. An invisible body may have only an invisible head; but a visible body, to be a body at all, must have also a visible head. The fact of a headship is part of the contents of the term.

Secondly, I came to see that there could be no reasonable doubt that *in the fifth century* the entire Christian world held to the Papal form of Christianity, the Patriarchate of Alexandria, the Patriarchate of Antioch, the Patriarchate of Constantinople all agreeing in the same form of administration, of an Episcopate equal in order, under the headship of the successor of S. Peter. And the true interpretation of the *fourth century* was, I felt, to be found in the universal belief of the fifth, grounding its belief, as that century did, on the tradition of the previous ages.

Further, I saw that in that fourth century (on whose testimony all Anglicans so implicitly rely) the same belief as to the successor of S. Peter was plainly held by those very saints, of whose works as an Anglican I had been specially fond. It was held by S. Chrysostom, S. Ambrose, and S. Cyprian.

Fourthly, I was convinced that, putting aside the extreme application of the theory, some kind of evolution is to be found in all developments of life. It could be no new thought to any one who had read Thomassinus, as I had been led to do some years ago, nor to any student of S. Thomas, my favourite author, nor to any one who had read S. Augustine on Genesis. Dr. Routh's celebrated saying, if it was really his, that there would be development of statement in the Church, carries with it the whole contention of Cardinal Newman; for development in statement of truth will naturally be coincident with development in the general life of the Church. I was prepared, therefore, to find something in the way of evolution in the Mystical Body of Christ. There would be growth; successive differentiations; such a thing as the Infant Church, as there was an Infant Saviour. I was prepared to see doctrines, held first in germ, gradually asserting their proper force and form, as the proportions of the Mystical Body enlarged. Amongst the Apostles themselves, all confirmed, as they were, in grace, there could be no need of a head for quite the same purposes as afterwards. And there could be little capacity of its exercise in days of persecution. Its true value would be discerned as the Church emerged from the era of tyranny and persecution and put out its expanding powers. The head, *ever there*, would come out to view, as need arose and opportunity favoured. And this I found to be actually the case. The headship of Peter is, as I shall presently show, clear enough in Holy Scripture and is exercised there; but, beyond Holy Scripture, it only appears in the scant records we possess on a few critical occasions during the first two centuries. In the third it becomes more marked. In the fourth it is making itself universally felt, and beginning to cement distant provinces under its binding authority. In the fifth it towers over the entire world, and is an acknowledged portion of that which had been 'heard from the beginning.'

Fifthly: and here, it seemed to me, was the true key to the difficulties of our Church of England life. Difficulties there must be in all Church life. But there is no parallel, unless it be in the history of the Donatists, to the peculiar nature of the Anglican position, in the whole of Church history. Yet all is perfectly explained when we consider our Lord's promise to Simon and the relation of Anglicans to the See of S. Peter. 'Simon, Simon,' said our Lord to the chief of the Apostles, 'Satan hath desired to have you' (notice the plural) 'that he may sift you' (plural) 'as wheat.' Thus our Lord passes from the singular to the plural, from Simon to the whole Apostolic College. And what follows? Does He say that He will pray for them all? That would be unnecessary only if there was one head amongst them with whom they were to be joined; and so our Lord says, 'But I have prayed for *thee* that thy faith fail not: and when thou art converted, strengthen thy brethren.' Could human words express more plainly the position which S. Peter would occupy in the future? Our Lord, by way of protecting His chosen band, prayed for one; and *that one* was to confirm the rest. And Peter's faith never failed him, even in the Passion, though his love and courage did. This, then, was to be the law of the Church's life; the rest would be safe, because the head was secured in his teaching by the prayer of the Lord for him.

Now the teaching of the Church of England has been, on the whole, simple heresy on all that concerns the life of the individual, ever since it split off from S. Peter's successor. Its Episcopate has shown itself as being no longer under the shelter of our Lord's prayer; as though it were no longer part of the 'brethren,' or episcopal brotherhood, strengthened by Peter. It has, in its pulpits, taught heresy on and off for centuries on the subject of Holy Baptism, Absolution, the Blessed Sacrament, Holy Orders; whilst the whole Episcopate in communion with the See of S. Peter has during those same centuries, throughout the whole world, taught one doctrine—and that, according to High Anglicans of the present time, the true one—concerning Baptism, the Eucharistic Sacrifice, the Gift in Holy Communion, and the general value of Orders. A perfectly supernatural *steadiness* has marked her path; whilst the Church of England has been unsteady, to say the least, on these momentous subjects, even if it has not been steadily wrong; so that for centuries not merely the Pope, but the idea of the Priest, as one commissioned to forgive sin and offer sacrifice, has been the horror of England, and her children, our ancestors (peace to their souls!), have gone to their graves without a suspicion as to the truth of these fundamental doctrines: denying them outright in good faith as no part of the everlasting Gospel. What a shocking state of things! And yet it is clear enough, from our Lord's words to S. Peter, that such might be expected to be the case where a religious community exists apart from the strengthening influence of the See of S. Peter.

It may be said that things are not as they were; they are steadily mending. Would to God that they were! But apart from the difficulty of proving the validity of Anglican Orders, it seems to me that there has been a steady descent *in this matter of obedience to authority* ever since the day of the Gorham Judgment. That judgment has not yet been honestly repudiated by the Church of England, in her corporate capacity, in the face of the Christian world. The truth is taught by those who like to teach it, but the blot remains. It may yet be denied, and the denier be admitted to the highest office in the Church of England. And this after all these years! The fact is, that having herself broken off from the centre of authority, the Church of England cannot speak authoritatively except so far as a State Court will permit. One of her Clergy may still go to prison for upholding the Eucharistic Sacrifice, and the Guardians of the Faith, the Shepherds, the Bishops as a body, will not lift a finger in the way of public decided remonstrance, on the ground *that they hold the doctrine at issue.* And this after more than fifty years have passed since what is called the Church movement began. At a time (last winter) when I was considering this question with an earnestness and desire to know the truth which I felt to be a special gift from God, one of my friends was told in public, by his own Bishop, that if he taught the doctrine concerning the Eucharistic Sacrifice, which you and I have always taught, he had better go elsewhere—*i.e.* to the Church of Rome. That Bishop has not been excommunicated for his heretical teaching on this subject, and never will be. He was perfectly within his rights. But he betrayed the Catholic Faith, as held by Saints and Martyrs since the Day of Pentecost. Could such a thing happen with any Bishop in communion with the See of S. Peter? Impossible. So that after fifty years the authorities of the Church of England have not settled who is right, who is in accord with her formularies, those who teach the Eucharistic Sacrifice, or those who stoutly deny it ; those who teach the Catholic Faith concerning everlasting punishment, or those who deny it. It is true that the (so-called) Ritualistic section has won its way to a position of sufferance. It has become a recognised party. But in so doing it has separated itself from the earlier Tractarian movement. The fundamental position of that movement was that their teaching was the authoritative teaching of the Church of England. So soon as it became evident that such was not the case, men like Newman, Wilberforce, Manning, Coleridge, and a host of others, felt that their position was no longer tenable. They could not belong to a party. It is sad to see a man like the venerable author of the 'Roman Question' sitting in judgment on such men and deciding on their moral status, attributing their convictions to moral weakness, when they acted on the intelligible principle that the first necessity of ecclesiastical life is submission to duly constituted authority. They began, we learn from the first named, with appealing to catenas of Anglican divines, they went on to catenas of the Fathers, and they found from the latter that they must, at the cost of all most dear to the human heart, take the authority to which they found the Fathers bowed, as their own guide ; and they saw that the movement in which they found themselves was a call back to their own Mother, whom they had lost so long, and who had at last won her way back to their docile hearts.

They went, and what did they leave behind ? What has been the course, on the whole, since then, of the religious community of which they were once members ?

Dr. Pusey writes thus in 1870, in a letter hitherto unpublished : 'Instead of one Phaethon, there have been thirty or three hundred : each guiding the chariot of the sun after his own fashion ; and the old father has been left in a very respectable seat in the chimney corner, treated very deferentially, as having been very useful in his day ; or the less antique and more malleable are taught to take a step here and a step there.

'Now the early Tractarians had a definite ideal, viz. to bring the Church of England practically up to her own standard, such as she took as her standard. This people understood in the main ; but now every one seems to be following his own course, each has his psalm, his interpretation. One stands as at a junction near Waterloo Bridge : train after train rushing along, one in this direction, another in that, until some seven or ten trains have swept past, each in a diagonal direction, some for a longer distance, some shorter, but each confident as to its own course, which also it comes to ; but they never see each other more, unless they come back again.

'The theory of the modern High Church seems to be, "Go as near to Rome as you can," only the "can" is a limit which to some has no limit. We, thirty-seven years ago, set out with the conviction that there was a Divine office for the Church of England ; that she had but to rouse herself and throw aside her drowsiness, and be in act what she was in theory. From this we did not swerve; we were sons, not patrons. We wished, by GOD's grace, to bring ourselves and others up to her. We held as a principle that nothing was to be done by majorities. We did not wish to act except upon her principles, and waited for her to act, when her hair "should be grown." And surely the state of the Western Church does imply that there is an office for her, if she could be one. But now people's only idea seems to be to gain a following each around himself, which they call Catholic, and to prepare, I suppose, for disruption. All who do not agree in all matters with them they despise as "Protestants," and bid them keep to themselves. They have no perception, apparently, to see what degree or aspect of truth there may be in persons who yet are in the main very much one with us: they take no account of any cloud which early education may have drawn over any mind, which prevents their speaking our language while they believe what we do. They treat all besides with contempt (take, *e.g.*, the "Church Times"). And whereas there never was a greater opportunity for union among ourselves, these are destroying all confidence in any one, except their own in themselves, which seems to be unbounded. . . . I wish there could be some unity of purpose, and so does ——. As it is, I fear that the young movement is ruining itself and the Church of England.'

And in 1884, another, of almost equal authority with Dr. Pusey on this subject, writes: 'High Church principles are more widely diffused than they were, but they are held in a much feebler and less emphatic form than was the case some years ago. . . . . is the modern type, and it is a very different type from that of the author of the "Christian Year." It differs alike in intellectual consistency and in moral intensity; but, in virtue of this, it is much more popular. Before his death Dr. Pusey noted this change with sorrow ; and since he has left us, as was natural, it has become more marked. . . . The change is far-reaching ; it promises to become, as far as the Church movement is concerned, little less than universal.'

All this, I repeat, is exactly what might be expected in a religious community, torn from the true Divinely guaranteed centre of authority. It quivers on with life which it has taken with it from the main body from which it has been torn off. It has its episcopal form of government ; so had the Nestorians, with, however, many more bishops and no doubt about its succession. It has its missionary efforts ; so had the Nestorians, but on a larger scale, or at least with greater effect. It has lasted nearly three centuries ; so did the Nestorians, only longer still. It may have its orders and valid sacraments ; so had the Nestorians, and so had the Donatists. But one thing it certainly does not possess, and that is the power to teach authoritatively one truth, one faith concerning those very matters which concern the sacramental life of the individual soul. It cannot even be said to teach with any authority as to the issue of our time of trial on earth, the truth which lay, as you and I believe, at the root of our Lord's practical teaching, and has been, and is to this day, the plain practical motive which, in addition to the supreme reason for holy living—the love of God—the Church throughout the world places before her children as a subduing thought in their hours of temptation, and as entering into their grateful recognition of a Saviour's love. The Church of England, I mean, is wavering even on the subject of hell.

In the last place in which I ministered as an Anglican clergyman (it was a small seaside place) I was in full communion with the following religious teachers :

One good and really learned man thanked GOD that the Church of England had never taught the doctrine of everlasting punishment, in which he sincerely disbelieved; another delighted in teaching the poor Italians to read their Bible instead of going to Mass; a third agreed with him; a fourth considered this a grievous sin, and felt it advisable to interpolate the Anglican Communion service with prayer from the Roman, or (which is the same thing) the Sarum Missal; a fifth, good as gold, and with all the charm of innocence, was vague as Maurice and Kingsley; a sixth would take the greatest trouble to get a (Roman) Catholic priest to attend a dying Catholic; a seventh had left the Church of England, or at least given up his ministry, on the ground that she had committed herself to a position of indifference on the subject of everlasting punishment. We were presided over by a Bishop, an amiable man, whose opinions on our points of disagreement we were never able to discover. Now I am not retailing scandals. These men were, I have every reason to suppose, men of blameless moral character. But here was the Church of England in miniature—failing in the one point without which a Church is no longer what the Church was when she came forth from the Upper Chamber in Jerusalem—an authoritative teacher of one faith. At the same time the faithful from all parts of the globe were pouring in their jubilee gifts to the successor of S. Peter, each gift (save a few, that represented Imperial and Royal respect, such as those from Germany and England) being an act of faith, and all these faithful from the four quarters of the globe are being taught on those matters that concern the life of the individual, one and one only faith—taught it definitely, taught it authoritatively; and their ancestors have been taught the same— and Gallicanism is no more; and you may see (as I have seen) a Strossmayer bringing his faithful to the feet of the occupant of the Fisherman's Throne ; and you may read how Père Gratry, whom you quote so approvingly, not only withdrew his opposition to the decrees of the Vatican Council, but in a beautiful letter to a friend explains why, and withdraws and regrets the passage that you quote ; and you may see the disciples of Rosmini submitting themselves with supernatural joy to the Holy See by anticipation : in short, as though our Lord would make His call to English Churchmen as loud and clear as it may be at this critical hour in the world's history, He has brought it about, in the ways of His providence, that there should be indeed signs and wonders following them that believe in Himself, the incarnate Lord, and in the authority which He has instituted to represent Himself.

The wonderful spectacle may be expressed in a parable from nature.

There is a mass of rock on one of our English coasts, which stands up from the sea and meets the eye at every turn of the headlands along that coast. Sometimes you see the great ocean tossing its wild waves against it hither and thither, destined, in all appearance, to submerge the covered mass. But the big waves break upon its sides ; the monsters of the deep thrust themselves in vain against it ; vessels have been known to go to pieces on it ; eagles and vultures strike their bills against it, and millions of parasites adhere to its sides but the rock stands there. There it has been, they say, for centuries past, and there it is to-day ; and we know that as we have seen it ourselves, so will our children's children see it too.

It is a symbol of what I seemed to see in the history of Christendom.

There is at this moment one, and only one, Apostolical **See** on the face of the globe. It has stood through these **near two thousand years.** Alone it has been honoured by a continuous transmission of its Episcopate. Other Apostolical Churches, venerable and holy, have sunk in the storms that from time to time have burst over the East. Lest they should plead the authority of their founders to break the sacred bond of Christian unity, our Lord willed that they should meet with tragic disasters and irremediable catastrophes. The See of S. Peter alone remains the one Apostolic See: remains, although Imperial persecutors, hordes of barbarians, faithless princes, rebellious republics, have passed over its body. It remains: and Almighty GOD has thus countersigned by its miraculous protection the promise of the Church's immortality—' Upon this Rock will I build my Church, . . . and the gates of hell shall not prevail against it.'[1]

In other words, we have had the fulfilment of our Lord's promise to Peter in the history of the See of Rome. For

WHAT IS THE PLAIN MEANING OF OUR LORD'S PROMISE TO PETER AT CÆSAREA PHILIPPI?

I am speaking of the primary meaning. In S. Augustine's writings we have a primary and a secondary interpretation—the secondary, struck out to meet a controversial emergency, unknown to the Church for more than three hundred and fifty years, not interfering with the primary, not holding its own in the Church, and never meant by S. Augustine to weaken the authority of the Roman See, in which, as we shall see, he clearly believed. It is of the primary meaning that we are now speaking.

Our blessed Lord in addressing His Apostle on that momentous occasion made use of two metaphors, that of a foundation and that of a key-bearer.

[1] Cf. Monsabré, *Conf. sur l'Eglise*.

What was actually said to Peter was this : 'Thou art Kipho (or Cephas); and upon this Kipho I will build my Church, and the gates of hell shall not prevail against it. And I will give unto thee the keys of the Kingdom of heaven : and whatsoever thou shalt bind on earth shall be bound in Heaven ; and whatsoever thou shalt loose on earth shall be loosed in Heaven.'

In the Greek there are two words for Kipho, or rock — the one masculine, the other feminine. The masculine word was therefore used, as was natural, in the Greek version, when our Lord said, 'Thou art Kipho;' and the feminine, when our Lord spoke of His Apostle as the foundation of His Church. It could not be otherwise in translating the one word, used by our Lord, into Greek, for the feminine word, as a name, would imply derision.

1. Now it is important to notice, that in the language of Holy Scripture, to be called anything by Almighty God is to be what we are called. The word of God is a creative word. We may, therefore, be sure that Peter would be what he was called, *i.e.* a rock. 'He was,' says S. Chrysostom, 'a rock in name and in deed.' In speaking of the call of S. Peter in S. John i., S. Gregory Nyssen says, 'by means of the change of his name, he is transformed into something more divine : instead of Simon, being both called and *having become* a rock (Peter).' And so S. Cyril of Alexandria on the same text in S. John says : 'With allusion to the Rock He transferred His name to Peter, for upon him He was about to found His Church.' So that we may explain our Lord's words in the history of his call: 'What thou shalt be called, thou shalt also be; thou shalt be called and thou shalt be, a rock.'

So that even if it were true that by the words 'this rock' in Matt. xvi., our Lord meant Himself alone, we have still to account for the first words, 'Thou art Peter.' Peter is, anyhow, constituted by our Lord a man with a new name, solemnly promised, solemnly given—a name which points to a *special* connection with Him, who is the Rock, in the building of the Church— a name not given to the other Apostles, but to Simon Bar-jona alone.

2. S. Peter does not at Cæsarea Philippi speak in the name of the other Apostles, in the sense of being their delegate. It was not according to the sacred record, that they all felt the same, but he alone spoke: but that his faith went beyond the rest and led them on. His dogmatic utterance stood by itself, the result of a special, personal revelation, and his reward is correspondingly personal. He represents them as being their leader: they followed him in his faith; like a band of soldiers, with their captain, they were, 'Peter, and those that were with him,' 'Peter and the rest'—as at the Cross there was 'the centurion and they that were with him'—the captain and the band. The revelation was made to him personally, and they had contributed nothing to this: 'Blessed art *thou* . . . flesh and blood hath not revealed it unto *thee*, but My Father.' Whatever it was, therefore, that took place, was clearly the reward of S. Peter's confession, and of his alone. The others joined themselves on to him, and shared afterwards in the reward, but not equally. The *same* was never said to them: only a portion of the promise was made over to them after the Resurrection. To Peter all was personal and fuller, and indicated some special relationship to our Lord in the building of His Church.

And his faith and his confession were himself: himself in action. These were the meritorious occasion, the formal cause, the divine origin, of our Lord's promise to him. They no more *excluded* himself than S. Jerome excluded the Apostle himself, when he said that 'not the body but the faith of Peter walked upon the waters.' And so some of the Fathers speak sometimes of the faith of the Apostle, sometimes of the Apostle himself, as the rock.

And now to consider the words 'this rock'—'on this rock I will build My Church.' It is not 'I am building,' as we should expect, if our Lord were speaking of Himself as the rock. Of course, there is a sense in which our Lord alone, or our Lord as confessed in His Two Natures and One Divine Person, is the rock on which the Church is built. But is it that truth which our Lord is revealing here? Or is it an instance of what S. Basil, speaking of this very subject, calls 'the proof of opulence, viz. to have and to give to others'?

'Now I ask you,' says S. Francis de Sales to the Calvinist ministers, 'what likelihood is there that our Lord would have made this grand preface: "Blessed art thou, Simon Bar-jona; because flesh and blood hath not revealed it unto thee, but My Father which is in heaven; and I say unto thee," &c., in order to say no more than "Thou art Peter," and then suddenly have changed His subject, and gone on to speak of something else? And again, when He says: "And on this rock I will build My Church," do you not see that He evidently speaks of the rock of which He had previously spoken? and of what other rock had He spoken but of Simon, to whom He had said: "Thou art Peter"? . . . . And this name of Peter was not the proper name of a man, but was only appropriated to Simon Bar-jona. This you will much better understand, if you take it in the language in which our Lord said it: He spoke not Latin, but Syriac. He therefore called him not Peter, but Cephas, thus: "Thou art Cephas, and on this Cephas I will build" . . . . there is no other Cephas spoken of in all this chapter but

Simon. On what ground, then, do we come to refer this relative "hanc" (this) to another Cephas besides the one who immediately precedes? You will say, Yes; but the Latin says, Thou art Petrus, and not, Thou art Petra: now this relative "hanc," which is feminine, cannot refer to Petrus, which is masculine . . . .'

The Saint says that the answer is that 'To accommodate the word to the person to whom it was given as a name, who was masculine, there is given it a corresponding termination, as the Greek does, which had put, "Thou art Πέτρος, and on this πέτρα." But it does not come out so well in Latin as in Greek, because in Latin "Petrus" does not mean exactly the same as "petra," but in Greek πέτρος and πέτρα is the very same thing. Similarly, in French "rocher" and "roche" is the same thing, yet still so that if I had to predicate either word of a man, I would rather apply to him the name of "rocher" than of "roche," to make the masculine word correspond with the masculine subject. I have only to add, on this interpretation, that nobody doubts that our Lord called S. Peter Cephas (for S. John records it most explicitly, and S. Paul to the Galatians), or that Cephas means a stone or a rock, as S. Jerome says.'

The Saint then remarks on the fact that 'to thee I will give the keys' is at any rate said to S. Peter, and that '*the foundation*' *and* '*the keys*' *are but two aspects of the same thing*; and he refers, as I shall presently do, to the express admission of the Council of Chalcedon, when the Catholic Church, 'even according to the admission of the ministers, was true and pure.' He then deals with a difficulty, on which some stress is laid by the venerable author of the 'Roman Question.' If the author of this volume is indeed one who has written so much that is beautiful on the Sacramental system, it is a painful surprise that he should now, in the decline of life, exhibit a virtual surrender of the fundamental principle of that system. The Papacy is, as it were, the Eucharist of Christ's government in His Church. It is His Presence within His own Institution which makes that institution to be effectual for its purposes. Christ alone is the Foundation of His Church, and yet the Apostles and Prophets are foundations too. Christ alone is the Head of His Church, and yet we never feared, even in the Anglican Communion, to talk of deference or resistance to the heads of the Church, or even to sign a document which pledged us to believe even a Gracious Lady to be, in some sense, head of the Church of England. And yet the venerable author of the 'Roman Question' can bring himself to quote the following passage, adopting the exposition of a comparative nobody in preference to that of a great saint the exposition of Tostatus in preference to that of S. Jerome (whom even the Articles of the Church of England quote with respect). It is with real pain that I append the quotation ('Roman Question,' p. 23): 'It is untrue' (says this Tostatus concerning S. Jerome's teaching that S. Peter is the rock on which Christ built His Church), 'because Christ is the sole foundation; according to 1 Cor. iii. 11, "other foundation can no man lay than that is laid, which is Jesus Christ."'

Withdraw, therefore, to your cell, great Saint of GOD! go on with your guidance of your religious houses at Bethlehem, with your tears and your study, and your earnest prayers; for when you come to interpret Holy Scripture, you are found capable of subverting the entire Gospel, and laying some other foundation than that is laid, which is Jesus Christ! And the 'Aged Priest' of the Church of England, writing on the 'Roman Question,' will echo the taunt of Tostatus—as though there were no such thing as the sacerdotal conception of the Christian ministry or the sacramental system; no priests, because there is but One Priest; no visible head, because there is but One Invisible Head—and will convict you of being a traitor to the unique glory and supreme headship of your Lord God and Saviour Jesus Christ!

Who is Tostatus, that we should heed him when he provides such poverty of exposition in depreciation of the Saint who gave us the Latin translation of the Bible? The Church does not hesitate to throw overboard the exposition of an Augustine, if it is not in accordance with the stream of tradition, or of a Cyprian, when it is contrary to the practice of the Church in dealing with the Baptism of heretics. Why should we defer to a Tostatus, who, so far from being, as the author of the 'Roman Question' asserts, 'of first-rate repute,' has a mark against his name, was controverted by Cardinal de Turrecremata, and his book placed on the Index, for other matters besides the subject of the Supremacy? Moreover, as S. Augustine said to some in his day, who were always quoting the name of Cyprian: 'Why do you take the authority of Cyprian for your schism, and reject his example for the peace of the Church?' So, and much more, we may say: 'Why do you quote one like Tostatus, and refuse to do as Tostatus did, who submitted himself and his writings to the Holy See?'

But let S. Francis, with his deep piety and great learning and unquestioned loyalty to his Divine Master, give the answer, as he gave it to the Calvinist ministers to whom he wrote on this very point, as follows:—

'Have you well considered the words of S. Paul? He will not have us recognise any foundation besides our Lord, but neither is S. Peter nor are the other Apostles foundations *besides* our Lord, they are subordinate to our Lord: their doctrine is none other than that of their Master, but their very Master's itself. Thus the supreme charge which S. Peter had in the militant

Church, by reason of which he is called foundation of the Church, as chief and governor, is not *beside* the authority of his Master, but is only a participation in this. So that he is not the foundation of this hierarchy *besides* our Lord, but rather in our Lord. . . . Our Lord then is foundation and S. Peter also, but with so notable a difference that in respect of the one the other may be said not to be it. For our Lord is foundation and founder; foundation without other foundation; foundation of the natural, Mosaic, and Evangelic Church; foundation perpetual and immortal; foundation of the militant and triumphant; foundation by His own nature; foundation of our faith, hope, and charity, and of the efficacy of the Sacraments. S. Peter is foundation, not founder, of the whole Church; foundation, but founded on another foundation, which is our Lord; foundation of the Evangelic Church alone; foundation subject to succession: foundation of the militant, not of the triumphant; foundation by participation, ministerial not absolute foundation: in fine, administrator and not Lord, and in no way the foundation of our faith, hope, and charity, nor of the efficacy of the Sacraments. A difference so great as this makes the one unable, in comparison, to be called a foundation by the side of the other; whilst, however, taken by itself, it can be called a foundation, in order to pay proper regard to the Holy Word. So, although he is the Good Shepherd, He gives us shepherds under Himself, between whom and His Majesty there is so great a difference that He declares Himself to be the only shepherd.

'At the same time it is not good reasoning to say: all the Apostles in general are called foundations of the Church, therefore S. Peter is only such in the same way as the others are. . . . For to whom has it ever been said, "Thou art Peter," &c.? . . . We have only to see for what general reason all the Apostles are called foundations of the Church; namely, because it is they who by their preaching have planted the faith and the Christian doctrine, in which, if we are to give some prerogative to any one of the Apostles, it will be to that one who said, "I have laboured more abundantly than all they."

'And it is in this sense that the passage of the Apocalypse is meant to be understood. For the twelve Apostles are called foundations of the heavenly Jerusalem, because they were the first who converted the world to the Christian religion, which was, as it were, to lay the foundations of the glory of men and the seeds of their happy immortality. But the passage of S. Paul seems to be understood not so much of the person of the Apostles as of their doctrine. For it is not said that we are built upon the Apostles, but upon the foundation of the Apostles—that is, upon the doctrine which they have announced. This is easy to see, because it is not only said that we are built upon the foundation of the Apostles, but also of the Prophets, and we know well that the Prophets have not otherwise been foundations of the Evangelical Church than by their doctrine. And in this matter all the Apostles seem to stand on a level, unless S. John and S. Paul come first for the excellence of their theology. It is then in this sense that all the Apostles are foundations of the Church; but in authority and government S. Peter precedes all the others as much as the head surpasses the members; for he has been appointed ordinary pastor and supreme head of the Church; the others have been delegated pastors intrusted with as full power and authority over all the rest of the Church as S. Peter, except that S. Peter was the head of them all and their pastor, as of all Christendom. Thus they were foundations of the Church equally with him as to the conversion of souls and as to doctrine; but as to the authority of governing they were so unequally, as S. Peter was the ordinary head not only of the rest of the whole Church, but of the Apostles also. For our Lord had built on him the whole of His Church, of which they were not only parts, but the principal and noble parts. "Although the strength of the Church," says S. Jerome, "is equally established on all the Apostles, yet amongst the twelve one is chosen that, a head being appointed, occasion of schism may be taken away." "There are, indeed," says S. Bernard to his Eugenius, and we can say as much of S. Peter for the same reason, "there are others who are custodians and pastors of flocks, but thou hast inherited a name as much the more glorious as it is more special."'

The Saint then deals with the bestowal of the keys of the Kingdom of Heaven on S. Peter. He observes that 'the ministers try as hard as they can to disturb the clear fountain of the Gospel, so that S. Peter may not be able to find his keys therein, and that we may turn disgusted from the water of the holy obedience which we owe to the vicar of our Lord. And therefore they have bethought them of saying that S. Peter had received this promise of our Lord in the name of the whole Church, without having received any particular privilege in his own person.'

This position of the ministers seems to be your own, as you maintain that S. Peter's position amongst the Apostles was only personal in the sense in which S. John's was (a position, as we shall presently see, contradicted *totidem verbis* by S. Chrysostom), and that it was no more meant to be an abiding fact in the Church's ministry than was S. John's (p. 33).

S. Francis replies to the ministers that 'if this is not violating Scripture, never did man violate it. For was it not to S. Peter that He was speaking? . . . . He does not say "*to it,*" but "*to thee*" *will I give.* If it is allowed thus to go surmising over clear words, there will be nothing in the Scriptures which cannot be twisted into any meaning whatever; though I do not deny that S. Peter in this place was speaking in his own name and in that of the whole Church, not, indeed, as delegated by the Church, or by the disciples (for we have not the shadow of a sign of this commission in the Scripture, and the revelation on which he founds his confession had been made to himself alone, unless the whole college of Apostles was named Simon Bar-jona), but as mouthpiece, prince, and head of the Church, and of the others, according to S. Chrysostom and S. Cyril on this place, and "on account of the primacy of his Apostolate," as S. Augustine says. It was then the whole Church that spoke in the person of S. Peter as in the person of its head, and not S. Peter that spoke in the person of the Church. For the body speaks only in its head, and the head speaks in itself, not in its body: and although S. Peter was not as yet head and prince of the Church, which office was only conferred on him after the resurrection of the Master, it was enough that he was already chosen out for it, and had a pledge of it. As also the other Apostles had not as yet the Apostolic power, travelling over all that blessed country rather as scholars with their tutor to learn the profound lessons which afterwards they taught to others, than as Apostles or Envoys, which they afterwards were throughout the whole world, when their sound went forth into all the earth. Neither do I deny that the *rest of the prelates* of the Church have a share in the *use* of the keys; and as for the Apostles, I own that they have every authority here. I say only that the giving of the keys is here promised principally to S. Peter, and for the benefit of the Church. . . . . But, one will ask me, what difference is there between the promise which our Lord here makes to S. Peter to give him the keys, and that which He made to the Apostles afterwards? For in truth it seems to have been but the same, because our Lord, explaining what He meant by the keys, said: "And whatsoever thou shalt bind upon earth, it shall be bound also in heaven; and whatsoever thou shalt loose," &c.—which is just what He said to the Apostles in general: "Whatsoever you shall bind," &c. If, then, He promises to all in general what He promises to Peter in particular, there will be no ground for saying that S. Peter is greater than any of the others by this promise.

'I answer that in the promise and in the execution of the promise our Lord always preferred S. Peter by expressions which oblige us to believe that he was made head of the Church. And as to the promise, I confess that by these words, "And whatsoever thou shalt loose," our Lord promised no more to S. Peter than He did to the others afterwards: "Whatsoever you shall bind," &c. For the words are the same in substance and in meaning in the two passages. I admit also that by these words: "And whatsoever thou shalt loose," said to S. Peter, He explains the preceding: "And I will give to thee the keys;" but *I deny that it is the same thing to promise the keys* and to say (only), "Whatsoever thou shalt loose." Let us then see what it is to promise the keys of the Kingdom of Heaven. And who knows not that when a master, going away from his house, leaves the keys with some one, what he does is to leave him the charge and governance thereof? When princes make their entrance into cities, the keys are presented to them as an acknowledgment of their sovereign authority.

'It is, then, the supreme authority which our Lord here promises to S. Peter; and, in fact, when the Scripture elsewhere wishes to speak of a sovereign authority, it has used similar terms. . .'

The Saint then refers to Rev. i. 17-18, and iii. 7, and compares Isaiah xxii., showing that the commandment given to Eliakim is parallel in every particular with that which our Lord gave to S. Peter, and he concludes: 'Such is what is meant by this promise of giving the keys to S. Peter, a promise which was never made to the other Apostles.

'But I say that it is not all one to promise the keys of the Kingdom and to say, "Whatsoever thou shalt loose," &c., although one is the explanation of the other. And what is the difference? Certainly *just that which there is between the possession of an authority and the exercise of it.* It may well happen that while a king lives, his queen, or his son, may have just as much power as the king himself to chastise, absolve, make gifts, grant favours: *such person will not, however, have the sceptre, but only the exercise of it.* He will, indeed, have the same authority, but *not in possession, only in use and exercise.* What he does will be valid, but he will not be head or king; he must recognise that his power is extraordinary, by commission and delegation, whereas the power of the king, which may be no greater, is ordinary, and is his own. So our Lord, promising the keys to S. Peter, remits to him *the ordinary authority*, and gives him *that office in ownership, the exercise of which he referred to when He said:* "*Whatsoever thou shalt loose,*" &c. Now afterwards, when He makes the same promise to the other Apostles, He does not give them the keys or the ordinary authority, but only gives them the use and exercise thereof. *This difference is taken from the very terms of the Scripture:* for to loose and to bind signifies but the action and exercise; to have the keys, the habit. . . . . See how different is the promise which our Lord made to S. Peter from that which He made to the other Apostles. The Apostles all have the same power as S. Peter, but not in the same rank, inasmuch as they have it as delegates and agents, but S. Peter as ordinary head and permanent officer. And in truth it was fitting that the Apostles, who were to plant the Church everywhere, should all have full power and entire authority as to the use of the keys and the exercise of their powers, while it was most necessary that one amongst them should have charge of the keys by office and dignity—"that the Church, which is one," as S. Cyprian says, "should by the word of the Lord be founded upon one who received the keys thereof."'

In this passage from S. Francis de Sales, all the difficulties raised by the author of the 'Roman Question,' and by yourself, as to the plain meaning of S. Matt. xvi. 16 19 seem to be answered, and that inimitably, by anticipation.

Next comes the question as to

THE TEACHING OF THE EARLY CHURCH.

You refer us to the rule of S. Vincent of Lerins, that the true faith is that which has been held in the Christian Church 'everywhere, always, and by all.' But what a difficulty there is in ascertaining this, without the assistance of the living voice of the Church! S. Cyprian erred about it, though so near the earliest times, and had to be set right by the living voice of the Church in Pope S. Stephen. So true is it, as Cardinal Newman has remarked, that however easy in its application the rule might be in the earliest times, when a man might almost ask the primitive centuries for their testimony, 'it is hardly available now, or effective of any satisfactory results. The solution it offers is as difficult as the original problem.'

For instance, the author of the 'Roman Question' gives what he calls an 'enumeration' of 'the Fathers' as witnesses against the Catholic interpretation of S. Matt. xvi. 16-19, quoting from Mr. Grueber (p. 23). In this 'enumeration' we have only eleven named. The earliest comes only from the middle of the fourth century! The passage is as follows: 'Mr. Grueber thus enumerates the Fathers as witnesses: "Some eminent among the Fathers, as S. Hilary of Poitiers, S. Epiphanius, S. Ambrose, S. Chrysostom, S. Isidore of Pelusium, S. Cyril of Alexandria, Theodoret, take the 'Rock' not as S. Peter only, but as the Faith, or S. Peter's faith" (which no one ever disputed), "or they hesitate between the two interpretations. Some again speak of Christ Himself as the Rock, as S. Jerome, S. Isidore, S. Augustine, S. Gregory the Great."'

This passage does not fairly represent the state of the case.

S. Hilary of Poitiers gives both interpretations, but gives no sign of hesitating between the two. One may fairly be considered the primary, the other the secondary interpretation—or one the literal, and the other the accommodated sense. In point of fact, S. Hilary in *De Trin. vi.* the best known passage, in which he speaks of the faith of S. Peter as the 'rock,' shows that he is not excluding, but including Peter in the rock; for he goes on to say that also 'this faith has the keys of the kingdom of Heaven.' Now no one doubts that S. Peter personally received the keys, though, of course, it is true also to say that his faith received them. His faith was the cause of his being the rock, and receiving the keys. The Church was to be built on his faith, and the keys were given to his faith, not excluding him. S. Hilary, therefore, speaks quite unhesitatingly of S. Peter as the *In Ps. 131.* 'foundation of the Church,' and as the 'firm rock on *Ps. 141.* which the Church was to be built,' as 'the Prince of the *I Matt. vii.* Apostleship,' as 'the happy foundation of the Church and the rock worthy of the building up of that which was to dissolve the infernal laws.'

The next witness, S. Epiphanius, twice calls S. Peter the rock, in one case adding, 'on which the Church was built,' in the other, 'on which the Church was in every way built.' Are we to suppose that Epiphanius contradicted himself?

S. Ambrose calls S. Peter both the foundation and the rock, and there is no sense of contradiction between this and his calling S. Peter's faith, or his confession, the rock, any more than, as already remarked, there is a contradiction in S. Jerome when he says that 'not the body, but the faith of Peter walked upon the waters'— his faith was the formal cause of his miraculous action.

S. Chrysostom, in one single passage, calls S. Peter, as well as his confession, the rock, showing that he considered both of them true—the one the cause of the other.

S. Cyril of Alexandria calls him 'the rock, upon whom the Lord was about to build His Church.'

Theodoret, in his letter to S. Leo appealing to be restored, is clear enough as to the supreme authority of S. Peter's See, and was one of those who (as we shall see) accepted the Council of Chalcedon's attribution of the term 'Rock' to the Saint, as S. Peter's successor.

S. Isidore of Pelusium, out of his 1,213 letters, of which his extant writings consist, only once deals with the text in hand, and says that Peter, inspired by our Lord, 'placed his confession, as a base and foundation, on which the Lord built His Church.' It was not, therefore, S. Peter's confession, apart from himself, that was the foundation. 'He laid the foundation,' says the Saint.

Thus, none of these seven witnesses are fairly witnesses at all. The question is not, as Mr. Grueber puts it, whether they included S. Peter's faith, or his confession; but whether they excluded S. Peter himself, which we have seen they did not.

Next as to those who, Mr. Grueber says, 'speak of Christ Himself as the Rock,' that is, if there is any relevance in the assertion, exclusively of S. Peter.

Four instances only are given.

First, S. Jerome. We have only to refer to a preceding paragraph on the very same page to see that S. Jerome at any rate cannot fairly be quoted as an instance of excluding S. Peter from the term 'rock.' Who does not remember S. Jerome's words speaking not only of Peter himself, but the 'chair of Peter'? 'On that Rock I know the Church is built.' There is no hesitation here. 'On that Rock I know the Church is built; whoso eats the Lamb outside this house is profane.' And this in the fourth century.

S. Isidore, by whom here, I presume, the writer means the Bishop of Seville, says, 'Peter in Christ, is the foundation of the Church. Cephas is the Princedom (principatus) and Head of the Body of Christ.' He is 'the Prince of the Apostles,' 'the pastor of the human race,' 'the rock of the Church,' 'the key-bearer of the kingdom.'

Life of S. Peter by S. Isidore.

There remain S. Augustine and S. Gregory.

Now S. Augustine gives both interpretations, but he does not say that either is to exclude the other, which is the point at issue. He speaks of his later interpretation in a certain tone of apology, as though it were an innovation, and gives a reason from the Latin translation, which S. Francis de Sales has shown to be quite untenable in view of the Greek and Syriac. But even from S. Augustine's suggestion nothing can be argued which would sustain the Anglican contention. In the course of a passage, much relied upon, he says, 'and so Peter, *named from this rock*, would represent the person of the Church, which is built upon this rock, and received the keys of the Kingdom of Heaven.' Now what S. Augustine understood by S. Peter representing the person of the Church is best shown from his forty-sixth sermon, when he says: 'For also Peter himself, to whom He commends His sheep *as another self*, He wished to make one with Himself, that so He might commend the sheep to him: that *he might be the head*, he bear the figure of the Body, that is, of the Church, and as husband and wife be two in one flesh.' Here is S. Peter's relationship to the Church portrayed in the most wonderful simile of all, and as S. Peter was to be 'the other self' of his Lord, he would still, even though the rock meant primarily our Lord, be 'another rock;' which indeed is not another, for He, our Lord, willed to make Peter 'one with Himself.'

Again, it is evident that S. Augustine was not there professing to give the traditional interpretation. He was not speaking as a witness to that, but hammering out a new meaning from the Latin. He doubtless felt that the truth of S. Peter's headship was secure enough on other grounds, seeing it had never yet been doubted.

Nor can we suppose that S. Augustine ever meant to contradict or retract what he said to the Donatists: 'Enumerate the priests from the See itself of Peter, and in that order of Fathers, see who succeeded to whom: this is the rock which the proud gates of hell overcome not.' S. Augustine never withdrew this. And no Roman Catholic could express the teaching of the Catholic Church more concisely than S. Augustine has done in this passage. He once puts the matter more tersely, but it loses from its very terseness: 'Peter, in whom alone He forms the Church.' Serm. 137.

Ps. in Part Donat

Lastly, S. Augustine's later suggestion, on which Anglicans rely, did not hold its ground in the Church. It disappeared almost altogether, to be revived by Luther.

As to S. Gregory the Great, the remaining witness, his words are plain enough : 'To all who know the Gospel, it is manifest that the charge of the whole Church was entrusted by the voice of the Lord to the holy Apostle Peter, chief of all the Apostles. For to him it is said, " Peter, lovest thou Me," &c. To him it is said, " Thou art Peter," &c.'

<small>Ep. lib. v. 20.</small>

Such is the 'enumeration' of 'the Fathers' as witnesses against the Roman claims from Holy Scripture produced by one who signs himself an 'Aged Priest.' It is a distressing chapter. S. Chrysostom is contradicted *totidem verbis*, p. 28. S. Augustine is misquoted, p. 25, and contradicted, p. 23. Tostatus is set against S. Jerome. Du Pin is quoted as arguing that 'govern My sheep,' and 'teach all nations,' are identical, p. 25. S. James's words at Jerusalem are made to mean what neither S. Jerome, nor S. Chrysostom, nor any known writing of any Father saw in them, p. 26. The contention between S. Peter and S. Paul is interpreted in a different way from what it is by the Fathers, p. 26. An argument is drawn from the word 'send,' which would be equally fatal to the superiority of S. Paul over the Church at Antioch, who 'sent' him, and which forgets that amongst the 'senders' was Peter himself, and that a body is often said to send, or commission, its head to represent itself; whilst even an uncertain reading, different from that which is used by Tertullian, Chrysostom, Ambrose, Augustine, Theodoret, Jerome, Irenæus, Gregory of Nyssa, is made to do duty as an argument, without reference to the reasons for which, if the reading were certain, the order of names might thus be placed ; and all this is called 'Holy Scripture as to Roman claims' ! Truly, when one so good, so justly venerated, as the author of the 'Roman Question,' can bring himself to deal with Holy Scripture and the Church's interpretation of it in this way, we may well emphasise the difficulties of applying the Rule of S. Vincent de Lerins, apart from the living voice of the Church.

And you yourself dispose very summarily of the traditional interpretation of this passage. You are content to say that 'Launoy, the learned French divine, is quoted as computing "that . . . seventeen fathers only understand that He (our Lord) founded the Church on S. Peter," and that a "candid" reader will see that S. Chrysostom and S. Augustine consider the matter of no very great importance.' Now who is this Launoy, this 'learned French divine,' whose investigations are given as sufficient to absolve others from going to the Fathers first-hand? Launoy was a writer of most equivocal reputation. Almost all his books were placed on the Index. He was committed to various errors on predestination and grace, besides his opposition to the Papacy. His Monday conferences became such a hotbed of democratic and anarchical theories that they were closed by royal order. He is accused of altering writers in quoting them with 'an incredible shamelessness.' He was an adherent of Richer, who, however, retracted his erroneous teaching concerning the succession of S. Peter (which ought to have been mentioned in the 'Roman Question,' p. 33). What authority, therefore, can a man like Launoy be on such a question as this? He is certainly wrong in this particular instance; for not seventeen of the Fathers, as Launoy says, but upwards of thirty in the first five centuries, tell us that the rock or foundation on which Christ built His Church was Peter.

Perhaps Launoy does what some Anglican writers do, viz. fix a date, arbitrarily chosen, beyond which the Church is no longer to be considered as one whole, but as a congeries of fragments, and then choose which fragment suits them best. Some take the first four centuries, and any one who lived after A.D. 401 can no longer be called a Father. The Church, it is said, was then pure; after that it is only to be discovered in a few favourite writers, and in some only of their writings. Only those who lived before S. Vincent de Lerins can be considered, according to some, to be sufficiently Primitive; for they see plainly that there is a difficulty about admitting the first six centuries to be pure and Primitive in their general deliverances on the subject of the Papacy. In fact, the difficulty of saying what is Primitive and what is not is really fatal to the idea that we can do without the living voice of the Church.

Your own little book seems to me quite the ablest defence of the Anglican position that has appeared, considering the small compass within which the subject is compressed. There is nothing in it that can be called harsh, with one exception (which I shall point out afterwards); and nothing that is not worthy of a scholar working at immense materials under the enormous disadvantage of all the while refusing the one key which would make that work simple and effective—I mean the guidance of the See of S. Peter. But it labours under the same difficulty of drawing an arbitrary limit as to the witnesses allowed to be competent. You turn out of court such a Saint as Leo the Great, and those who agreed with him! you speak of the Fathers 'excepting those of the Papal school in and after the fifth century'! And we find elsewhere that S. Leo is the 'Father' of this Papal school.

But I would ask in all earnestness: If S. Leo, and those who taught as he did, sinned against the Vincentian rule; if they are to be considered only a 'school of thought,' where are we to find the main volume of the Church's tradition? How are we to get at the 'always, everywhere, and by all' which is to be the rule of our faith?

This 'Papal school,' of which you speak, has, at any rate, held its ground for 1,400 years; it is a 'school' with which for at least centuries the course of Christianity was identified; it is a 'school' which numbers amongst its adherents at this hour upwards of 1,200 bishops, besides a galaxy of theologians, scholars, not a few scientists, innumerable saintly souls in every sphere of life; to which, in its present august representative, nearly the whole world has paid its respects in the shape of gifts, which it must have cost upwards of 40,000*l.* to house, and arrange, and exhibit; it is a 'school' which has its missionaries in every quarter of the globe, and has had its martyrs within our own generation; a 'school' which, *at the era of the English Reformation*, had its Saints, such as S. John of God, S. Camillus de Lellis, S. Philip Neri, S. Ignatius of Loyola, S. Francis Xavier, S. Jerome Emilian, S. Charles Borromeo, S. Peter of Alcantara, S. Thomas of Villanuova, S. Francis Borgia, S. Aloysius Gonzaga, S. John of the Cross, S. Francis of Sales, S. Jane of France, S. Catharine of Siena, S. Jane Frances of Chantal, and S. Teresa of Spain—heroes and heroines, some of them not only conspicuous for extraordinary holiness of life, but illustrious also for having created such communities as the Society of Jesus, the Oratorians, the Oblates, the Theatines, the barefooted Carmelites, the Order of the Pious Schools, the Fatebenefratelli, and the congregations for special aid to the dying! Such was the outburst of sanctity in the very century in which men like Barlow, and others, whose characters no one respects, were separating themselves from the rest of the Catholic world, and starting a ministry which succeeded in stamping out from England both the idea of the Sacrifice of the Altar and the sacrifice of the celibate life! It is a 'school,' this Papal school, which in the following century produced a S. Vincent de Paul, S. Rose of Lima, S. Mary Magdalen of Pazzi, and others too numerous to mention, whose very names are unknown to your English hagiography; besides, in that same sixteenth century, our own B. Fisher and Thomas More. It is a 'school' which has had signs and wonders following them that believe it during the last few centuries, as all along the Church's history; in truth, if it were indeed originated by S. Leo, it has fallen to the lot of that 'real saint' (as you justly call him) to originate something more powerful, and holy, and universal, and permanent than did S. Peter, or S. Paul, or S. John. Nay, I might go further—for, indeed, it is the simple truth—that if this 'Papal school,' as you call it, is not the Church of Christ, but only a portion weighted with a claim which is monstrous blasphemy if it is not vital truth—then, indeed, the gates of hell have prevailed against the Church which Christ built, and the promises are of none effect.

For myself, I believe in GOD the Father Almighty, and in Jesus Christ, His only Son, and in the Holy Catholic Church—which I could not do if His Fatherly Providence had failed the Church for 1,400 years, and one man had originated a 'school,' which has taken the place of the Church which the Son built for the home of believers, and if the Catholic Church had to be sought as some invisible thing underneath an outward universal lie, with an inward unity which never expressed itself on this fundamental question with the authority of an outward living voice.

No, indeed; I prefer to be with S. Leo in my understanding of the centuries that preceded him. And this the more, since

THE COUNCIL OF CHALCEDON ADOPTED S. LEO'S ESTIMATE OF HIS OFFICIAL RELATIONSHIP TOWARDS THE WHOLE CHURCH.

S. Leo taught that S. Peter was constituted by our Lord the Head of the Apostolic College, and that he, as successor of S. Peter in the See of Rome, was invested with the responsibilities of the supreme government of the Church. That supremacy could not, of course, be exercised with the same facilities and frequency as in after times, when the means of intercommunication increased, but directly the Church appeared before the world with her organised life of Patriarchal and Metropolitical jurisdiction, and Conciliar action, all was seen to have flowed from that Chief of the Apostles, to whom the keys were given. His action in the regions round Rome became the accepted norm of the Church's action elsewhere—accepted as such by the Council of Nicæa. Three Patriarchates emerge to view, each of them tracing their succession of Bishops to S. Peter, and the Prince of these Patriarchs is the occupant of the See of Rome. No other Apostle was permitted to leave behind him an Episcopal succession save Peter only. 'For who does not know,' asks 'S. Gregory the Great,' 'that the Holy Church has been established on the solidity of the Prince of the Apostles, who expressed in his name the firmness, being called Peter from the Rock; to whom the Truth said, "I will give to thee the keys of the Kingdom of Heaven"? and again, "Thou, when thou art converted, confirm thy brethren;" and a third time, "Simon, son of Jona, lovest thou Me? Feed My sheep." And thus, though there be many Apostles, yet, in virtue of its very principate, only the See of the Prince of the Apostles, which is the See of one in three places, received supreme

Rome.

Alexandria.

Antioch.

authority. For he made that See sovereign, which he honoured by resting in it, and there ending the present life. He distinguished the See to which he sent his disciple, the Evangelist. He strengthened that in which he sat himself for seven years, though he was to leave it.'

Peter, says S. Leo, 'was watered with streams so copious from the very Fountain of all graces, that while nothing has passed to others without his participation, yet he received many special privileges of his own. . . . Out of the whole world Peter alone is chosen to preside over the calling of the Gentiles, and over all the Apostles, and the collected Fathers of the Church; so that, though there be among the people of GOD many priests and many shepherds, yet Peter rules all by immediate commission, whom Christ also rules by sovereign power. Beloved, it is a great and wonderful participation of His own power, which the Divine condescendance gave to this man: and if He willed that other rulers should enjoy aught together with him, yet never did He give, save through him, what He denied not to others.' And again, '"Thou art Peter:" that is, whilst I am the immutable rock—I, the Corner Stone who make both one; I, the Foundation beside which no one can lay another—yet thou also art a Rock, because by My virtue thou art firmly planted, so that whatever is peculiar to Me by power, is to thee by participation common with Me.' And in speaking of the keys the Saint says: 'The privilege of this power did indeed pass on to the other Apostles, and the order of this decree spread out to all the rulers of the Church, but not without purpose. What is intended for all is put into the hands of one. For therefore is this entrusted to Peter singularly, because all the rulers of the Church are invested with the figure of Peter.' And then he speaks of himself sitting in the seat of S. Peter.

Such is the doctrine of the great S. Leo, whose teaching on the Incarnation at a most critical hour in the Church's life was accepted by an Œcumenical Council, his volume placed only second to Holy Scripture itself, and of whose clear, full enunciation of the revealed truth concerning that fundamental article of our faith the same Council said, 'Peter hath spoken by Leo.'

Now, before considering how the Council of Chalcedon accepted S. Leo's estimate of his relationship to the whole Church as S. Peter's successor, as given above in an address to the assembled Bishops of all Italy, let us notice this important point. It was no new teaching. S. Leo had been preceded, to speak of no others, by S. Boniface I., who had given the following historical summary of what had happened with regard to his own See of Rome in the fourth century, himself writing in the beginning of the fifth. Such an account must be considered of the highest value. He is speaking of the fact, as he considered it, that the care of the Universal Church had been laid upon Peter by our Lord, and that the Bishops of Rome had succeeded to that care; and he proceeds: 'We must prove by instances that the greatest Eastern Churches, in important matters, which required greater discussion, have always consulted the Roman See, and, as often as need arose, asked its help. Athanasius and Peter, of holy memory, Bishops of the Church of Alexandria, asked the help of this See. When the Church of Antioch had been in trouble a long time, so that there was continual passing to and fro for this, first under Meletius, afterwards under Flavian, it is notorious that the Apostolic See was consulted. By whose authority, after many things done by our Church, every one knows that Flavian received the grace of communion, which he had gone without for ever had not writings gone from hence respecting it. The Emperor

Theodosius, of merciful memory, considering the ordination of Nestorius to want ratification, because it was not according to our rule, sent an embassy of Councillors and Bishops, and solicited a letter of communion to be regularly despatched to him from the Roman See, to confirm his Episcopate. A short time since, under my predecessor Innocent, of blessed memory, the Pontiffs of the Eastern Churches, grieving at their severance *from the Communion of blessed Peter*, asked by their Legates for reconciliation, as your charity remembers.'

And so the Greek historian Sozomen: 'The Bishop of the Romans, having inquired into the accusation against each' (S. Athanasius, Paul, Bishop of Constantinople, Marcellus of Ancyra, and Asclepas of Gaza), 'when he found them all agreeing with the doctrine of the Nicene Synod, admitted them to communion as agreeing with him. And inasmuch as the care of all belonged to him on account of the rank of his See, he restored to each his Church.'

Here was tradition, *and* the living voice to decide who was in accord with tradition and who was not.

Thus S. Boniface answers for the century that preceded him; whilst Innocent speaks of the 'Apostolic See, unto which, as unto the head of the Churches, reference was made,' and refers the authority of his See to S. Peter, as accepted by the Synod of Nicæa; and S. Xystus III. tells John of Antioch that 'the blessed Peter, in his successors, has delivered that which he received;' and S. Celestine speaks of himself as 'we, on whom, in the holy Apostle Peter, Christ conferred the necessity of being concerned as regards all, when He gave him the keys of opening and shutting;' and S. Zosimus had traced the authority of the Apostolic See to the tradition of the Fathers, interpreting thus the promise of our Lord to S. Peter.

Marginal notes: Ep. 17, ad Rufum. Ep. 6, ad S. Joan. Ep. 3. Perigen. et Episc. per Illyr.

And these are all the Popes who preceded S. Leo in the fifth century : S. Innocent, S. Zosimus, S. Boniface, S. Celestine, S. Sixtus III. ; and thus the 'Papal School,' as you call it, of the fifth century, of which you call S. Leo the father, had for its adherents all the previous heads of that Church of the Romans to which, said S. Cyprian, 'faithlessness can have no access.' And yet all these Saints erred on such a fundamental point as the Charter of the Christian Church ! and we may revise their history in this nineteenth century ! and we may accuse Saints of 'unscrupulousness,' as you accuse the glorious Leo, whom till now history has called 'the Great' ! Is this the nineteenth century notion of sanctity ? Is it history at all ?

This was not the attitude of the Council of Chalcedon towards S. Leo. You call its letter to him 'complimentary ;' and my friend the Rev. Nehemiah Goreh, formerly one of the Cowley Fathers, calls it 'adulatory.' Well, better 'compliment' than depreciate a Saint, and accuse him of unscrupulousness in the most fundamental acts of his life. Better address him with 'adulation' than with condemnation. Certainly, however, the Eastern Bishops of the following century did not take the public utterances of the Council, in presence of S. Leo's assertions, as compliments or adulation, but as solemn, serious affirmations, intimately affecting their own position as Bishops, and expressing Divine truth. And surely the history of the Council, as a whole, does not admit of such a contention as that its members meant nothing but flattery when they addressed S. Leo as having had the guardianship of the Vine entrusted to him by our Saviour.

For it was after they had listened, without a word of protest, to S. Leo's description of his Divinely constituted authority, as read to the whole Council by his Legates :

'Leo, most holy and blessed Archbishop of great and elder Rome, by us, and by the holy Council, together with the blessed Apostle Peter, *who is the rock and ground of the Catholic Church,* and the foundation of the right faith, hath stripped him' (*i.e.* the Patriarch of Alexandria) 'as well of the rank of Bishop, as also hath severed him from all sacerdotal ministry'—it was *after this* that the Council solemnly addressed S. Leo as having been 'entrusted by our Saviour with the guardianship of the Vine.'

So that this Council accepted the relationship between S. Peter and S. Leo asserted by the Legates, and hears the Apostle called, without amazement and without protest, 'the rock and ground of the Catholic Church;' and after all S. Leo's authoritative action through his Legates, and after the position of head of the Church had been assigned to him by the Emperor, it approaches him with the solemn declaration that, whilst the holy, murdered Archbishop of Constantinople is a 'plant of the Vine,' *he*, on the contrary, is 'the very person entrusted by the Saviour with the guardianship of the Vine.'

Cf. Allies, Per Crucem, &c.

Now, to take first the acceptance of the expression that S. Peter is the rock or foundation of the Church (of course, under our Lord), it must be remembered that it was an expression which already had a history. It cannot be said to have been used as some of the Fathers use expressions concerning the Holy Trinity and the Incarnation in early times, without any consciousness of their being liable to distortion. The expression had already been used as the ground of important decrees, and been made the starting-point of far-reaching lines of conduct by previous Popes, and even by S. Leo himself. It had a context, and one that laid on the Fathers of the Council the obligation of not adding to the cumulative weight of such a long line of utterances. For it is precisely in its cumulative power that the evidence for the particular meaning of the expression lies. It is part of a body of proof. It is not like an occasional expression used by S. Chrysostom about S. Paul, to whom he had such a special devotion. These had no history before them, and have had none after them. They are in keeping, and that is all, with the high position assigned to S. Paul by Papal utterances of to-day, placing him, in some sense, above the Twelve (saving only S. Peter), as being the Apostle of the uncircumcision, S. Peter's coadjutor in establishing the Church in Rome, and being venerated as one of the twin Patrons of the Holy See. But to admit such an expression as the rock in application to S. Peter was to set its seal on a long line of teaching. And then to address S. Leo as the very person entrusted by our Saviour with the guardianship of the Vine, after all that he had done and said previously to the Council and, by his Legates, in the Council, would be, if adulation or compliment, base and unworthy to the last degree, and is indeed to a Catholic mind wholly unimaginable. They must have been aware that they were dealing with part of the deposit of truth, or favouring a fundamental heresy.

And so it is this declaration on the part of the Council that ought, in all reason, to govern our view of the 28th Canon. It is perhaps here that we are confronting most thoroughly the only logical basis of Anglicanism. For Anglicans it is an absolute necessity to interpret the 28th Canon as giving the full account and the entire reason of the Primacy of the Bishop of Rome. Consequently it is a universal assumption, in which you yourself share, that the 28th Canon gives the view of the Council of Chalcedon as to the *only* reason why Rome should take precedence of Constantinople, Alexandria, and Antioch. That reason is to be found, according to Anglicans, in the mere fact that Rome was the Imperial city, and that the Bishop of Rome obtained a natural precedency, confirmed to him, if not bestowed upon him, by the Councils of the Church. His precedency, according to Anglican teaching, can have no proper connection with any relationship to S. Peter.

But, first, I would ask this: is it not at least intelligible that the desire of the Council (or rather the Bishops of the Council after the Council had closed) to raise Constantinople above the Sees of Alexandria and Antioch, on the ground that it was new Rome, and that the Fathers of a previous Council had sanctioned the 'prerogatives' of the throne of the elder Rome, because that city ruled—is it not, I say, at least intelligible that all this had to do with the patriarchal incidents of the See of Rome, and did not touch the question of its relationship to S. Peter, and the pastoral commission given to him? Constantinople, they pleaded, should be the second Patriarchate, as Rome was the first; but there was something more than being a Patriarch, and with this they did not pretend to deal. They expressly say in their synodical letter to Leo, after speaking of him as 'the constituted interpreter to all of blessed Peter,' as 'the head of the members,' including themselves in the members, as 'the person entrusted by our Saviour with the guardianship of the Vine,' that they are persuaded that he will 'extend his wonted care to the Church of Constantinople, and enlighten it with his Apostolic ray.' 'Honour, then, we pray you, our judgment, with your decree, that as we have been united to our Head in agreeing upon what was right, so the Head, too' (*i.e.* you, S. Leo), 'may confirm the becoming act of the children.'

All these Bishops were, according to their own

expression; the children of the Holy Father, the occupant of the See of Rome! What is this but the teaching of the Church of Rome at this hour at its very core?

And so the Archbishop of Constantinople was, according to their desire, to be the Patriarch, *with Rome's permission*, next in honour to Rome; but S. Leo was still to extend his 'wonted care' to that Patriarchate. There was, then, something over and above the dignity of Patriarch belonging to the Bishop of Rome, and this was acknowledged, not given, by the Council; just as at Nice no confirmation was given to the usage of the Church of Rome; but, on the contrary, the usage of Alexandria was confirmed, because it had the authority of Rome. And, curiously enough, in this very Council a different word is used of Rome ($\pi\rho\omega\tau\epsilon\iota\alpha$), when speaking of her deposing the Patriarch of Alexandria, from that which is used ($\pi\rho\epsilon\sigma\beta\epsilon\iota\alpha$) when speaking of the dignity of which Constantinople might bear the image, and almost possess the equivalent.

This, then, is at least intelligible—that the Council, even in their abortive Canon, repudiated as it was by S. Leo, did not touch on that relationship of the Pope to the rest of the Church, which flowed to him as successor of S. Peter, but only a certain dignity and rank which could be all but possessed by other Sees—the rank of Patriarch.

But what is not intelligible is that the Council should use or admit terms, well known and well defined already by the person to whom they were applied, and claimed as an inalienable possession by all his predecessors in that century, to go no further should use or admit them in some entirely different sense from that in which they had been already used, in the very Council itself, without a word to intimate the different usage. The

Canon could not, even on the supposition that it meant what Anglicans imagine it to mean, be considered sufficient to counteract the effect of their use or admission of such solemn terms as the rock, applied to S. Peter, and the guardian of the Vine, to S. Leo; for similar Canons had had no such effect. No Pope, no Emperor, had read the previous Canons of the Council of Constantinople or of Nice as interfering with the claim made by the Popes, and admitted by so many Saints, as to a special relationship between the Bishop of Rome and the Apostle S. Peter, and a special relationship between that Apostle and the Divine Head of the Church. To pass over such expressions, then, as S. Leo used of himself through his Legates, and to use such expressions as the guardian of the Vine and head of the Bishops, of the saintly Bishop of Rome, would have been a wrong done to the Church; it would have been using on a most solemn occasion, in most public manner, expressions which must in the necessity of the case inflict an irreparable injury on the faith, unless they were part of the deposit of truth. They could not be ignorant of their significance. Consider only what had taken place during the previous twenty years or so.

The Papal Legate (Philip) had uttered these plain statements in the Œcumenical Council at Ephesus :—

'We return thanks to the holy and venerable Council, that the letters of our holy Pope having been read to you, you have joined yourselves as holy members to a holy head. For your Blessedness is not ignorant that the blessed Apostle Peter is the head of the whole faith, and of the Apostles likewise.'

Here is a point-blank contradiction of the position assumed by yourself and by the venerable author of the 'Roman Question.'

But further: after hearing the acts against Nestorius

read, the Legate says: 'It is doubtful to no one, but rather *known to all ages*, that holy and most blessed Peter, *prince and head of the Apostles*, pillar of the faith, and *foundation* of the Catholic Church, received from our Lord Jesus Christ, viour and Redeemer of the human race, the keys of the Kingdom of Heaven, and that the power of loosing and binding sins was given to him, *who to this very time and for ever lives and exercises judgment in his successors.* And so our most blessed Pope Celestine, the Bishop his successor in due order, and holding his place, has sent to this holy Council us to represent him.'

Now here, again, is the most emphatic point-blank contradiction conceivable of your own position and that of the whole Anglican Communion. Words could not be plainer. If this claim is accepted in an Œcumenical Council, logic, honesty, and loyalty to our Divine Lord demand that we should either accept the entire Protestant basis of repudiating the Œcumenical Councils, or that we should acknowledge in the Holy See, in the Bishop of Rome, the one supreme authority, representative of our Lord, left by Him here on earth.

Was this tremendous claim, this *nomen blasphemiæ*, or vital truth, repudiated or taken as a matter of course? *Everything for an Anglican turns upon this.*

Let us see. What followed? S. Cyril was president, by special commission from S. Celestine the Pope. And S. Cyril having heard this plain statement of the 'Apostolic organisation of the Church,' moved, notwithstanding, that he and the other Legates, 'since they had fulfilled what was ordered them' by Pope S. Celestine, should set their hands to the deposition of Nestorius; 'and the holy Council said: Inasmuch as Arcadius and Projectus, Legates, and Philip, Presbyter and Legate of the Apostolic See, have said *what is fitting*,' although they had said it with the accompaniment we have quoted, 'it follows that they should also subscribe and confirm the acts.'

And it was *after all this*—after the Church had had twenty years to consider matters—that the Fathers of the Council of Chalcedon listened to the assertion that the Apostle Peter is 'the rock and ground of the Catholic Church, and the foundation of the right faith,' and that they addressed S. Leo as 'entrusted by the Saviour with the guardianship of the Vine.'

It was after the Empress Galla Placidia had written to her son, the Emperor Theodosius, urging him to direct that the matter of Flavian 'be transferred to the judgment of a Council and the Apostolic See, in which he who was first worthy to receive the heavenly keys ordained the Princedom of the Episcopate.'

It was after the Emperor Valentinian had issued an edict with the following terms : 'Since, therefore, the *merit of S. Peter*, who is the chief of the Episcopal coronet, and the dignity of the Roman city, moreover the authority of a sacred Synod, have made firm the Primacy of the Apostolic See,' &c. ; where we see two sources of dignity mentioned—the merit of S. Peter, whose successor the Bishop of Rome was acknowledged to be, and the dignity of the place as the Imperial residence —one divine, the other human ; that is to say, one pointing to an immediate commission from the Lord, in short, to the scene at Cæsarea Philippi, the other to the concurrence of Providential ordering in the course of the world.

It was after all this, when the doctrine of the authority belonging to the occupant of the See of Rome as the successor of S. Peter was expressing itself so frequently and so uniformly, and when this vital matter had come to the front of the Church's teaching—when, owing to the centrifugal forces in the Church, through its extension, having increased, the centripetal force naturally came into greater play, and the headship became more conspicuous as the body emerged from the confusing incidents of persecution it was at such a crisis in the Church's life that an Œcumenical Council solemnly, publicly, in a studied letter, addresses the Bishop of Rome, and describes his official position in the Church of GOD as that of 'the very person entrusted by our Saviour with the guardianship of the Vine.'

Cf. Allies, Per Crucem, &c.

It is surely quite impossible to explain the fact, which you admit, that S. Cyril of Alexandria in some sense recognised 'the universal Pastorate of the Roman Bishop' (p. 46) by attributing his witness not to conviction of the truth, but to his fear of the rising claim of Constantinople,' *and* to his being 'under circumstances when interest put strong pressure on belief.' S. Cyril acted with the whole Council. Surely it is idle to explain away the witness of other Bishops on a matter of such concern by calling them 'individual Oriental Bishops, especially appellants to Rome, who wished to say what was pleasant' (p. 46). Surely it is not enough to urge that 'Oriental writers were much given to verbose compliments in addressing distinguished people,' and to insinuate that that solemn public utterance of the Fathers of Chalcedon, in view of all the claims that had been made by Saints, in the face of contemporaneous history, endorsed as it was by S. Cyril, was 'the language of rhetoric and compliment.'

And surely the Canon which they proposed could never have been intended to contradict, by a side wind, terms used in the very letter which recommended it to S. Leo's notice. Surely, too, if not merely the Patriarchal position of the Bishop of Rome, but his Primacy over the whole Church, had been attacked by the Canon,

rested as that Primacy was on his successorship to
S. Peter, S. Leo, of all men, would never have shrunk
from reiterating the statement, which Popes before him,
and Emperors, and Patriarchs had made, that his supremacy, with all its fearful responsibilities and burdens, was
due to the scenes at Cæsarea Philippi and the Sea of
Tiberias, and therefore of Divine origin.

But, further, there is one point which I do not find
noticed in your account of this matter, and which is
positively misrepresented by the author of the 'Roman
Question.' He makes the strange statement that 'the
Fathers of that Council (six hundred and thirty Bishops)
did not feel that any superiority of government belonged
to the Roman See on that account'—*i.e.* because it was the
chair of Peter, 'for they distinctly refused to accede to
Leo's demands, and against the Roman Legates decided
on giving the Patriarchal dignity to Constantinople,
which was the point to which the Pope's contention
referred' (p. 32). It is difficult to know how to deal
with a statement like this. What were 'Leo's demands'?
He had demanded the deposition of Dioscorus, and had
been obeyed. In the absence of his Legates, it was proposed that Constantinople should be raised above Alexandria and Antioch, and after the Legates refused their
assent, the Bishops approached S. Leo with their petition
that he would, as their 'head,' confirm their proposal.
It was not a demand on S. Leo's part at all. He simply
refused. And what happened? Why, that the proposed
Canon did not win its way to a place in the collection of
the Church's Canons for near four hundred years. It
did not obtain the force of law. It would have been a
pure misfortune for the Church if it had. It was a misfortune when it did, in the time of the miserable Photius.
The fact is that the attempt to pass the 28th Canon
represented mere earthly ambition. It was the sin of

pride which set it going, and the Erastianism of the East that nearly brought it to a successful issue. It was through Imperial influence that the Bishops were led to make the attempt. It was the high-water mark of an evil influence in the Church. It was the result of that tendency on the part of the Bishops to be the tools of an Emperor which marred their witness for GOD on the mystery of the Incarnation, and led to their ruin. Tradition was against the Bishops. They were setting at naught the Council of Nicæa. Where was the living voice to decide the bent of tradition? It was found in Leo. To Leo we owe it that the old Patriarchal Sees of Alexandria and Antioch did not succumb, so soon as they would otherwise have done, to the growing ambition of Constantinople. Sitting on the throne of S. Peter, he simply refused his consent to the Canon. He could not quell the carnal pride of New Rome; but the Canon failed at once to be part of the Church's law. He refused his consent on the ground of that ecclesiastical position of his, with its tremendous responsibilities, which placed him, as the Fathers of the Council stated, above all Patriarchs and all Councils. He tells the Empress, to whom he writes, that he does so by virtue of the prerogatives of his See. 'What has been obtained from the Bishops, disregarding the Nicene Council, we annul by the authority of the Apostle S. Peter.' Ep. cv.

Thus, as at a most critical moment of her existence he had saved the Church from having a Council forced upon her as Œcumenical, which tampered with the doctrine of the Incarnation, so now he saved the Church, for we know not how long, from being submerged by the carnal pride of the Imperial slaves at Constantinople, the Bishops of that unfortunate See.

And it is on this Canon, this summary of earthly ambition, this attempt at assisting an Emperor to further his designs of lowering the influence of Alexandria and Antioch—this Canon, which for centuries was refused entrance into the authorised list of the Church's Canons, owing to the courageous determination of the Roman Pontiff, to the pure high faith of the Saint who occupied the See of S. Peter and won the name of 'great'—on this Canon, which represented a tendency that had grown, as S. Leo pointed out, through the 'connivance' of seventy years, and was destined to be the ruin of the See of Constantinople—it is, I say, on this Canon that you rely to overthrow the statements of the Council to the effect that the Church was built on Peter, and that the occupant of the See of Rome inherits, as Peter's successor, the 'Principate of the Apostolate' (Aug.).

The Canon itself did not really touch the question of the Primacy of Rome, but only alluded to its Patriarchal jurisdiction: it was aimed simply at moving Alexandria and Antioch down, and it failed in coming to the birth, through the determination of the Saint, who could face Bishops, carried away for the moment by Imperial pressure, as boldly as he was soon to face an adversary, all but at his doors, the 'Scourge of GOD.' Attila was on his way to Rome, and was to be confronted by the saintly, lion-hearted Bishop, and the city so far saved. It required a higher courage to resist the proposed 28th Canon: but S. Leo was equal to both.

I conclude, then, that a Universal Pastorate over the Church was recognised, at the Council of Chalcedon, as belonging to the successor of S. Peter, given to him and his successors by our risen Lord; and that the volume of tradition which the Fathers of Chalcedon accepted, and expressed and swelled by their utterances and action in the Council, should determine the meaning of their abortive Canon, and not *vice versâ*; that the proposed Canon did not refer to the Primacy over the Church, but to the Patriarchal position of the Bishop of Rome, the Primacy being unquestioned; and that the Canon, even so, did not establish its footing in the Church's law at that time, or for centuries afterwards. The suggestion was obtained from the Bishops through Imperial influences, and was repudiated by Leo. 'What has been obtained from the Bishops, disregarding the Nicene Council, we annul by the authority of the Apostle S. Peter.'

Thus the witness of the fifth century is clear as to the Church's belief that our Lord commissioned S. Peter and his successors to feed and shepherd His sheep. And this witness is given universally as having been the constant tradition of the Church. And so Bishop Fisher and blessed Thomas More died for a truth which is contained in Holy Scripture as interpreted by the early Church. For the witness of the fifth century includes that of the fourth. There is no consciousness of any novelty in the thought that to S. Peter were given the keys in a peculiar, pre-eminent way, and that his was the pre-eminent commission to govern the sheep of Christ's fold. Occasional remonstrances (and they were few indeed) against some particular exercise of that commission on the part of the Holy See prove nothing at all against the universal belief that peculiar authority to govern was resident in the 'Successor of the Fisherman,' as S. Jerome called the Bishop of Rome. How, then, can the Anglican Church defend herself against the charge of sinning against the Vincentian rule? If the volume of tradition be taken as a whole for the first thousand years of the Church's life, who can doubt which way that volume speaks? If by an arbitrary assumption (and what assumption can be more arbitrary?) we limit the true, pure life of the Church to the first four centuries, still we have the voice of the fifth century deciding that her predecessor, the fourth, was, like herself, a witness for the inborn authority of S. Peter's See. And surely she could look into the fourth with better sight than we can in the nineteenth century. When the Calvinist ministers assumed that they knew the primitive Church better than the intervening centuries did, S. Francis de Sales remarks that the early Church must have had a long speaking-tube indeed to make itself audible to Luther across the centuries without those centuries hearing what it said. And surely there is something bordering on the absurd in the supposition that we know better than the fifth century what was the teaching of the fourth.

And here I will add a word as to the *consentient witness of the Popes* to the responsibility laid upon them. If this office of Universal Teacher and head of the Church be divine, we should expect that those who held it would be made aware of its Divine institution. We can hardly suppose the existence of a Priesthood unconscious of itself, unaware of its sacerdotal powers for any length of time. It would be a Priesthood given up to a perpetual neglect of its very purpose in life. And we should find it difficult indeed to imagine a headship ordained by our Lord over His Church without its possessors being conscious of their authority and responsibilities. On the other hand, the sense of its possession by men of varied character, great ability, and recognised piety would of itself go far to make us feel that it could hardly be an untruth.

Now we have a long series of decretal letters written by the Popes from the fourth century onwards; and from the first letter extant down to the last, all along the ages, these letters bear the same stamp, witness to the same consciousness of the same responsibility on the part of the writers towards the whole Church, as occasion demanded its fulfilment. The author of the 'Throne of the Fisherman,' in that invaluable work, cites a remark made by the learned editor of these letters. It is this: 'Of so many Pontiffs famous for doctrine and sanctity, whom even to suspect of claiming what did not belong to them would be the height of rashness, not a single one can be found who did not believe that the prerogative had been granted to him or to his Church; while among all the Churches founded by the other Apostles or their successors, no single one can be found who ventured to call himself the head of the whole Church. Either the Popes claimed what was their right, by the gift of Christ, or they were one and all impostors from the beginning.'

I see no way out of this dilemma. And I do not envy the man who can choose the latter alternative.

We have seen, then, what the Council of Chalcedon thought of the See of S. Peter, and how the Bishops ended with going to it as humble suitors to obtain its confirmation for their proposed Canon, and failed in their suit. They did not afterwards say, 'Then, if we cannot have the consent of the successor of S. Peter, we will do without it.' They did not think they could be good Catholics, and yet separate from that See. Only Dioscorus, the heretic, ventured on that. And yet all these Bishops were Eastern—that is to say, precisely those who would be least likely to defer to such a headship, if it were not grounded on Holy Scripture and immemorial tradition. In fact, wherever we look throughout the East we find the same faith as to the position of S. Peter and his successors in the See of Rome. Let us take S. Chrysostom as a doctor, Antioch as a See, Armenia as a country, and the East in general as it expressed itself up to the time of the great schism.

I shall show, then, I hope, that beyond controversy

S. CHRYSOSTOM DISTINCTLY TAUGHT THE SUPREMACY OF S. PETER.

But first I feel compelled to touch on a personal matter. It was your reference to my dealing with S. Chrysostom that led me to write this letter to you. S. Chrysostom has been my favourite Father throughout life. I read him eagerly within the walls of my college as an undergraduate. It always seemed to me that in S. Chrysostom you have the highest flights of eloquence under the complete control of a mind full of dogmatic precision. There is a fascination to the ear in the very run of his Greek, but his eloquence is always full of some truth to which it is strictly subordinate. What can you find in Cicero, even in Demosthenes, to equal in point of human eloquence the Saint's sermons on the Ascension? Where in all secular literature will you find any description of any scene more enthralling than his picture in his sermon at Antioch of the gradual approach of the awful pageant of the Last Day? Yet his highest flights are guided and chastened by the precision of a theologian. He is at once orator and doctor of the Church. I always indeed felt that he spoke of S. Peter in a singular way, but I comforted myself with the delusion that he spoke of S. Paul in similar terms. But there was one portion of S. Chrysostom's writings whose acquaintance I made only a few years ago, and unfortunately through a translation. And I was misled by this translation. It was the discovery of this that gave me the first decided shock, of late, as to my position as an Anglican. S. Chrysostom, I saw, was really against us. The perusal of a letter by a very eminent Anglican divine, containing what I found to be some certainly unhistorical statements, made me feel that further investigation was a duty. Up to the last I thought something would come to light to turn the scale, until the day came when I saw that we were in schism. Orders or no orders was not the question; everything must hang on jurisdiction. And the day came when I felt I could no longer approach an Anglican altar. It would be a deliberate act of schism on my part to exercise orders (if I possessed them) apart from the See of S. Peter.

> O gift of gifts ! O gift of faith !
>   My God, how can it be
> That Thou, who art discerning love,
>   Shouldst give that gift to me ?
>   . . . . there was a day
> The Spirit came and left that gift,
>   And went upon His way.

There are convictions too clear, too strong, to allow of one who believes in everlasting punishment dallying with them. I believed in that doctrine, and could not think of adding to all my other sins that of schism. If any one deserved that punishment it was myself. Yet here was my Lord calling me to receive forgiveness of sins in His Holy Catholic Church, and, if I persevere in His grace, in the end everlasting life. By His unutterable mercy I was not disobedient to the Heavenly Vision.

I say this much because it has been said that my conversion was too sudden to be true. I believe in sudden conversions ; but in this case it was not without preparatory convictions. And amongst these was the conviction that S. Chrysostom condemned a fundamental point of Anglican teaching, viz. the idea that all the Apostles were equal, except in natural qualities. The history of the Council of Chalcedon finished my intellectual conversion, but S. Chrysostom began it.

Until five years ago I had only read some parts of

S. Chrysostom on the Acts, and (as I have said) I then read his Commentary in a translation, and I quoted from it in a pamphlet addressed to Bishop Meurin (S. J.), of Bombay.

My pamphlet was well received, and is referred to by yourself in a note (p. 34), in which you say: 'On Bishop Meurin's inconceivably misleading and perverse quotation of the words "all the multitude held their peace" (Acts xv. 12), I need only refer to Father Rivington's pamphlet, "Verify your Quotations" (p. 4), and his apposite references to S. Chrysostom's Commentary.'

In that pamphlet I sum up my references to S. Chrysostom with saying: 'It is not possible to imagine a more point-blank contradiction than there is between your Lordship's comment on this passage in the Acts and that of S. Chrysostom.'

The Bishop had quoted the passage in Acts xv. 12, 'And all the multitude held their peace,' as an instance of the deference paid to S. Peter in the Council at Jerusalem, and had likened it to the present order of the Catholic Church, in which, when the successor of S. Peter speaks as such, on a matter of faith, the multitude hold their peace. I contended that the multitude held their peace only because some one else was going to speak, since the verse goes on, 'and listened to Barnabas and Paul.'

But I am persuaded that I was wrong. And what can one do better in this life than own that one was wrong on finding it out?

On this particular point I was misled by the translation in the Library of the Fathers, edited by Dr. Pusey.

That translation bears all the marks of the most painstaking accuracy; but it has, nevertheless, been guilty of a singular slip in this particular instance, the result of which is that it makes the passage tell in favour of the Anglican theory that S. James presided at the

Council of Jerusalem and was superior to S. Peter. I did the same, and brought S. Chrysostom to bear on Bishop Meurin.

My mistake was this:—According to the Oxford edition, S. Chrysostom says: 'No word speaks John here, no word the Apostles here, but held their peace, for James was invested with the chief rule.' This looks like a plain contradiction of Bishop Meurin's comment on the same passage.

But, in the original, the word 'James' does not occur. It is 'he;' and a word is used which may quite naturally refer to S. Peter, who has been the prominent subject of S. Chrysostom's previous sentence.

My 'apposite reference' therefore was simply a misquotation. There was no contradiction between Bishop Meurin and S. Chrysostom.

Bishop Meurin's quotation, so far from being what you call 'inconceivably misleading and perverse,' is, in point of fact, only a reproduction of S. Jerome's comment on the passage, who says: 'And all the multitude held their peace, and S. James the Apostle and all the ancients (*presbyteri*) together adopted his sentence'— *i.e.* S. Peter's. And he goes on to say that, besides this proof of S. Peter's authority, 'so high an authority was Peter, that Paul wrote in his letter, "Then three years after, I came to Jerusalem to see Peter and stayed with him fifteen days."'

I was, therefore, completely in the wrong. Indeed, I do not see how it is possible to mistake S. Chrysostom's belief in the supremacy of S. Peter as being identical with the teaching of Rome to-day.

I would ask any one who reads this letter seriously to weigh the following account of S. Chrysostom's teaching.

But, first, considering that S. Chrysostom was specially devoted to S. Paul, and that his eloquence always rises to its highest pitch when on the theme of S. Paul's glories, let us bear in mind what the teaching of the Church is on the relationship between SS. Peter and Paul. According to Catholic teaching, S. Paul holds quite a unique position, different from that of the twelve; and has a special relationship towards the See of Rome. 'Into that See,' according to Tertullian, those two Apostles 'poured all their doctrine' (a very important assertion, occurring as it does in such a very early writer); and there is a certain equality between S. Peter and S. Paul, not exclusive of a certain subordination and subjection on the part of S. Paul in the supreme power and government of the Universal Church, so that, as S. Chrysostom notices, as well as S. Jerome, S. Paul went up to 'see' (ἱστορῆσαι—not a mere friendly visit) Peter after his conversion. The division or work between them referred to preaching and the Apostolate only; nor was it so fixed as to prevent Peter from preaching to the Gentiles and Paul to the Jews. S. Paul's attitude at Antioch is explained by S. Chrysostom in perfect conformity with this : it is explained by the Twelve being equally Apostles, and does not touch the question of jurisdiction. At Rome itself, S. Paul together with S. Peter founded the Church; and he was Peter's coadjutor in the government of that Church, and exercised extraordinary episcopal power with the consent of Peter. Consequently the Roman Pontiffs call themselves the successors of SS. Peter and Paul. In convoking Councils, and indeed in every Papal Bull, they use the words, 'by the authority of the Apostles Peter and Paul, and by our own authority.' They are the Patron Saints of the See. Their likeness appears on the seals of the Pontiffs, and sometimes Peter, sometimes Paul, is on the right hand, to show the perfect equality between them, in respect of the Apostolate. A mystical reason is given for this, viz. that sometimes it is wished to note that the one Apostle was called by our Lord on earth, the other from Heaven. This is given by S. Thomas, with no feeling that it could be perverted as an argument against the Primacy of S. Peter. Indeed, in pictures, the right hand is not necessarily the side of honour, as it sometimes depends on whether you are supposed to look with, or at, the picture, and it has to be remembered that the right hand was not invariably connected with honour, even in assemblies; for in the Council of Chalcedon, Dioscorus sat on the right hand after his deposition, and the Legate of the Holy See on the left. Anyhow, the pictures of which the author of the 'Roman Question' speaks, in which SS. Peter and Paul are portrayed on a level, are in strict accordance with the present teaching of the Holy See, which places the two Apostles on a perfect level in respect of their Apostolate. The particular picture which the writer mentions as having led Mr. Hemans to renounce his faith, and which he himself calls 'remarkable,' witnesses to two things—first, that there was a certain equality between S. Peter and S. Paul; and secondly, that they were above the rest of the Twelve. In what respect S. Paul was above the rest it is easy to feel, though difficult to define; in what sense S. Peter was above them, according to S. Chrysostom, we shall presently plainly see. But there is a mosaic at Rome which affords a complete contradiction to the conclusion drawn by the author of the 'Roman Question' from this fresco in the catacomb of SS. Nero and Achilles. There is a mosaic inscription which is considered to be, beyond question, of the fifth century, written on the arch erected by the Empress Galla Placidia. It has, on the right-hand side, on which S. Paul is, a description of him, as the chosen vessel of honour for the Gentiles; whilst, on the left hand, *on the same level only*, stands S. Peter, with this inscription :—

> Voce Dei fis Petre Dei Petra culmen honoris
> Aulæ cœlestis splendor et homne decus.

'Homne' is the old form of 'omne.'

So that the Empress, in placing S. Peter on the left hand, and on the same level with S. Paul, did not consider that she was in any way detracting from S. Peter's singular prerogative, whom she calls 'the rock,' 'the highest point of honour.' So dangerous was it in Mr. Hemans to argue from a fresco. The Empress's mosaic inscription remains to this day, and forms part of the splendid new Church of S. Paul's, 'without the walls' of Rome—fit symbol of the unchanging faith of nineteen hundred years.

Now in S. Chrysostom we find S. Paul's glories sung in what you rightly call 'glowing language.' He is called, as every Apostle is, 'the teacher of the world,' as, indeed, is S. John the Baptist in the prologue to S. John's Gospel. He is called 'the voice of Christ,' as indeed every minister of the Word is. He is called 'the tongue of the world,' 'the founder of the Church,' as is every Apostle. He is called 'the wise architect,' and 'the common Father.' Expressions equally glorious are used, though more sparingly, of S. John. And on all this you remark, 'In what vast letters would these expressions be printed in Allnatt's "Cathedra Petri" did they but refer to S. Peter!'

But pardon me if I say that Mr. Allnatt could have produced similar expressions about S. Peter, only he would have considered them pointless. Why? Because *the* point is this : that the noteworthy expressions used of S. Peter are those that refer to his relationship to the other Apostles. And no similar ones to these are found relating to S. Paul. There are no expressions about S. Paul that in any way imply a superiority over the other *Apostles*; there are about S. Peter.

For instance, S. Chrysostom does not *simply* speak of S. Peter as being entrusted with the whole world, as he does of S. Paul, and as might be said of every Apostle; but he speaks of him as 'having become the *first of the Apostles*, and to have entrusted to him the whole world.' He is 'the Coryphæus of the Apostles;' and was 'declared to have power and to go beyond *all the rest of the Apostles*;' he is 'the head of the Apostles, the first in the Church;' he is '*that unbroken rock, that immovable foundation*, the great Apostle, the first of the disciples.' Christ put into his hands 'the presidency of the Universal Church.' 'Great,' says S. Chrysostom again, 'was God's consideration towards this city (Antioch), as He manifested by deeds; inasmuch as Peter, who was set over the habitable world, into whose hands he put the keys of Heaven, to whom He entrusted to do, and to support, all things,' &c. So, again, Peter is '*the leader of the choir of the Apostles*, the mouth of the disciples, the pillar of the Church, the buttress of the faith, *the foundation of the confession*, the fisherman of the universe, he who raised up our race from the depths of error even unto Heaven' (with which compare the language used of our Lady by the Church). He was 'for this called Peter, because he had an unshaken and immovable faith.' The Saint speaks of Flavian as 'another Peter, who, having succeeded to his virtue, has also had allotted to him his chair. For this is also one privilege of our city, that it received in the beginning for its teacher *the chief of the Apostles*. For it was befitting that that city which before the rest of the world was crowned with the name of Christian, should receive as shepherd the first of the Apostles.' 'Not of Peter only, *the chief of those holy*

Hom. Adv. Judæos.

De Sacerdotio, l. ii. c. 2.

Hom. 3. De Pænit.

Hom. 3. De P.en.

In S. Ign. M.

Hom. in Paralyt.

Hom. 2 in Inscr.

F

men, but of all the Apostles absolutely was Paul the servant' in his own estimation; and 'he (*i.e.* S. Paul) who was thus disposed towards all, knew also *how great a precedence* it was necessary for Peter to enjoy; and he *reverenced him most of all men.* ... The whole world was looking to him (Paul); the solicitudes of the Churches throughout the earth rested on his soul; a thousand affairs engaged him every day; on all sides there surrounded him appointments, commands, corrections, counsels, exhortations, teachings, the administration of countless matters; and, putting aside all these, he went to Jerusalem, and there was no other motive for that journey but this, to see Peter. ... Thus he honoured him, and held him before all.'

<small>Hom. in faciem restit.</small>

S. Chrysostom's whole explanation of S. Paul's resistance to S. Peter at Antioch amounts to this: that S. Paul resisted his superior on a matter of conduct, of practical expediency, not on a matter of faith—a course which might be pursued by any Saint without lack of faith in the infallibility of the Church's Head, as defined by the Vatican decree.

S. Peter is, according to S. Chrysostom, 'the first of the Apostles, the foundation of the Church, *the leader of the choir of the disciples.*'

<small>Adv. eos qui scandal..</small>

You will notice that the expressions I place in *italics* are not such as the Saint uses of the Apostle S. Paul, nor of any other Apostle, though along with such expressions there are eulogies like those applied to S. Paul. S. Peter is 'that leader of the choir;' 'the leader of the choir, the mouth of the Apostles, *the head of that brotherhood He set over the world*, the foundation of the Church.' 'The first of all, and the Coryphæus is Peter.' In the very passage in which he interprets the Rock as the faith of Peter's confession he shows that it is Peter, *as* thus believing and thus confessing, who is the Rock; 'For

<small>In Ps. 129.

In illud Hoc scitote, n. 4, p. 282 (Migne).

In Matt. Hom. 32.</small>

those things which are peculiar to God alone to loose sins, and to make the Church incapable of overthrow in so great an assault of waves, and to exhibit a fisherman more solid than any rock, when the whole world is battling —these things He promises Himself to give.' And 'He committed to the hands of a mortal man the authority over all things in Heaven when He gave him the keys.'

On Matt. xvi. 1.

Again, '"Give to them for Me and thee." Dost thou see the exceeding greatness of the honour?' The tribute money due from the little band of disciples was paid by Peter, as their head. And so S. Chrysostom goes on. '"In that hour," when He had honoured him (Peter) above all. For of James, too, and John, one was a first-born' (alluding to the opinion that the tax was for the firstborn and representative of the family), '*but no such thing had He done for them.* They being ashamed to acknowledge the feeling which they experienced, they do not say indeed openly, On what account hast Thou honoured Peter above us? and, is he greater than we are? for they were ashamed; but they ask indefinitely, Who, then, is greater? For when they saw the three honoured above them, they suffered nothing of this kind, but because this matter of honour had come round to one, then they were vexed. And not this only, but putting together many other things, that feeling was kindled. For to him also He had said, "To thee will I give the keys," and "Blessed art thou, Simon Bar-jona," and here "give to them for Me and thee."'

S. Chrys. in loco.

They rightly argued, according to S. Chrysostom, that our Lord was making Peter the head of the Apostolic College; they were wrong in feeling jealous. Our Lord, in His answer, did not deny the pre-eminence of that 'greater one,' about which they asked, but pointed out what his character ought to be.

And then S. Chrysostom compares S. John's behaviour

on this occasion with his changed behaviour after the resurrection. All feeling of envy had then disappeared. 'This same John . . . . everywhere gives up the first place to Peter.'

Then, in the account of the Last Supper, S. Chrysostom is careful to point out, that if Peter beckoned to John to know of whom our Lord spake, it was not because John was greater, but the other way. 'That thou mightest not think that he beckoned to him as though he (John) were greater, he says that the thing took place because of that great love.'

And, after the resurrection, on 'Feed My sheep,' S. Chrysostom remarks, 'Why, then, passing by the others, does He converse with Peter on these things? He was the chosen one of the Apostles, and the mouth of the disciples, and the leader of the choir. On this account Paul also went up on a time to see him, rather than the others. And withal, to show him that he must thenceforward have confidence, as the denial was done away with, *He puts into his hand the presidency over the brethren.*' (It is obvious that the brethren are the Apostles.) 'And if any one should say, How then did James receive the throne of Jerusalem? this I would answer, that He appointed this man (Peter) teacher, not of that throne, but of the world.'

And further on, ' He who then (at the Last Supper) did not dare to question Jesus, but committed the office to another, he was entrusted *with the presidency over the brethren*, and not only does not commit to another what relates to himself, but himself now puts a question to his Master concerning another. John is silent, but Peter speaks.'

Thus far S. Chrysostom's estimate of S. Peter's relation to the other Apostles in the Gospel history. Can any one doubt what that is? Is it not very different from the explanation given in your book? (p. 33), and is not the quotation from Mr. Palmer, as given by the author of the 'Roman Question' (p. 25), *positively unfair*? He says: 'This is the interpretation given by S. Chrysostom, who explains our Lord's words thus: If thou lovest Me, protect the brethren, and now show that warm affection which thou hast always manifested, and in which thou hast rejoiced.' S. Chrysostom says much more than this, which I can only characterise as a serious *suppressio veri*.

But still more important is the position assigned by S. Chrysostom to S. Peter in the Acts of the Apostles.

The idea commonly entertained by Anglicans is that the part played by S. Peter in the Acts was that of a fervent, forward, impulsive nature, taking the lead of the rest by reason of natural pre-eminence, but without an official position; with no authority from our Lord, but simply as a matter of course, by reason of his commanding ways and special fervour. If, however, there is one thing more than another on which S. Augustine and S. Chrysostom insist, it is the humility and reticence of Peter as to his dignity and rights. So his marvellous humility in the scene at Antioch with the novice Apostle of the Gentiles is enlarged upon as the humility of one who, when opposed on a matter of personal conduct, of practical expediency, did not say, as he might have said, 'I am your Prince, your Head, your Primate; you have no right to address me so;' but he listened to what S. Paul had to say, thought it over, and adopted his suggestions. S. Augustine and S. Chrysostom are full of his praise on this account. In fact, S. Paul occupies something of the position towards S. Peter that S. Bernard did towards Pope Eugenius III. S. Bernard had no hesitation in speaking his mind, in spite of his sense of the exalted dignity of the Pontiff whom he addressed.

S. Paul was, of course, an Apostle, and, as such, of equal fellowship and honour in regard to the 'sacerdotium' with S. Peter; but S. Peter was his superior. The courage of the one was exhibited in speaking out what he felt to be right on an important practical matter; the humility and graciousness of the other, in listening gladly to what his brother Apostle, more practically acquainted with the matter in hand through the recency of his conversion, and his peculiar relation to his past religion, had to say. But Anglican writers lay stress only on S. Peter's qualities of courage, fervour, faith. They miss what S. Chrysostom adds, that these qualities were not the only cause of his taking the lead, but the Divinely bestowed attributes of one chosen by our Lord for the office of head and leader.

Your own position is very difficult to grasp. S. Peter, you admit, was 'the leader—the Coryphæus of the Apostolic band' (p. 34). Surely this means a great deal in a supernatural society? To what was the leadership due? Had it no connection with his being singled out so often by our Lord in the Gospels? Was it not, considering that fact, a Divine appointment? Did it not point to a law of the Church's life? 'He' (you say), 'as holding the keys of the Kingdom of Heaven, opened the door of the Gentiles.' Surely to no mortal man has it ever been given to exercise a prerogative of higher importance, and surely this was not a matter of personal moral qualities, but the exercise of a Divine office. Did he then resign the keys? You say that 'he occupies no governing position in the Council at Jerusalem.' And the author of the 'Roman Question' is plainer still He asserts that 'there is no single instance of any act of superior authority attributed to him (Peter) which in any degree places him above his brother Apostles. It is impossible but that there must have been an exercise of such power, had it existed.' He then quotes some instances of what he considers proofs of mere equality (each one of which has been explained in a different sense by S. Chrysostom), even going so far as to base an argument on Gal. ii. 9.

Barrow, besides being exceedingly inaccurate, is quite offensive; admitting a sort of primacy, which he calls a 'womanish prerogative;' and seeing in 'this conceit little solidity and as little harm.'

Now, so perfectly untrue is it that S. Peter did not act as one possessing an official position, and as possessed of real jurisdiction, that, as a matter of fact, there are instances recorded in the Acts of the Apostles of each and every form of jurisdiction being exercised by him.

He exercises the prerogative of initiation in the filling up of the Apostolic College. What could be more significant?

<small>See Allies, Per Crucem ad Lucem, vol. i.</small>

He defends the Apostolic College, and gives the first exposition of the Christian Revelation as the authoritative teacher.

He pronounces the first excommunication.

He goes with S. John (sent, as a chapter sometimes sends its head), but was the evident principal, to open the gates of Heaven to Samaria.

He secures the Catholicity of the Church in opening, of his own authority, the Kingdom of Heaven to the Gentiles at large.

He issues the first ecclesiastical judgment, and sets the model of ecclesiastical discipline.

He exercises the administrative powers of his Primacy to an extent that not even S. Paul exercised his office (cp. Acts ix. 31 with xv. 36). 'Like a general he went surveying the ranks,' says S. Chrysostom.

He occupies the first position at the first Council at Jerusalem, and gives the sentence, which is subscribed by the rest, first by S. James.

What fuller evidence can be needed of the official position held by S. Peter? And this authoritative position is confirmed by miracles. It is S. Peter who is so constantly working miracles; where with others, still as leader—often by himself. His very shadow healed the sick. Is anything too hard to believe of this glorious Saint, this embodiment of his Incarnate Lord as Governor of the Church, this sacrament of the administrative power of the one Lord over all? The Acts of the Apostles are divided into two parts: one, the account of the Church's organisation; the other, the history of its wider missionary enterprise; the one, the narrative of the Apostles in common, the other, the biography of a single missionary Apostle; and the one is, more or less, the history of S. Peter, the other of S. Paul. The one builds up the Church, the other spreads it; it is built on Peter, spread by Paul.

Now as to the Council of Jerusalem. It was, perhaps we may say, the second occasion on which there had been a regular formal assembly of the Apostles. At the first S. Peter called on the Apostles to elect one in place of Judas, to supply the number of twelve in the Apostolic College. On that occasion he acts as the appointed teacher of all; he tells them what *must* be done; he prescribes the form, and the election is made. *In loco.* S. Chrysostom says: 'Might not Peter by himself have elected?' Now here is a startling question, coming from one who had so much to do with Antioch, occurring in the sober commentary of a Doctor of the Church, *à propos* of the Church's constitution. I would ask the venerable author of the 'Roman Question' what answer he would have given to this question. He must have replied in the words of his book (p. 25), that 'there is *no one single* instance of *any* act of superior authority attributed to him (Peter), which *in any degree* places him above his brother Apostles'—a sentence which immediately follows the quotation from S. Chrysostom, which I have already called a *suppressio veri*. But when S. Chrysostom—S. Chrysostom, on whom Anglicans have so much relied; S. Chrysostom, who cannot belong to the 'Papal school' of which you call S. Leo the Father; S. Chrysostom, not in a burst of eloquence, not in a sermon descriptive of the glories of an Apostle; S. Chrysostom, who must have known better than most the Apostolical tradition of the Church of Antioch— when S. Chrysostom asks the question, 'Might not Peter by himself have elected?' he answers categorically, emphatically, 'Certainly.'

Is it possible to avoid the force of this statement? Is it possible not to see that in the fourth century a Doctor of the Church- and such a Doctor! - held a view of S. Peter's relationship to the other Apostles, and to the whole Church, which is repudiated by yourself and others, like the author of the 'Roman Question,' as fatal to the Anglican theory? The only reason why S. Peter does not act upon the authority which he possessed was 'that he might not seem partial.' It was his gracious use of authority which S. Chrysostom admires. Peter, he says, 'first acts with authority in the matter, *as himself having all put into his hands*; for to him Christ said, "And thou, in thy turn, one day confirm thy brethren."' Already he had given the same reason why Peter rose up in the midst of the disciples. 'As being ardent;' but is that all? No; that is all that some would see, but S. Chrysostom says, '*both* as being ardent, *and entrusted by Christ with the flock, and as the first of the choir.*'

And so S. Chrysostom says of the Council at Jerusalem, that it was really assembled by S. Peter's permission. It is, I think, difficult to read S. Jerome, and S. Chrysostom, and S. Augustine on S. Peter, and not to feel that they were in possession of a traditional interpretation of such matters as this, which fits in with Holy Scripture, though it is not forced upon us by the surface view of the sacred words. So here S. Chrysostom says plainly that S. Peter first allowed an inquiry about the matter to be made. He called the Council, and, consequently, the Apostles and elders came together to consider the matter. In that Council S. Peter acted as the legislative authority; he determined the law, and the rest followed. 'That which was required to be established by a law, namely, that the law was not to be kept, was introduced by Peter,' says S. Chrysostom; 'but about the domestic practice (which concerned the converts from the Synagogue), and which was received from olden times, he (James) speaks.' And *S. Chrysostom, though S. Luke's language was his own, sees no authoritative delivery of the Council's sentence in S. James's saying* that he judged 'that we trouble not them which from amongst the Gentiles are turned to GOD.' Where you say 'the formal authority, the formal "I decide" (Acts xv. 10) comes from S. James;' and where the author of the 'Roman Question' actually sees the judgment of a Bishop, not of an Apostle, given as superior to that of all the Apostles (cf. p. 26, line 1, with p. 31, last line), S. Chrysostom sees something *quite different*. S. James is not, according to him, exercising his authority in comparison with the other Apostles in uttering those words (questionably translated 'my sentence is'), but he is recommending S. Peter's decision to his own people on his own declaration, rather than by reference to the old law. The emphasis is on the 'I,' in contrast with the law.

And so S. Jerome, writing to S. Augustine, says that after Peter had 'spoken with his wonted freedom "all the multitude held their peace," *and S. James the Apostle and all the ancients* (presbyteri) *together adopted his sentence.*' And S. Augustine, in his reply, does not quarrel with S. Jerome's interpretation, which is also Bishop Meurin's. And so S. Francis de Sales writes of the Council : ' If we consider who presided, we shall find that it was S. Peter who first gives sentence, and is then followed by the rest, as S. Jerome says.'

I may remark before passing on that the translation in the Oxford edition of S. Chrysostom makes the Saint say that 'S. James's speech puts the completion to the matter under discussion.' But the Greek word for 'matter under discussion' is 'pragma,' which would be better translated 'business,' or 'proceedings.' The matter under *discussion* was already decided by Peter in the judgment of S. James, and his proclamation of the decision is not a sanction or confirmation which belongs to a superior, at least the terms do not compel this, but a simple concurrence with S. Peter's decision, with which S. James brings the 'proceedings' to a close.

I conclude that, if we are to look to Holy Scripture for the law of the Church's life, we find that as that Church came forth from the Upper Chamber at Pentecost, it came with a 'form of unity' which is to be found to-day only in the Holy Roman Catholic Church.

And what is the traditional teaching of that Church in which S. Chrysostom spent so much of his time ?

THE SYRIAN CHURCH OF ANTIOCH.

We could hardly have a more important witness on this subject than that Antioch where 'the disciples were first called Christians' (Acts xi. 26) ; that Church founded by Peter before he established himself in the capital of the Cæsars—that Apostolical See, which was in honour throughout the east and west, when Byzantium was only a portion of the diocese of Thrace, subject to the Metropolitan of Heraclea. Of the occupant of this See, S. Gregory the Great writes: 'I receive with pleasure what is said of the Chair of Peter by him, who sits in it himself.' Antioch was always considered the Chair of S. Peter, in a sense only subordinate to that in which Rome was held to be S. Peter's See. So S. Innocent writes almost within the fourth century (A.D. 402 was the date of his election): 'We note that this privilege was given to Antioch, not so much on account of the city's magnificence, as because it is known to be the first seat of the first Apostle, where the Christian religion received its name, where a great meeting of Apostles was held, and which would not yield to the See of the city of Rome, except that the latter rejoices in having received and retained to the end that honour which the former obtained only in transition.'

It may be noticed in passing that, through the whole Arian controversy, Rome and Alexandria took side against Antioch and Constantinople. But this did not prevent Antioch from bearing witness to the supremacy of Rome as the See of S. Peter. From the Syriac Codices in the Vatican library, Cyril Beynam Benni, Archbishop of Mossul (Nineveh), has traced for us the creed of that Church from the fourth century, and in the 'Prænotanda' we are assured that he collected and examined two hundred documents. His authorities are: the Syriac Liturgy, the Syro-Chaldæan Liturgy, Nestorian Synods, Canones Nicæni, vulgo Arabici, the Maronite Patriarch, Josephus II., S. Ephrem Syrus (A.D. 379), S. James of Serug (A.D. 452).

There is a version of S. Ignatius's letter to the Romans, which one of these documents gives, that is interesting, as throwing some additional light on S. Ignatius's enthusiastic encomiums of the Church of Rome. He says:

'The God-robed Ignatius to that most beloved Church, whose greatness *is the greatness of the Most High*, and of His only begotten Son Jesus Christ ; to that Church which is enlightened by the all-hallowing and most beloved will of God, and by the charity of Jesus Christ our Lord; to that Church which hath the first See within the precincts of Rome ; the most worthy of God, worthy of majesty, worthy of blessing and glory, *praiseworthy for her purity, seated in the principal See of Charity within the law of Christ.*' Commentators on this passage, in their eagerness to define the exact meaning of the words 'which hath the first See within the precincts of Rome,' are apt to overlook the way in which S. Ignatius looks upon this 'first See in the region of the Romans,' or 'within the precincts of Rome,' as so specially enlightened, so specially worthy of God, and 'as seated in the principal See of Charity within the law of Christ,' as though the first See within the region of the Romans were not first there only, but also throughout the world.

This, however, by the way. The witness of the Syrian Church of Antioch becomes perfectly clear before and during the time of the Council of Chalcedon, and shows how the conviction of the supremacy of S. Peter's See permeated the Church.

From the mass of evidence take the following : S. Ephrem (A.D. 379), speaking of Moses and Peter meeting at the Transfiguration, compares their relationship to the two covenants. 'There were both the prince of the Old and the prince of the New Testament confronting one another. There the saintly Moses beheld the sanctified Simon, the steward of the Father, the procurator of the Son. He who forced the sea asunder to let the people walk across the parted waves, beheld him who raised the tabernacle and built the Church.' It seems quite a common, natural thing to compare S. Peter with Moses (*see* S. James of Serug, 'Hom. de Transfig.'). Again: 'Then Peter deservedly received the Vicariate over His people.' And again : 'Blessed art thou, O Simon Kipho, who keepest the keys fashioned by the Holy Ghost. Great and ineffable word is thine which binds and looses in heaven and on earth. O blessed flock entrusted to thy care! Oh ! how rapidly hath it grown ! For while thou didst fix the cross over the waters, the sheep, enamoured of it, brought forth saints and holy virgins of every class. Oh ! blessed art thou *who didst hold the place of head* and tongue in the body of thy brethren,' &c.

S. James of Serug (452–521 A.D.), a contemporary of the Council of Chalcedon, says : '(John) did not go in (to the sepulchre) until the perfect Simon arrived. He waited for the arrival of him who was carrying the Keys of the Church ; of him who, as Steward of the House, was to open and enter it first. . . . Simon Peter, the head of the structures, came up and entered before him : that he might be built first into the edifice of the Apostleship: The spiritual child duti-fully yielded to his worthy elder: That, as he is in the foundation, he might also be first in his preaching.' Again: 'Thou art Kipho : down in the foundations of the great house I will set thee : upon thee I will build My elected Church. . . . (Christ) entered the house ' (cf. 'He came unto His own '), 'chose a stone, and set the foundation. . . . The great Apostle was the foundation of the Great House. . . . The Bridegroom chose it, His Father carved it in that revelation, and the Holy Ghost had it finished and settled in the foundation of the Church.' And again: 'Thy strength is that of a rock, here (I say) thou art a rock. And upon thee I will build My Church.' ' He blessed him, and had His Church built upon that Apostle ; . . . he was to keep the whole fabric from shrinking.'

There is a document, too, containing the account of a Nestorian Synod of Bishops under their Patriarch Dadishoo, A.D. 430, from which it appears that they clung to the general conviction of the Church as to the supremacy of S. Peter. It says: 'One is His (Christ's) faithful Vicar, Simon Bar-jona, who is named Kipho (stone), to whom (Christ) Himself made the promise, saying: "Upon this stone I will build My Church;" and again: "To thee I will give the keys of the heavenly kingdom." Christ, in truth, did not say to all the Apostles, "I will build upon you, I will give you." . . . Although to each Disciple was given the priestly office, the singular primacy, which is a spiritual paternity, has not been given to all, but to a single one, as to a faithful Vicar of the one true God, that he should rule and guide all, and be over all his brethren.'

Again: 'Now all perfection should prevail in the Holy Church; so that as one is the veritable Father; one His Son, our Saviour Jesus Christ; one His Spirit, the Paraclete; so also one is His faithful Vicar, Simon Bar-jona, who has been called (Kipho) the Rock, as (Christ) Himself had promised to him, saying, "Upon this Rock I will build My Church." And again: "To thee I will give the keys of the kingdom of heaven."'

And a Chaldæan Synod in the next century adopts the same reason: 'Thus it seemed good unto the Holy Ghost to bring together every order in such a manner as to have one set first above all, who should rule the rulers as well as the ruled; one with whom all should inwardly be coherent, as limbs with the head, whence the intelligence proceeds,' &c.

The Syro-Chaldæan Liturgy, in the Office of the Apostles Peter and Paul, says: 'Here is Simon, whom the Lord thrice called upon (saying), "Feed Me My rams and My gentle sheep. I intrust thee with the keys of

My spiritual treasury, that thou mayest bind and loose on earth and in heaven. *I will instal thee Vicar of the heavenly kingdom* ; rule justly, and govern the children of thy household."'

And the Syriac Liturgy : 'Blessed art thou, Peter. The Son of God hath settled thee in the foundation of His Church, that thou mayest bear the weight of the whole house, as He beareth the weight of the whole world.'

Again, the Syro-Chaldæan Liturgy has : ' He (Christ) saw his sincere affection and made him head of His flock.'

And, 'Simon, the Head of the Apostles, the Foundation, the Ruler, the Pastor, and the Governor of the Church of Christ, to whom his Lord bore witness, saying, "Thou art a rock (Kipho), and upon this rock (Kipho) I will build My Church : " to him also the Lord said, " Feed the little sheep of My flock, feed My lambs, feed My sheep ; graze them in the green fields of faith."'

And, not to weary, John Maro, the first Maronite Patriarch, writes, two hundred years before the Greek schism : 'And as a Patriarch has authority over his subjects, the Roman (Pontiff) has authority over all Patriarchs, in the same manner as Peter had it over all chiefs of Christianity, and over all Churches, for he is the successor of Christ, placed over His Church, over His flock, over all people. If any one refuses to observe these statutes, let him be anathema.'

There is something I would remark here in passing, viz. that in all writers for the first six or seven centuries (and, of course, after that too), when S. Peter is spoken of, it is so frequently said, 'to whom were given the keys ;' whereas this epithet, so to call it, is rarely applied to other Apostles. They had, as S. Francis says above, the *use* of the keys ; but S. Peter is spoken of as the one who possessed them; just as Tertullian, in speaking of S. Peter and S. John as both inspired, describes S. John as 'the most beloved of the Lord, who leaned upon His breast,' &c., but S. Peter as him 'who is called the "Rock whereon the Church was to be built," who obtained "the keys of the kingdom of heaven,"' &c. Thus from the very earliest times S. Peter is spoken of as having a special relation to the keys. The other Apostles had theirs, but Peter had his, and it was unique. De Præscr. n. 22.

From Antioch we will turn to

ARMENIA.

And I am the more anxious to touch on the Armenian witness to the Papal supremacy, because many Church of England people are under a complete delusion as to the lineage of a number of Armenian Bishops who call themselves the Armenian Church. In past times the Armenians were seldom free from heresy, except when in communion with the See of Rome. So long as they were in communion with Rome they accepted the orthodox doctrine of the Incarnation, and on each occasion of their reconciliation with the Holy See they have expressed their adherence to the decrees of the Council of Chalcedon. Mr. Brisco Owen's speech at the Church Congress at Wolverhampton, quoted with approval by the author of the 'Roman Question,' would convey, I fear, to most a misleading impression. One would gather from it that the Armenians, as a body, severed themselves externally from the Catholic Church merely by reason of a mistake in the translation of the word 'Nature,' as used by the Fathers of Chalcedon. And one would suppose that they had remained separate ever since. Else why allude to this supposed cause of separation? Now, whereas Mr. Owen says, 'As the Armenians were not present at the Council of Chalcedon, they could only judge of its decrees from a letter which Pope Leo had written with regard to them,' the real truth is that, sixteen years previously to the Council of Chalcedon, their Patriarch Isaac had published a declaration of faith identical with that part of the Council of Ephesus which dealt with the Eutychian heresy by anticipation, *using the same terms as were afterwards used at the Council of Chalcedon*; that they were fully acquainted with the course matters took in the Council, and that the Armenian Church *was represented* by some of its Bishops, who were in concert with the orthodox Bishops at the Council, and who subscribed the decrees of the Council against Eutyches and brought back to Armenia a report of their proceedings; and Armenia accepted with quite a vehement enthusiasm the faith which these orthodox Bishops brought with them, *and held it for ninety years.* It was only when some heretics and schismatics, intruders, disturbed the peace of Armenia that the pretence about not understanding the terms used by the Council was got up and a schism ensued. But Armenia was more than once reconciled to Rome, and thereby the Catholic doctrine of the Incarnation established; and, later on, the representatives of the Armenian Church, though arriving just too late for the actual Council of Florence, were yet included amongst those who had signed the Profession of Faith, which proclaimed the Supremacy, by Divine institution, of the See of S. Peter. Those to whom in some parts the Church of England holds out the right hand of fellowship are tainted with heresy and schism—the former, it is true, to some extent now disavowed, but the latter connected with a disgraceful history. They separated themselves from what is now, alas! a smaller body, but is the true 'remnant' which has held on all along to the See of Rome, their original mother, and to the orthodox faith, in the midst of terrible religious persecutions.

Now the early faith of the Armenian Church as to the supremacy of S. Peter's See is given by its Patriarch in a remarkable letter, professing to give the tradition received from S. Gregory the Illuminator, which thus carries us up to the beginning of the fourth century. The letter itself, giving the traditional belief of the Patriarchate of Armenia, was written A.D. 426. S. Isaac, the author of the letter, a man of the very highest account in the Armenian Church and nation, was Patriarch from A.D. 390 to 440, the latter being the year in which S. Leo ascended the throne of S. Peter. In 426, this saintly man, who went through so much for his faith, wrote thus in a document which is of the very highest value, written in Greek, which may be thus translated: 'The precept of GOD commends to us, not a Church built of stones and wood, but the human race built on a rock by faith in the truth. Wherefore the true faith is the Church which gathers us together and builds in the unit of the knowledge of the Son of GOD; for He Himsel the Life-giver, teaches us, saying to St. Peter: "Thou art Peter, and on this Rock I will build My Church, and the gates of hell shall not prevail against thee."' (Notice the substitution, by way of comment, of 'thee' for 'it.')
'Now when we hear Peter called a rock, what are we to understand to be said? That it is like a stone amongst stones? Far from it; but it is a man using reason, the head of the Apostolical band; and since he with immovable faith confessed Christ, the Son of the living GOD, He obtained the blessing, and was called Rock. So, too, those who are built on it are not inanimate stones, but men, sharers in the same faith, since the Holy Scriptures do not hesitate often and often, where there is need, to call our Lord and Saviour by this name.'

See Archbp. Balgy, Hist. Doctr. Cathol. inter Armenos. Vienna, 1878.

Here we have the Patriarch of Armenia professing to give the traditional belief of the Church to the effect that S. Peter is the rock, and the Church is built on him, and that he is the head of the Apostolical band. Thus we have witnesses from Antioch, witnesses from Armenia, and, as we shall presently see, witnesses from Constantinople —witnesses from exactly where we should least expect to find them; and S. Leo in the West, in his plainest utterances, does not go beyond the affidavits of these various competent witnesses from the East.

There is, however, another document which shall depose to the faith of the East a little later on, A.D. 519— three centuries before the unscrupulous Photius accomplished his schism. It is known as

THE FORMULA OF POPE HORMISDAS, OR THE PROFESSION OF FAITH SIGNED BY THE ORIENTALS,

when John, Patriarch of Constantinople, the Emperor Justin, and a synod of forty Greek Bishops, begged the Pope to send Legates to Constantinople and terminate divisions, which dated back from the Council of Chalcedon. On March, A.D. 519, the Papal Legates entered the city amidst extraordinary enthusiasm, the Prelates and grandees of the Empire preceded them in state; the streets were lined with thousands of Greeks bearing lighted tapers in their hands; the Emperor himself welcomed them with every token of cordiality; and the day of solemn reconciliation was Holy Thursday of the same year. Now this Profession of Faith did much more than meet the controversies of the day. Its opening and closing sentences were repeatedly borrowed by the Greeks in after times, the only difference being that, as new heretics made their appearance, their names, too, appeared in this favourite formula. It was signed and sent to Pope Hormisdas; signed and sent to Pope Agapetus; it was signed and sent to Pope S. Nicolas I. If we turn to Harduin's 'Acta Conciliorum,' we see it sent in substance to Pope Adrian II. by the 8th Œcumenical Council, with special condemnation of Photius and Gregory of Syracuse. As early as A.D. 546, Rusticus, a contemporary writer, says that this Profession of Faith had been signed probably by 2,500 Bishops! It opens with the declaration that ' in the Apostolic See (Rome) religion *has ever been kept immaculate*. Wherefore, desiring never to be parted from that faith and hope, we excommunicate all heretics, and in particular Nestorius, Eutyches, Dioscorus, Timothy, Acasius. . . . We receive and approve *all the letters of Pope Leo*, following in all things the Apostolic See, and professing all its decrees.'

Here apparently each Bishop inserted, and spoke in, the name of his Diocese:—' I hope to be worthy to be in that one communion with you which the Apostolic See enjoins, in which is the full and real solidity of Christian religion; promising also that the names of those who are separated from the Communion of the Catholic Church, *that is, those who are not united in one mind to the Apostolic See*, shall not be recited in the Holy Mysteries. This my profession I have subscribed with my own hand and presented to thee, Hormisdas, holy and venerable Pope of the city of Rome.'

Are we not, by this time, in possession of the mind of the Church? There is one more document I will quote before returning to the earlier ages, and that shall be the well-known formal definition in which, later on, *the Latin and Greek Churches united*. It runs thus: 'We define that the Holy Apostolic See and the Roman Pontiff possess Primacy over the whole world, and that the Roman Pontiff himself is the successor of Blessed Peter, the Prince of the Apostles, and the true Vicar of Christ, the Head of the whole Church, and the Father and Teacher of all Christians; and that to him, in the person of Blessed Peter, full power has been given by our Lord Jesus Christ to feed, rule, govern the Universal Church, even as also is contained in the Acts of the Œcumenical Councils and in the Sacred Canons.'

A question suggests itself. How could the Greeks, after some of the above declarations, start away from this faith? The answer would involve a volume. But one thing is certain, viz. that the point of dispute, in its origin, had nothing whatever to do with this doctrine of the supremacy of S. Peter's See. And here I adopt the words of an unpublished manuscript written in answer to the assertion by an Anglican divine that the Greek schism was due to the supposed fact that Rome 'endeavoured to impose upon the East the Papal jurisdiction, which was in reality the product of political and social causes that operated powerfully on Western Europe after the fall of the Roman Empire. The question of the dual Procession was the mere πρόθεσις of that quarrel: the Papal Supremacy was the true cause.'

We have seen how the East based its belief in Papal jurisdiction on our Lord's words to S. Peter. And it is in accord with this that Photius, in his list of errors committed by Rome, omits altogether the question of Papal Supremacy. So far from impugning that, this founder of the schism began by begging Pope S. Nicolas to *confirm* him in the Patriarchate of Constantinople; and he also sought *letters of confirmation* from Pope John VIII. as late as A.D. 877. To conciliate S. Nicolas, he addressed to him an elaborate profession of faith, declaring that he wished to make 'a perfect and indestructible chain with his Holiness; that he accepted the Seven General Councils, anathematising those whom they anathematised,

Jager's Histoire de Photius, p. 435. Paris, 1844.

embracing and honouring those whom they honoured, and that in sending that "Profession of Faith" to his Holiness, he had special need of the Pontiff's prayers.' Moreover, he joined the Emperor in despatching to Rome the most magnificent presents—a paten of pure gold, adorned with diamonds and precious stones; huge Oriental fans, enriched with costly stones; chasubles and other robes of the rarest workmanship; together with an altar carpet, or probably an antependium, fringed with purest gold and decorated with stones. If presents and protestations had been able to seal the Pope's lips there would have been no controversy about the 'Supremacy.' S. Nicolas did not neglect to praise Photius for his Catholicity, nor to blame him for his gross misconduct. The heresiarch had violated the ecclesiastical canons: he occupied the chair of a Patriarch who at this moment was in chains: in his letter to the Pope he pretended that the lawful owner of the See had resigned, whereas neither threats, nor blows, nor imprisonment had induced the brave old Patriarch to abdicate. Here is not the place to give details of the battle between Rome and Constantinople; the Pope insisted on fair play, a fair trial for the Patriarch Ignatius who had been wronged: but for a period Photius managed to have his own way in the East. He flattered the passions of his Sovereign, Michael 'the drunkard;' he bribed the Papal Legates; falsified the Papal letters; forged the signatures of Bishops for his ambitious ends; and when sentence had been passed upon him by S. Nicolas, he urged the besotted Emperor to threaten to send an army to Rome and to repudiate the Pope's supremacy. In Harduin's fifth volume of 'Acta' we have S. Nicolas's reply to the Emperor, and the following extract must suffice for our present purpose: 'If you will not hear us, we must treat you as Jesus Christ commanded us to treat those who

margin notes:
Hefele, Histoire des Conciles, tom. v. p. 446.
Harduin, tom. v. p. 126.
See letter of Photius, Jager, l. c.
Harduin's Acta Conc. tom. v. p. 754, &c., and cf. pp. 215, 189.
P. 152.

refuse to hear the Church. For the privileges of the Roman Church, confirmed to Blessed Peter by the mouth of Christ Himself, established in the Church, guarded from antiquity, proclaimed by holy Œcumenical Councils, and ever respected by every Church, cannot, in anything whatever, be either diminished, or violated, or changed; because human efforts cannot overturn what is founded, strengthened, and supported by GOD Himself. The privileges of this See are perpetual, rooted, planted by a Divine Hand; they may be wounded, but not transplanted; violated, but not exterminated. *Thanks be to God, they continue where they were before your reign; they will subsist after you*; and as long as the Christian name shall be preached they will continue without diminution. These privileges granted to this Holy Church by Christ, not by Synods, . . . oblige us to have a pastoral solicitude for all the Churches of GOD,' &c.

Here, then, is the real origin of the schismatical Greek Church—ambition, hypocrisy, fraud, revenge. On the death of S. Ignatius the Holy See yielded to the petition of the Orientals and allowed Photius to become Patriarch of Constantinople. For the purpose of confirming him in his See, a large Synod of Eastern Bishops assembled in Constantinople. The Papal letter was read and approved, *as far as ecclesiastical matters were concerned*, and in it the doctrine of Papal Supremacy was plainly affirmed.

But, so far as peace was concerned, it was in vain. Revolt was followed by reconciliation, and reconciliation by fresh revolts in the tenth and eleventh centuries. Such Oriental prelates as Macarius of Nicomedia, Euthymius of Constantinople, and Joseph of Ephesus, laboured sincerely for ecclesiastical unity. Such emperors as Alexis, Commenus Manuel and Michael Palæologus distin-

guished themselves as defenders of communion with
Rome. At the General Council of Lyons, in 1274, the
last-named emperor signed a 'confession of faith,' declaring that 'the Holy Roman Church hath full and
supreme Primacy and Principality over the whole Catholic
Church,' the principality having been vested 'by our Lord
Himself in Blessed Peter, Prince and Head, whose successor is the Bishop of Rome in fulness of jurisdiction.'
Six-and-twenty Metropolitans subscribed a declaration of the 'Prelates'—or the Sacramentum Græcorum—setting forth 'the primacy of ancient Rome,' and that 'the Pope was the first and highest Bishop of all Churches;' and three years later the Patriarch of Constantinople, in the name of the Holy Synod of that city, assured Pope John XXI. of his 'pure and perfect obedience to the Holy See.' But oaths were taken and broken continually by the fickle East; though the three Patriarchs of Jerusalem, Antioch, and Alexandria accepted the definitions of the Council of Florence, and the aged Patriarch of Constantinople, who died during the Council, before his soul passed into eternity signed his adhesion to the Catholic doctrine of the Procession of the Holy Ghost, and 'submitted himself humbly to the ruling of Holy Church;' though the Armenian, Ethiopian, and Jacobite Bishops subsequently sent in their adhesion to the Council; though the Patriarch of the Syrians, the Metropolitan of the Maronites, and the Metropolitan of the Chaldæan Nestorians combined in confessing the supremacy of Rome—still, disputes, insurrections, schisms scourged the land until the capture of Constantinople by the Turks; and under Mahomet II., A.D. 1453, all relations between the East and West were forcibly severed, and S. Sophia's shrine became a Turkish mosque! What the schism in the East has ended in, to what a condition the Greek Church has sunk, may be best gathered from

[margin: Harduin's Acta, tom. vii. p. 695.]
[margin: L. c. pp. 700-702.]
[margin: Harduin, tom. ix. p. 953.]

sank into Erastianism.

_{The Church and the Churches, Eng. trans. p. 126.}

two incidents related by Dr. Dollinger: 'Pius IX., in his evangelical letter to the prelates of the East in the year 1848, reminded them of their want of religious unity; and thereupon the Patriarch answered in his own name and in that of the Synod, "In disputed or difficult questions, the three Patriarchs discuss the matter with the Patriarch of Constantinople, because that city is the seat of empire, and because he is the President of the Synod. If they cannot agree, the affair is, according to ancient precedent and usage, referred for decision to the head of the (Turkish) Government."'

_{Dollinger's Pope of Rome and the Eastern Popes, Eng. trans. p. 112.}

Again, a certain Greek 'mentions also a case in which a decision was really given The Armenian Clergy had a dispute with the Greek Priests concerning the custom of mixing water with the sacramental wine; and the dispute was finally brought before the Turkish Reis-Effendi, who accordingly gave his decision: 'Wine is an impure drink, condemned by the Koran; pure water, therefore, should be used.'

And this is part of that Greek Church whose separation from Rome used to be such a support to myself and others in our isolated condition as Anglicans cut off from the communion of Rome.

SS. MELETIUS AND CYPRIAN NOT EXCOMMUNICATED.

There remains still almost the *pièce de résistance* with many English Churchmen—viz. the supposition that certain saintly men were not in communion with the Holy See and yet were canonised; and that there was an independence of Rome in Africa in the time of S. Augustine sufficient to justify a comparison between their relations and the rupture between Rome and England since the sixteenth century.

And this latter contention is emphasised by the author of the 'Roman Question' in a paragraph (p. 34) in which he compares the relationship between Rome and Africa to that which exists between England and her 'daughter colonies' of Australia and New Zealand. But S. Augustine himself by no means recognises this close relationship. He is rather fond of speaking of 'that root of the Eastern Churches, whence the Gospel came to Africa.' And, indeed, the relationship never could be at all of the same kind, what with weekly mails, telegraphic communication, all manner of intercourse, commercial and other, in these days of rapid movement, whilst Augustine, from the lack of constant media of communication, exhibited sheer ignorance about the Canons of the Council of Sardica, which would be impossible in days like these. Add to which, the entire difference of races necessarily led to a measure of autonomy, of which Rome, in her wisdom, was patient in days of distress, when the difficulties of government were sufficiently great, but which would be quite out of place with countries more contiguous, and races more closely connected, and means of intercourse indefinitely multiplied.

Ep. 52 and 43.

But how often in my Anglican ministry have I rung the changes on Cyprian, Meletius, Augustine—Cyprian and Stephen, Meletius and Damasus, Augustine and Zorimus! I find the same note struck in your own book; it is a sort of refrain in the dirge that you chant over what I must call the funeral of the Church; for, indeed, the Church of Christ as Christ founded it, with a promise that the gates of hell should not prevail against it, is gently lowered to her grave by your theory of perpetual schism as the universal feature of her sick and palsied frame. It is perhaps here that the most fundamental difference between the Catholic and the Anglican conception of the Church is to be found. With you the Church is ever in error; I mean the visible Church. S. Francis de Sales says of the Calvinist ministers, 'When they declare the visible Church can err, they dishonour the Church to which our Lord directs us in our difficulties, and which S. Paul calls the pillar and ground of the truth; for it is only of the visible Church that these testimonies can be understood, unless we should say that our Lord directed us to address ourselves to an invisible and unperceivable thing, a thing utterly unknown, or that S. Paul instructed his Timothy to converse in a society of which he had no knowledge.' You do not go as far as this, but you are not far off it. I cannot find any successor of Peter in your book who did not act from unworthy motives and make a mistake as to the very nature of his office, Saints although they be. I find only a Church in which the unity of love has been always broken all round; though somehow, in a way that I cannot grasp, the unity of faith (you hold) has been preserved (p. 68)—preserved, you contend, in spite of 'an irrational and unhistoric claim' (p. 69), 'sacrificing the claims of truth and mercy and love' (p. 67) made for fifteen hundred years by the largest and most powerful portion of Christendom; a unity of faith preserved (you declare) in spite of this gigantic error (as you must consider it) touching the very vitals of all religion, laying another foundation of authority than that is laid; a unity of fath preserved, although 'the schismatic spirit' (you admit) 'was at work in the Reformation in England,' and 'the deprival of the Marian prelates in England introduced a certain degree of irregularity into the circumstances of Parker's consecration' (p. 89); a unity of faith preserved in spite of the 'blank conservatism' 'and the ambition which centred round the See of Constantinople.' Why, it is a picture which might be summed up by saying, 'Beautiful bride of Christ, thou hast been altogether faithless to thy Lord: the gates of hell have prevailed against thee: the promises of thy spouse have proved of none effect; and on thy brow should be written not Israel, but Ichabod. The finger of Divine Providence has written of thee on the wall of history, "Mene, Mene, Tekel, Upharsin."'

'Was the Prince of this world,' asks S. Francis, 'driven out with rod of the cross for a period of three or four hundred years to return and reign for a thousand?'

No, indeed; the fact is, to put things at their lowest, that the great S. Cyprian did not die out of communion with the See of S. Peter; that S. Meletius never suffered a formal excommunication; and that S. Augustine, through all his eagerness to maintain a system, as it were, of courts of first instance, still deferred to the Holy See as the final authority, as inheritor of the promises to S. Peter.

And first, to return to the city of Antioch. Where is there any evidence that in all the troubles that beset the See of Antioch Meletius was ever excommunicated? There is positively none. His canonisation is *primâ facie* evidence that he *died* in communion with Rome; his presidency at a General Council proves that he was *then living* in communion with Rome; his subscription to the Epistle of the Roman Synod two years previously proves it to demonstration. And S. Jerome's words to the Pope imply that S. Meletius either told a falsehood or was in communion with Rome, though not supported as against Paulinus. Ep. 16, ad Damasum.

Dr. Pusey's statement on this subject is still less true than your own when he says of S. Meletius that 'when departed he was owned to be a Saint by those who, in his lifetime, owned him not as a Bishop.' The statement can only refer to Rome and the West to have any point in it. But he was unquestionably owned as a Bishop when his subscription to the exposition of the faith of the Roman Synod was deposited in the Roman archives; his signature, thus formally accepted, bears the title of 'Bishop of Antioch.' This simple fact disposes of the entire argument drawn from S. Meletius's relationship to Rome to cover the relationship of England to the Holy See. S. Meletius was never excommunicated; he was, before he died, in formal communion with Rome. Moreover, in speaking of him as 'remaining out of communion with the West and Egypt,' you ignore the fact that, according to S. Basil, S. Athanasius, whom I presume you mean by Egypt, had actually decided to enter into communion with him, but was prevented by some accidental circumstances. This transitory, exceptional incident therefore, in the Church of Antioch, was very different from the formal severance between England and Rome. S. Meletius never rebelled, England did. The truth is, that in the Antiochean dispute Rome seems to have acted with great caution. She showed her keenness for the orthodox faith in sympathising with the horror of so many at Antioch at the idea of being placed under a Bishop who, like Meletius, good as he was, yet had dallied with Arianism. At the same time, while she favoured Paulinus, his rival, as did the great Athanasius, she never seems to have gone the length of excommunicating Meletius, who was where he was through no self-seeking, and in no arrogant spirit; she gave the matter time and room to heal itself, if so it might be. Consequently Meletius could claim still to be in a sort of communion with Rome, as S. Jerome implies, and interchanges of counsel and advice actually took place between him and the West on other matters. No one who has read ever so little of the life and character of Meletius can suppose for a moment that he would have looked to Rome, and claimed to be in communion with Rome, if he held anything like the Anglican view of the See of Rome, or if he had been formally severed from her communion. That he did so claim to be in *some sort* of communion with Rome we have S. Jerome's witness, as I have said. S. Jerome, true to the constant rule of his whole life, only sought to know who was in communion with Rome, to settle with whom he would be in communion himself; but he found that Meletius, as well as Paulinus, was considered to be in communion with her. We do not know what answer S. Jerome received. Probably it was to the effect that he should hold communion with Paulinus and his followers, but that, for all that, Rome had not actually excommunicated the others. This might seem illogical, but it was the logic of charity, and a measure of prudence. And Rome had the supernatural gift of love and the cardinal virtue of prudence.

We come now to Cyprian, a household word with all English Churchmen. 'Remember Cyprian' is almost as universal a motto as 'Remember Mitchelstown' with certain politicians. 'I am willing to be with S. Cyprian;' 'Our position is that of S. Cyprian;' 'If Cyprian could die out of communion with the See of Rome, and yet be a Saint, surely our case, as Anglicans, out of communion as we are with the Holy See, cannot be called unprecedented.'

What, then, were S. Cyprian's dogmatic statements as to the relation of S. Peter to the rest of the Apostles, and the relation of his successors to the Church at large?

I cannot see how any Anglican could adopt his statements as to either with any logical consistency.

There is a passage in the 'Roman Question' in which the writer says: 'I believe S. Cyprian's view of unity to be the true view, viz. that the Church's unity rests on the unity of the Episcopate; that the Episcopate is essentially one, and undivided; and that each Apostolically consecrated Bishop being in direct communion with our Lord and the channel of His grace, the life-blood of the Church's Sacramental existence uninterruptedly continues to flow to each member, through this divinely appointed means.' So far (supposing the writer to except those Apostolically consecrated Bishops who are excommunicate) he is at one with every Catholic divine. The question between us comes further on. How is this one Episcopate officered? How is it kept together when occasion of division arises? Has this one Episcopate (whose members are all equal in the fellowship and honour of Order) any head? Did it arise as a tree from its root? Does it still grow as a tree with its spreading branches, all the branches in communion with *a root, in the same order of life*? Has it a visible, Sacramental head, or is it not, after all, in the strictest sense a body, having no head, in the same order of life, *i.e.* the visible and temporal? Here is the question which supervenes. And on this important part of the question the venerable author, in common with yourself (p. 56), is, it seems to me, at variance with S. Cyprian. For he goes on to say (p. 2) that 'S. Cyprian recognised S. Peter as the symbol of unity by Divine grace; but that he at the same time made it clear that not Rome, nor any one Episcopal See, but the entire collective Episcopate, are represented under the symbolic character ascribed by our Lord to S. Peter.' And you say (p. 56) that 'the theory of the See of S. Peter held by the African theologians of the third and fourth centuries, while it makes the Roman See amongst other Churches the symbol of unity, as Peter was amongst the Apostles, does not involve any distinctive authority in the Roman See.'

But how could Peter be a symbol of unity, unless

he bore a special relationship to the other Apostles? He would be a symbol of the solitary, not of unity. And could that relationship be nothing more than what Dr. Barrow profanely calls 'a womanish prerogative,' a mere name, with no right, no authority, no authorised position in the movement of the Church's life, nothing but the honour of receiving some praise, with no practical issue? or did he take precedence of the rest by Divine authority? S. Chrysostom, as we have seen, says that he did. And this is the real question. Whatever its extent, it cannot be, to use again the great Anglican theologian Dr. Barrow's flippant words, as quoted by yourself, 'a conceit, in which there is little solidity and as little harm.' Whatever it was that our Lord made S. Peter, it must have been something tremendously real, very vital, quite supernatural; for it was a subject of His own prophecy; it was ushered in, in His promise, by the declaration that the Apostle was the subject of a special Divine revelation; and it was solemnly conferred at the Sea of Tiberias. Was it making him *only* a symbol? A symbol must rest on something. And was S. Peter, *by himself*, and not as the source of a stream, a symbol of unity?

Now S. Cyprian says that S. Peter was not merely a symbol of unity, not merely, as you put it, that his See was 'the symbol of Episcopacy in which all Bishops equally share,' but he says more; he says that, 'in order to manifest unity, He has by His own authority so placed the *source of the same unity as to begin from one*.' What can really be clearer than that this is not the case of a mere symbol, but *the very creation of an actual source*? Not that S. Peter differed from the others in point of Order, if one may so speak of the Apostolate, for 'certainly the other Apostles also were what Peter was'—*i.e.* not the source of unity, but, nevertheless, Apostles, with immediate commission from our Lord, and with personal inspiration, 'endued with an equal fellowship of honour and power.' They were to sit on twelve thrones. But we are not to suppose from this that there was no visible source where unity took its rise, no head, no root and womb of the Church; for S. Cyprian goes on to say that, in spite of the Apostles' equal fellowship in honour and power, there is something further; there is still the fact that S. Peter's relation is peculiar—for, as he goes on to say, '*but* a commencement is made from unity, that the Church may be set forth as "one."' S. Cyprian begins with saying that our Lord has so placed the 'source' of the same unity as to begin with one; then he interrupts himself to give the Apostles their due glory, but *returns* to the original source of unity, viz. S. Peter as Divinely placed there by our Lord. In his quotation on p. 7 the writer of the 'Roman Question' omits the preface to this argument of S. Cyprian's, which, nevertheless, governs the whole of the passage. S. Cyprian says—and it is much to be noted in view of English history—that 'falling away from the Church and schism will exist so long as there is no regard to the *source* of truth, no looking to the *head*, nor keeping the doctrine of a Heavenly Master.' He then says that there is an easy proof to a faithful mind. And, in giving the easy proof, he goes at once to Peter, and our Lord's promise to him. And then, after the passage concerning this oneness of the Episcopate, under its one head, he likens the Church to a *stream flowing from its source*, which we have seen is S. Peter ('so placed the source of unity as to begin from one')—to a body with its head full of light—to a mother with her Divine fruitfulness—'one head, one source, one mother.' These are favourite expressions with S. Cyprian. The successor of S. Peter and his See are with him the 'root and womb' of the Catholic Church. The Church of the Romans is the *'Chair of Peter*, and the principal Church whence the unity of the priesthood *took its rise.*' 'From this, through the changes of times and succession, the ordinations of Bishops, and the *principle of the Church* descends, so that the Church is constituted upon Bishops.' 'GOD is One, and Christ is One, and the Church One, and One the chair founded upon a rock by the Lord's voice.' 'One Church founded by Christ the Lord upon Peter, the origin and principle of unity.' 'To Peter first, upon whom he built the Church, and from whom He instituted and set forth the origin of unity.' Or, as S. Optatus says in the same century (and to his view of unity you especially refer your readers in one passage, saying that the 'most exact theory that we have is that propounded and developed by the great theologians S. Cyprian, S. Optatus, and S. Augustine' [p. 36]), 'You cannot deny that you know that the chair of Peter first of all was fixed in the city of Rome, in which Peter, the head of all the Apostles, sat; whence, too, he was named Cephas; in which single chair unity was to be observed by all, so that the rest of the Apostles should not each maintain a chair to themselves, and that forthwith he should be a schismatic and a sinner who against that singular chair set up another.' And again: 'For the good of unity, blessed Peter both deserved to be preferred to all the Apostles, and alone received the keys of the Kingdom of Heaven, which were afterwards to be communicated to the rest.' Or, as S. Pacian puts it to another Donatist, 'He spake to one, that from one He might shape out unity.'

<small>Ep. 55, ad Corn.</small>
<small>Ep. 38 Lapsis.</small>
<small>Ep. 40. ad Plebem.</small>
<small>Ep. 70. ad Januar.</small>
<small>Ep. 43, ad Corn.</small>
<small>De Schism. Donat. i. 10</small>
<small>Ep. iii.</small>

S. Cyprian, therefore, held that S. Peter was a source, not a symbol only; that he had a Primacy given to him by our Lord Himself; and we know that, when speaking of Cornelius having succeeded Fabian, on the death of the latter, in the See of Rome, he says, 'when

<small>Ep. 52, ad Anton.</small>

the place of Fabian, that is, when the place of Peter ... was vacant.' The place of Peter! Here is the whole question in one short phrase. Even if the expression 'head' in the passage on which we have commented above be referred to our Lord, we have in S. Cyprian the doctrine that Peter is not (I repeat) merely a symbol, but the *source* of unity; as streams, he says, have their multiplicity of waters, but are kept one, 'their unity is preserved in the source itself,' which source he has said in the same passage is S. Peter, and that the place of the Pope is the 'place of Peter,' or, as he calls it elsewhere, 'the chair (or See) of Peter.'

<small>Ep. 55, ad Corn.</small>

Evidently there is a chasm between the teaching of S. Cyprian on the subject of unity and anything which will cover the Anglican position. The Protestant historian Mosheim has felt constrained to remark that 'Cyprian and the rest cannot have known the corollaries which follow from their precepts about the Church. For no one is so blind as not to see that between a certain unity of the Universal Church terminating in the Roman Pontiff, and such a community as we have described out of Irenæus and Cyprian, there is scarcely so much room as between hall and chambers, or between hand and fingers.' Indeed, from the passage we have just quoted, it will be seen there is not even the space supposed by Mosheim: the teaching of Rome now and the teaching of S. Cyprian in the third century are simply and perfectly identical. The place of Fabian the Pope = 'the place of Peter;' the See of Rome = 'the chair of Peter.'

Does, then, S. Cyprian in his Episcopal life, in his actual attitude towards the Holy See, contradict his formal teaching about Peter being 'the source of unity'? A man's life is not always as true as his teaching. Did S. Cyprian fail, under the provocation and stress of circumstances?

Now let us remember that, because S. Paul had to fight for his authority, it does not follow that his Apostleship was doubtful; and because he wrote to Timothy and Titus, 'Let no man despise you,' it cannot be said that they were not Bishops, or that they were guilty of innovation or usurpation. If S. Cyprian *had* for a while resisted the authority of Rome, resistance would not cover the Anglican position. S. Cyprian, however, through the greater part of his life was most deferential to the occupant of S. Peter's See. He held, indeed, the strongest opinion concerning the authority of every Bishop in communion with the rest of the world. A Bishop out of communion with the rest of the Catholic world had, according to him, 'neither the power nor the honour of a Bishop.' But a Bishop in communion with the Catholic Church had to look forward to a judgment in which no one but his Divine Lord was judge. 'Each Prelate hath, in the government of his Church, his own choice and free will, hereafter to give account of his conduct to the Lord.' So he speaks when he invites the Bishops of his Province to give their opinion in his presence, without respect of persons, and, perhaps, wishing them also not to regard further consequences. Not that he considered that there was no one on earth to judge a Bishop, so far as judgment on earth could go. This would be to extinguish the authority even of Provincial and General Councils, which he could never have meant, although some Protestant writers, in quoting the above passage by way of proving that Cyprian acknowledged no one above himself, really land the Saint in a state of opposition to all the Constitutions and Canons of the Church. He had indeed his own authority to uphold in his Province. He was not only Bishop of Carthage, but Primate of Africa; and he must have held, n accordance with all Catholic teaching at that time, that the Metropolitan was the source of mission and jurisdiction within his Province. He tells us that no one amongst the Bishops of Africa, 'no one of us,' called himself 'Bishop of Bishops;' but he writes thus to the Bishop of Rome, urging him to secure the deposition of the Bishop of Arles: 'Let letters be addressed *from thee to the Province*, and to the people dwelling at Arles, *whereby Marcianus being excommunicated*, another may be substituted in his room, and the flock of Christ . . . be again collected together. . . . Signify plainly to us who has been substituted in Arles in the room of Marcianus, that we may know to whom we should direct our brethren, and to whom write.' It is clear from this that S. Cyprian's expression as to the Episcopate being 'a whole in which each enjoys full possession,' did not interfere with his holding that one Bishop could be superior to another in point of jurisdiction. It is also clear from this that S. Cyprian was at this time on the best of terms with S. Stephen the Pope.

<small>S. Cyprian's Works Clarke's Tr.), vol. i. p. 2.</small>

Did he, then, suffer excommunication from this same Pope? This is asserted by yourself, and by the author of the 'Roman Question;' and his relationship to Rome is consequently compared to the relationship between Rome and England.

If so, it would have been only during the years 254-7. The above friendly letter to S. Stephen was written A.D. 254. S. Stephen gained his heavenly crown A.D. 257, having been beheaded in his pontifical chair whilst celebrating the holy mysteries. S. Cyprian followed him A.D. 258; and, as Tillemont remarks, 'The Roman Church has always shown such great veneration for S. Cyprian, that there *can be no doubt* that he *died* in unity with her, not only through the disposition of his heart, but also through external communion.'

During those three years was there any interruption of

outward communion between S. Stephen and S. Cyprian? There *may have been* such for some short period; and that is the most that can be said. There is *no* positive evidence that there was.

But let us suppose for a moment that there was such a temporary interruption of communion. Can it for a moment be compared with the severance of England from the Holy See? Would it imply that there was a place within the bosom of the Church for those who separate on the grounds that England did in the time of Henry VIII., or again under Elizabeth, *with all that change of doctrine*, altering the number of Sacraments, dropping one altogether, changing the mode of ordination; accusing, in public documents to be signed by her clergy, the See of Rome of idolatry and her teaching on Justification, on the Sacraments, on the Government of the Church, of heresy? Why, you might as well compare a passing thunderstorm on a summer's day, which rolls about amongst the mountains and shakes a house or two in the city, to an earthquake which changes the whole features of a region and permanently severs continents; you might as well compare a breakfast quarrel with its reconciliation at lunch, to a civil war which ends in a permanently separate rule, as compare S. Cyprian's 'brotherly altercation' (as S. Augustine calls it) to the position adopted by England for three hundred years towards the Holy See.

But there is *no* evidence that S. Cyprian was *ever* under excommunication; much less that he died out of communion with the See of Rome. Eusebius does not mention it, nor even hint at it. S. Augustine's language does not favour it; indeed, it seems to negative the idea: 'Vicit tamen pax Christi in cordibus eorum, ut in tali disceptatione nullum inter eos malum schismatis oriretur.' Elsewhere he says that it may not unsuitably be be-

Ep. ad Vincent.

lieved of such a man that he corrected his opinion. Indeed, S. Augustine says that either there was a mistake, and 'his opinion was other than has been said; or else he afterwards corrected it by the rule of truth; or else he entirely covered over this spot (so to speak) in his most pure breast with the abundance of charity, whilst he most abundantly defended the unity of the Church which was increasing in all the world, and most perseveringly maintained the bond of peace.' Our own Venerable Bede, though he does not give his authority, states it as a fact that, through the abundance of his good work, 'Cyprian merited to be speedily corrected and to be brought back to the Universal law of the Holy Church by the instruction of spiritual men.'

And, indeed, it seems evident from one of his Epistles that S. Cyprian had friendly communication with Rome at the time of the persecution under Valerian, in which the Pope S. Stephen suffered martyrdom, and this 'persecution' commenced in 257.

What S. Cyprian's action in the matter of the rebaptization of heretics shows is this—that on a matter of discipline, new, as he thought, to the Church, he felt it open to him to contest the judgment of the Pope. And so far, of course, he was strictly within his rights. S. Stephen did not issue any *ex cathedrâ* decision as to the speculative question. He only insisted that the discipline hitherto in vogue should be maintained. S. Cyprian in this matter was, we know, very wrong; S. Stephen the Pope was right. The Church has ever since acted on S. Stephen's ruling. She never rebaptizes heretics, unless there is a doubt about the validity of the form used. S. Cyprian would have rebaptized them all. S. Stephen threatened to excommunicate all who adopted the new departure. There is no evidence that he ever proceeded to execute his threat. There is, indeed, one disgraceful letter, written by Firmilian, which has been taken to imply that he did. But as the very sentence in which the statement occurs contains a most exaggerated account of the situation, we may feel ourselves at liberty to regard this statement also as exaggerated. Dr. Pusey makes much of this miserable letter of Firmilian's, but he fails to draw one obvious conclusion, which is that it contains a witness to the fact that S. Stephen held that his position called upon him to exercise authority over even the Primate of Africa, and all who sided with him, and that this right in itself was not once contested, but only the propriety of its exercise in that particular instance. Dr. Pusey speaks of Firmilian as 'one now counted a Saint;' but he has never obtained that place in the Roman Calendar. And he quotes Firmilian's saying about S. Stephen : 'While thinking that all may be excommunicated by him, he excommunicated himself alone.' Yet S. Stephen was right, and S. Cyprian and Firmilian were wrong, and S. Augustine, as we have seen, hopes that S. Cyprian corrected his error in this matter. The whole letter of Firmilian is so unbecoming from any one Bishop to any other, that it has been doubted whether it is genuine. Only a Latin copy is extant, bound up with S. Cyprian's letters. Firmilian's assertion was, indeed, flagrantly false, for it is notorious that S. Stephen did not stand alone. S. Augustine says that S. Cyprian's party consisted of 'some fifty Orientals, and seventy or a few more Africans, against many hundreds of Bishops, to whom this error was displeasing, throughout the whole world.' It has been well said of Firmilian's letter that 'it was not a Saintly one, whoever was its author.' But it bears witness to the existence of the authority of the Holy See, for it speaks ironically of S. Stephen preserving humility *primo in loco* (in the position of Primate), and shows in the very sentence quoted by Dr. Pusey that he held the same conviction concerning his own responsibilities in the middle of the third century that S. Leo did in the middle of the fifth century.

In fact, the whole controversy tells in favour of Papal Supremacy. It shows that truth must be Rome-marked, as metal must be Hall-marked, if we are to be sure that it *is* truth. S. Cyprian, insisting on rebaptizing heretics, could claim in his favour the Synod of Carthage, under Agrippinus, the Synod of Iconium under Firmilian, together with the contemporary Synod under Synnada. Nevertheless, Antiquity was against him; Apostolical tradition was against him; the practice of the Universal Church could be said to be against him. Where was the living voice, the present authority to decide which way Antiquity, Apostolical tradition, and the practice of the Church went? It was found in S. Stephen.

And if Rome had no jurisdiction over Africa and Asia Minor, why did not the Prelates of those Provinces smile at Rome's threats, instead of growing so uneasy about excommunication? Why did they have recourse to every argument *except* the argument that Stephen was an usurper, and that the Bishops of Africa were independent of him? For Firmilian's angry remonstrance did not amount to that. It bitterly resented the particular exercise; it did not question the right in the abstract.

He says that the Pontiff contended 'that he holds the succession of Peter' (this in the middle of the third century) 'upon whom the foundations of the Church were laid,' and that he 'proclaims that he occupies by succession the chair of Peter;' but Firmilian does not appear to dispute either of these statements, but wishes the Pope to act up to this exalted position by allowing heretics to be rebaptized. I may notice, in passing, that if Firmilian's letter is genuine, it is absolutely conclusive against a statement made by the author of the 'Roman Question,' p. 36, that 'four hundred years had elapsed since the foundation of the Roman See, without any sign of such an authority being possessed by it,' *i.e.* of an authority derived from S. Peter. S. Stephen claimed it, according to Firmilian, in the third century.

S. Cyprian himself does not seem to doubt that the arm of a Pope stretched to Africa as readily as to Gaul. He can appeal to the direct judgment of GOD, but not as setting aside the office of the Pontiff, only to encourage the Bishops to speak their minds. His own argument against Stephen showed that, *without Stephen*, he himself was nowhere. For when he endeavoured to prove that 'Remission' was impossible *outside the Church*, he contended that *in the Church* there was 'Remission.' How? 'For, first of all, the Lord gave the power to *Peter, upon whom He built His Church*, and whom He appointed and showed,' not the symbol, but 'the *source* of unity; the power, namely, that whatsoever he loosed,' &c. <small>Clarke's Cyprian, vol. i. p. 264.</small>

And elsewhere, complaining of Pope Stephen, he indirectly assumes his Primacy, for he dwells, by contrast, on the patience of Peter when Paul disputed with *him.* Peter did not *say* to Paul that he 'held the Primacy.' <small>Ibid. p 255.</small> The remark would be irrelevant unless, in Cyprian's opinion, S. Peter did hold the Primacy, and was succeeded in it by S. Stephen. Just as S. Gregory says of the same incident in S. Peter's life, 'he is reproved by his inferior, and he is not impatient of the reproof; he does not remind him (S. Paul) that it is he (S. Peter) who has received the keys.' <small>Lib. ii. in Ezek. hom. xviii.</small>

In conclusion, we must remember that S. Stephen was a Martyr Pope, as S. Cyprian was a Martyr Bishop. *Heretics* and *Schismatics* have thought it heroic that Carthage disputed with Rome; but *Fathers* and *Doctors* have felt that Cyprian's conduct called for apology rather than for approbation. The immortal Augustine exclaims: 'I will not review what he poured out against Stephen, under irritation.' When the Donatists invoked the name of Cyprian against S. Augustine, the great doctor bade them remember of his brother of Carthage that 'he was cleansed by the pruning-knife of martyrdom, if in this matter there was need of purification.' And when the same heretics worried S. Augustine with their stale interminable refrain, 'Cyprian,' turning upon them he said, with tremendous energy: 'You are, indeed, accustomed to object to us the letters of Cyprian, the opinion of Cyprian, the Council of Cyprian. Why do you take the authority of Cyprian for your schism, and reject his example for the peace of the Church?'

S. Vincent of Lerins considers that the whole incident redounds to the glory of S. Stephen, 'thinking it fit that he should surpass all others in the devotedness of his faith, as much as he excelled them *by the authority of his station*. Finally, in the epistle which was sent to Africa, he decreed in these words that 'No innovation should be admitted, but that what was handed down should be retained.' What force had the African Council or decree? None, through the mercy of God.'

S. Cyprian misinterpreted the tradition of the Church: the living voice of the Church in S. Stephen set him right.

It is simply, then, beyond dispute that S. Stephen, long before the Council of Nice, claimed authority over Africa by virtue of his succession from S. Peter; that S. Cyprian sent him the acts of the African Synod, and compared him to S. Peter, and spoke of the Church as built upon Peter, and of S. Peter as the source of unity; and though restive under the exercise of the Pope's authority in one important matter, in which he (Cyprian) was mistaken, he never denied it in itself; and if he said

[margin: S. Jer. Dial. adv. Lucif.]

violent things about its particular exercise and the judgment concerning the Church's tradition, he has either, *according to S. Augustine,* been misrepresented and his letters forged, or he was cleansed by the sickle of his passion. Of the idea that he died out of communion with the See of Rome there is no evidence; that he was ever formally excommunicated is but a baseless dream.

What, then, of S. Augustine himself? Did he, in the whole case of Apiarius, the priest, who appealed to Rome, deny the jurisdiction of the Pope altogether over Africa; or did he simply demur to the extent to which the exercise of that jurisdiction was being carried by the reigning Pope? Did his entreaty that the archives of Alexandria, Antioch, and Constantinople should be consulted as to the authenticity of the Canons which Zosimus (following his predecessor's frequent expression) quoted as Canons of Nicæa, amount to more than this, viz. that *since the Pope did not, in this matter, see fit to rest the matter on his own authority as S. Peter's successor,* but, as it were, said, 'The Bishops themselves have acquiesced in my interpretation of the extent of my authority,' S. Augustine felt at liberty to inquire whether this was really so? And does it not make all the difference, that Zosimus did not, as many seem to imagine, address a document himself to the African fathers, but S. Augustine is combating the message which the Legates brought? Zosimus was not pointing out the source of his own authority, but bidding the Legates inform the Africans of the plan for its exercise which had been acquiesced in by a Council of Bishops—a Council of such importance, viz. that of Sardica, that its Canons were bound up with the Canons of the Council of Nicæa, and did actually in the event determine the Church's action for the future.

Let it be remembered, too, that the whole question debated between S. Augustine and the Legates did not touch the authority of the Pope on matters of faith; he and his fellow-Bishops simply expostulated against what they thought the undue exercise of a right of appeal, which in itself, in some form and measure, none of them denied. They thought that national discipline was in danger, and they contended for a measure of autonomy which would better secure that discipline. But they give no sign of having ever dreamt of entire independence.

As regards the authority of the See of S. Peter on matters of faith, S. Augustine is most explicit and emphatic. He tells the Donatists that the Bishop of Carthage could afford to disregard the opposition with which he met, because he was united by letters of communion with the rest of the world, not only 'with the other lands whence the Gospel came to Africa itself,' but 'with the Roman Church, in which the principate of the Apostolic See hath ever been in force.' He is speaking of a time anterior to the Council of Nice, and therefore does not suppose that the Council of Nice gave to the 'Apostolic See' that 'princedom' of which he speaks, for before that Council it 'was in force,' yea, it 'was always in force.'

<small>De Util. Cred. 17.</small>

It is S. Augustine who asks: 'Shall we then hesitate to hide ourselves in the bosom of the Church, which, even by the confession of the human race, hath obtained possession of supreme authority from the Apostolic See, by the succession of Bishops,' &c.?

It is S. Augustine who was held to the Church, as by other things, so also 'by that succession of priests from the chair itself of the Apostle Peter, to whom the Lord after His Resurrection commended His sheep to be fed,' and who speaks of Anastasius, Bishop of Rome, as 'sitting in the chair of Peter.' He it is who says the cause of Pelagianism was at an end when the answer

<small>Ep. Fund. Man. 5. Ep. 55. Generoso.</small>

came back from the Apostolic See, which has been well summarised. 'Roma locuta est: causa finita est.' S. Augustine it is who says that amongst the Apostles 'Peter alone merited to bear the person of the Church,' and that to the Church 'were the keys of the Kingdom of Heaven given when given to Peter,' and who explains the meaning of S. Cyprian's words about a commencement being made from unity, when he says of Peter, that he was 'the oneness in many,' and again 'therefore one in the name of all, because he is the unity in all.'

But, above all, his observations on the Letters of S. Innocent I. are conclusive as to his formed teaching on the authority of the Holy See. S. Innocent had written to the Council of Carthage, speaking of the African bishops: 'Knowing what is due to the Apostolic See, since all we who are placed in this position desire to follow the Apostle himself, from whom the very Episcopate and all the authority of this title sprung,' and further on: 'Ye resolve that these regulations should not be trodden under foot, while they (the Fathers), in pursuance of no human but a Divine sentence, have decreed, viz. that whatever was being carried on, although in the most distant and remote provinces, should not be terminated before it was brought to the knowledge of this See, by the full authority of which the just sentence should be confirmed, and that thence all other churches might derive what they should order.'

Now here is a contention touching the root of the matter absolutely fatal to the Anglican position.

And again, speaking of the Church under a favourite simile of the Fathers, as many streams from one fountain and of the 'Apostolic fountain,' S. Innocent, addressing the Council of Numidia, says: 'Especially so often as a matter of faith is under discussion, I conceive that all our brethren and fellow Bishops can only refer to Peter, that is, the source of their own name and honour, just as your affection hath now referred, for what may benefit all Churches in common throughout the whole world. For the inventors of evils must necessarily become more cautious when they see that at the reference of a double synod they have been severed from ecclesiastical communion by *our sentence.*'

Now what must you yourself; what must the author of the 'Roman Question;' what must Dr. Pusey have said in reviewing these letters of S. Innocent I.? You must have repudiated his estimate of the position assigned to him by our Lord.

S. Augustine does pass them under review, and S. Augustine says: 'He answered to all as was right and as it became the prelate of the Apostolical See.'

Certainly the relationship between Rome and England bears no resemblance to the relationship between Rome and Africa in the days of Augustine, and the principles of authority laid down in S. Augustine's formal teaching contains the most emphatic condemnation of the position of the Church of England that words can convey.

There is, indeed, a most curious coincidence in the use made by yourself, and by Dr. Pusey, of a simile, which happens to have been also used by S. Augustine in reference to the same subject, but with an exactly opposite application.

You compare the separate bodies of religionists to the stream which 'went out of Eden to water the garden: and from thence it was parted and became into four heads.' You compare the 'various Churches,' as they are sometimes called, to these parted streams, flowing out of Paradise—'they still before the throne of God are one Holy Catholic Apostolic Church.'

S. Augustine, on the contrary, says: 'For the streams too, as Scripture witnesses, flowed broadly from the fountain of Paradise, even outside of it; since they are mentioned by name, and all know through what lands they flow, and that they were placed outside of Paradise: not, however, that the happiness of the life which is mentioned in Paradise is to be found in Mesopotamia or in Egypt, whither these streams reached. Thus it is that though the water of Paradise be outside of Paradise, the blessedness is only within Paradise. So, therefore, the Church's baptism may be outside the Church; but the gift of a blessed life is only to be found within the Church, which likewise is founded upon the rock, and has received the keys of binding and loosening.'

Thus whilst Dr. Pusey is content to be in one of the streams outside of Paradise, which, though parted, he considers still to be one, S. Augustine looks upon those parted streams as failing to impart the blessed life which is found only in Paradise, that is, within the Church.

I conclude, then, this entire appeal to the Fathers with adopting S. Jerome's words.

I am not surprised that every effort is made (as, for instance, by the author of the 'Roman Question,' p. 23) to evacuate S. Jerome's witness to the magisterium of S. Peter's successor of its tremendous significance. S. Jerome, of all men, might be expected to be an important witness for or against the Papal form of Christianity. Living in the full blaze of all the difficulties that beset the exercise of that magisterium, in the very sunshine of Scriptural study, under the illuminating influence of an austere virginal life of prayer and spiritual guidance, and in Palestine at Bethlehem, and yet in full correspondence with the West, his witness is, of course, of quite exceptional importance. And it is of the clearest and most emphatic character. When, for instance, some came to him in Antioch, and the question was whether he should hold communion with them or not, what did he do? He desired to know which of them was in communion with the See of S. Peter. That was all he asked, all he desired to know. He says to Pope Damasus: 'I speak with *the successor of the Fisherman*, and the disciple of the Cross. I, following no chief, save Christ, am counted in communion with your blessedness, that is, *with the chair of Peter*. On that Rock I know the Church is built.' And again: 'I cry out, if any one is joined with the chair of Peter, he is mine.'

<small>Plain Reasons, S.P.C.K.</small>

And let us note that if Damasus had been, as Dr. Littledale profanely calls him, 'a murderous rioter,' these words of S. Jerome are an indefinitely more valuable witness to the necessity of communion with the See of Peter. Even if occupied by a 'murderous rioter,' it would still, in the Saint's opinion, be necessary to be in communion with him, as the successor of S. Peter.

I am not surprised, therefore, that you should be anxious to discredit S. Jerome's witness. It is really fatal to the Anglican position. But I am surprised that, in endeavouring to do so, you should not merely fall into a serious mistake in your quotation, but also level a sweeping and very severe accusation against the whole body of 'Roman controversialists'!

<small>P. 56.</small>

You accuse them of unfairness in not quoting the passage in S. Jerome which speaks of the various Sees of 'Rome and Eugubium, and Constantinople and Rhegium, and Alexandria and Tanis,' as being of the same 'merit and sacerdotium.'

And yet why should they quote it? What has it to do with the question of the jurisdiction of one See over another—*i.e.* with the question between Rome and England? You do not surely suppose that all Sees are equal in point of *jurisdiction*, or that S. Jerome thought so? You do not, for instance, suppose that there is no difference between Constantinople and Rhegium, or no kind of jurisdiction attaching to a Patriarch?

Yet the only point in quoting this passage of S. Jerome would lie in the supposition that he states that all Sees are *thus* equal. Else what has it to do with the matter in hand?

But a more serious matter is, that you have given to the whole letter a meaning for which there is no evidence whatever. You speak of S. Jerome's being pressed with the authority of Rome, and, *under such pressure*, pleading the equality of all Sees, and, consequently, repudiating the authority of Rome.

It would be strange, indeed, if S. Jerome, 'later in life,' as you say (though there is no proof that it was later in life), pressed with the authority of the Roman See, which, you say, he did not like, should have used 'exactly the opposite tone.'

But in this letter to which you refer, for proof of these statements, he does no such thing. There is, unfortunately, no evidence forthcoming as to the time of the Saint's life at which this letter was written, except that it was after a visit to Rome. We know how S. Jerome once at least, when at Rome, sided with the Bishop of Rome in his endeavour to correct a state of things in the city due to the haughtiness of the Clergy. And this particular letter deals with certain local customs with which it looks as if the Bishop of Rome had some difficulty in dealing. The Saint speaks of what he had seen done in the absence of the Bishop; how the deacons took precedence of Priests. We know how difficult it is to deal with such customs as he mentions. The deacons, from their fewness in number in the city of Rome, had acquired a great social position, and hence on occasion behaved as though superior to the Priests. S. Jerome tells us in this letter that he had seen them pronounce a benediction at private houses before a Priest. And so he argues thus : He points out the difference between a Priest and a deacon *all over the world* ; he speaks of the Sacerdotal power in which a Priest excels a deacon, and this, he says, is the same everywhere, whether a Priest is rich or poor. A Bishop, according to S. Jerome, differed from a Priest only in the power of ordaining. As he says: 'Wherever a Bishop is, whether at Rome, or Gubbio, or Constantinople, &c., he is of the same "meritum," and the same priesthood ; the power of wealth or the depth of poverty does not make a Bishop higher or lower, but all are successors of the Apostles.' His argument, therefore, is this : The Sacerdotium (which, in its fulness in the Episcopate, constitutes its possessor anywhere and under whatever circumstances of poverty or the like a successor of the Apostles) makes all the difference between a Priest and a deacon ; and therefore a deacon should never take precedence of a Priest.

So that the quotation has no bearing on the relationship between various Sees in respect of jurisdiction. No one supposes that Gubbio, Reggio, and Tanis were considered equal with Rome, Constantinople, and Alexandria in that respect.

It would, therefore, have been an insult on the part of 'Roman controversialists' to suppose that any Anglican would have been misled by such a sentence in S. Jerome's letter. And it is matter for regret that you should have gone so far as to add that S. Jerome wrote the letter under the pressure of authority which he disliked, when all the evidence goes to show that he wrote in support of authority with which he sympathised.

A Catholic, then, adopts as his own the words of S. Jerome :

'I speak with the successor of the Fisherman, and the

disciple of the Cross. I, following none as the first, but Christ, am associated in communion with thy blessedness, that is, with *the chair of Peter. On that rock the Church is built, I know.* Whoso shall eat the Lamb outside this house is profane.'

APPENDIX.

THE FORGED DECRETALS.

Is there any foundation for the contention that the authority of the Pope as supreme head of the Church under Christ owed its establishment to these Decretals?

What was the history of these spurious Decretals?

They consist of a collection of Papal decisions, partly genuine, partly false ; forged not in Rome but in France ; not in the interest of Rome so much as in the interest of Bishops, probably by a man who had suffered, and felt that his only chance of redress was to be found in the cautious, impartial judgment which was synonymous with Papal decisions. He wanted that authority, which clearly (I suppose I may say unquestionably, for anyone who has read them) was *already acknowledged* as supreme, to be invoked more often, and as a matter of obligation in a larger number of cases. It is so untrue that the Holy See caught at their support, that there is positive evidence to the contrary. The S.P.C.K. has endorsed a gross misrepresentation on this point, and cruelly distributed translations of it amongst the faithful of other lands besides our own. It occurs in Dr. Littledale's 'Plain Reasons,' who has the hardihood to assert that these Decretals 'were eagerly seized on by Pope Nicolas I. . . . to aid in revolutionising the Church, as he, in fact, largely succeeded in doing' (p. 117). The fact is, that when for the first time these Decretals were quoted to Pope Nicolas, he made *no use* of them in his reply, which he based on other considerations.[1] And there is no evidence that he ever used them at all. The popular Protestant notion is that some Pope, or Popes, looking about for some support to their authority, forged these Decretals, or had them forged, or connived at their forgery, or, as Dr. Littledale, with his usual inaccuracy, says, 'eagerly seized on them' when they appeared. There is not a word of truth in all this. For some reason or other the Pope did not use them when they first appeared. One might have expected otherwise. For, considering the state of literary criticism, the lack of our modern critical apparatus, there would have been nothing surprising in the Pope's accepting them as genuine at once, agreeing as they did, in the main, with the state of things already established. Dr. Littledale's notion that Popes could have at once consulted their own archives and settled the matter implies an entire ignorance of the state of the case. Papal Decretals were not necessarily confined to the Papal archives; and there was nothing in these Decretals to startle or suggest inquiry.

This latter statement can be easily proved by considering whether the essential features of Papal authority were in existence at some given date before the pseudo-Decretals stole into acceptance. I have already shown that they were. But it is worth while insisting on this point. Let us take the history of a Pope who lived more than two hundred years before the pseudo-Decretals were forged—the history of Gregory the Great.[2] If the Papal claims, in their essence, were made and admitted in the

[1] See an article on this subject in the *Month*, March 1881.
[2] I am indebted for much that follows to Fr. S. Smith's *Alleged Antiquity of Anglicanism.*

time of Gregory the Great, the Protestant contention falls to the ground. Gregory the Great lived much more than two hundred years before the pseudo-Decretals appeared, and a great deal longer still before they can be shown to have been adopted into the collection used by the Popes.

Now S. Gregory says that he 'knows not what Bishop is not subject to the Apostolic See.'

Nothing in the false Decretals goes beyond this. Therefore the doctrine of the subjection of all Sees to the See of S. Peter did not originate with the false Decretals.

Let us look at S. Gregory's act to see his practical interpretation of this doctrine, and its recognition by others.

He rebukes the Metropolitan of Ravenna for wearing the symbol of authority at times when he should not. It was a delicate matter, touching the comparative authority of the Pope and Metropolitan. The plea which the Metropolitan preferred was not one which repudiated Gregory's right to interfere. The whole case reveals a claim and admission of the claim to interfere, as decided and ample as any suggested by the false Decretals.

In France the Bishop of Arles is made his 'vicegerent,' and rules are given by which he is to be bound in the exercise of his metropolitical authority. All the Bishops of Gaul are exhorted by Gregory to render obedience to Vergilius. Could the false Decretals go further than this?

England was, we know, considered by S. Gregory to be under his jurisdiction.

In the province of Illyria he appoints a papal Vicar, and places all the other Bishops under him. And when he acts contrary to what S. Gregory considers right, the Saint writes to him :—' By the authority of Blessed Peter,

Prince of the Apostles, we cancel and annul the decrees which you have passed.' (Ep. liii. c. 6.)

What was there for Pope Nicolas to revolutionise, or the false Decretals to establish after this? They could only insist on some minor and comparatively inconsiderable points.

Passing from West to East, we find that the Patriarchs of the East are held to be under his jurisdiction, and that 'his claims met with recognition, though not with invariable obedience.'

He says, for instance, ' As to what they say about the Church of Constantinople, who is there that doubts about its subjection to the Apostolic See? As the most pious Sovereign the Emperor *and our brother the Bishop of that city* assiduously profess.'

What, I ask again, could the forged Decretals teach, after this, except some comparatively insignificant issues?

And S. Gregory *acted* on this teaching in the East. In Asia Minor he reversed the sentence of the Patriarch of Constantinople in the case of a certain Athanasius, and he writes to a friend, 'If I find that the canons are not observed at the bidding of the Apostolic See, Almighty God will show me how to treat those who contemn Him.'

So it is in writing to John, Patriarch of Constantinople, that, whilst refusing the title of Œcumenical Bishop, which seemed to Gregory's humble soul to savour of Antichrist, he uses the words quoted above, 'I know not what Bishop is not subject to the Apostolic See.' And he tells him that if he should refuse to amend, he has commissioned his representative not to celebrate mass with him, 'with the intention that if this wicked and impious pride cannot be cured by shame, I may proceed to severe measures according to the canons.' This was of a Patriarch of Constantinople.

Thus S. Gregory acts upon the whole Catholic world; and on the principle that there is no Bishop that is not subject to his See. And the Catholic world sees no novelty in his claim.

It must be sufficiently clear from all this, that there was nothing of real importance for false Decretals to inaugurate in the way of teaching on the supremacy of the See of Rome. It was taught and acted upon throughout the world more than two centuries before their fabrication. It was taught and acted upon by S. Gregory, and accepted in East and West. And in this single fact, the Anglican contention concerning the pseudo-Isidorian Decretals simply falls to the ground.

In these Decretals, as Fr. Sydney Smith remarks, 'there is very little of any moment which is original. The fraud consists in assigning the language of a later period to writers of an earlier one'—though sometimes the case is actually the reverse. 'And the purpose of securing the clergy against the accusations made in the interest of avarice, which is avowed in the preface, is stamped on the text from end to end.' 'It is not the assertion of Papal power which is uppermost in the writer's mind—it is not here that he reveals any consciousness of any adversary to be convinced or refuted.'

A LIST OF
KEGAN PAUL, TRENCH, TRÜBNER & CO.'S
(LIMITED)
PUBLICATIONS.

7.90.

57 and 59, Ludgate Hill; and 1, Paternoster Square,
London.

A LIST OF
KEGAN PAUL, TRENCH, TRÜBNER & CO.'S
(LIMITED)
PUBLICATIONS.

CONTENTS.

	PAGE		PAGE
GENERAL LITERATURE.	2	TRÜBNER'S ORIENTAL SERIES	68
THEOLOGY AND PHILOSOPHY.	31	MILITARY WORKS.	72
ENGLISH AND FOREIGN PHILOSOPHICAL LIBRARY	42	EDUCATIONAL	73
		POETRY.	80
SCIENCE	44	NOVELS AND TALES	84
INTERNATIONAL SCIENTIFIC SERIES	48	BOOKS FOR THE YOUNG	87
		PERIODICALS.	88
ORIENTAL, EGYPTIAN, ETC..	52		

GENERAL LITERATURE.

Actors, Eminent. Edited by WILLIAM ARCHER. Crown 8vo, 2s. 6d. each.
    I. **William Charles Macready.** By WILLIAM ARCHER.
    II. **Thomas Betterton.** By. R. W. LOWE.

ADAMS, W. H. Davenport.—**The White King**; or, Charles the First, and Men and Women, Life and Manners, etc., in the First Half of the Seventeenth Century. 2 vols. Demy 8vo, 21s.

AGASSIZ, Louis.—An Essay on Classification. 8vo, 12s.

ALLIBONE, S. A.—A Critical Dictionary of English Literature and British and American Authors. From the Earliest Accounts to the latter half of the Nineteenth Century. 3 vols. Royal 8vo, £5 8s.

Amateur Mechanic's Workshop (The). A Treatise containing Plain and Concise Directions for the Manipulation of Wood and Metals. By the Author of "The Lathe and its Uses." Sixth Edition. Numerous Woodcuts. Demy 8vo, 6s.

American Almanac and Treasury of Facts, Statistical, Financial, and Political. Edited by AINSWORTH R. SPOFFORD. Published Yearly. Crown 8vo, 7s. 6d. each.

AMOS, *Professor Sheldon.*—**The History and Principles of the Civil Law of Rome.** An aid to the Study of Scientific and Comparative Jurisprudence. Demy 8vo, 16s.

ANDERSON, *William.*—**Practical Mercantile Correspondence.** A Collection of Modern Letters of Business, with Notes, Critical and Explanatory, and an Appendix. Thirtieth Edition. Crown 8vo, 3s. 6d.

ANDERSON, *W.,* and TUGMAN, *J. E.*—**Mercantile Correspondence.** A Collection of Letters in Portuguese and English, treating of the system of Business in the principal Cities of the World. With Introduction and Notes. 12mo, 6s.

Antiquarian Magazine and Bibliographer (The). Edited by EDWARD WALFORD, M.A., and G. W. REDWAY, F.R.H.S. Complete in 12 vols. £3 nett.

ARISTOTLE.—**The Nicomachean Ethics of Aristotle.** Translated by F. H. PETERS, M.A. Third Edition. Crown 8vo, 6s.

ARMITAGE, *Edward, R.A.*—**Lectures on Painting:** Delivered to the Students of the Royal Academy. Crown 8vo, 7s. 6d.

AUBERTIN, *J. J.*—**A Flight to Mexico.** With 7 full-page Illustrations and a Railway Map of Mexico. Crown 8vo, 7s. 6d.

Six Months in Cape Colony and Natal. With Illustrations and Map. Crown 8vo, 6s.

A Fight with Distances. Illustrations and Maps. Crown 8vo, 7s. 6d.

Australia, The Year-Book of, for 1889. Published under the auspices of the Governments of the Australian Colonies. With Maps. Demy 8vo, 10s. 6d.

AXON, *W. E. A.*—**The Mechanic's Friend.** A Collection of Receipts and Practical Suggestions relating to Aquaria, Bronzing, Cements, Drawing, Dyes, Electricity, Gilding, Glass-working, etc. Numerous Woodcuts. Edited by W. E. A. AXON. Crown 8vo, 3s. 6d.

Bacon-Shakespeare Question Answered (The). By C. STOPES. Second Edition. Demy 8vo, 6s.

BAGEHOT, *Walter.*—**The English Constitution.** Fifth Edition. Crown 8vo, 7s. 6d.

Lombard Street. A Description of the Money Market. Ninth Edition. Crown 8vo, 7s. 6d.

Essays on Parliamentary Reform. Crown 8vo, 5s.

Some Articles on the Depreciation of Silver, and Topics connected with it. Demy 8vo, 5s.

BALL, V.—**The Diamonds, Coal, and Gold of India.** Their Mode of Occurrence and Distribution. Fcap. 8vo, 5*s.*

A Manual of the Geology of India. Part III. Economic Geology. Royal 8vo, 10*s.*

BARNES, William.—**A Glossary of the Dorset Dialect.** With a Grammar of its Word-Shapening and Wording. Demy 8vo, sewed, 6*s.*

BARTLETT, J. R.—**Dictionary of Americanisms.** A Glossary of Words and Phrases colloquially used in the United States. Fourth Edition. 8vo, 21*s.*

BARTON, G. B.—**The History of New South Wales.** From the Records. Vol. I. Illustrated with Maps, Portraits, and Sketches. Demy 8vo, cloth, 15*s.*; half-morocco, 20*s.*

BAUGHAN, Rosa.—**The Influence of the Stars.** A Treatise on Astrology, Chiromancy, and Physiognomy. Demy 8vo, 5*s.*

BEARD, Charles, LL.D.—**Martin Luther and the Reformation in Germany until the Close of the Diet of Worms.** Demy 8vo, 16*s.*

Becket, Thomas, Martyr-Patriot. By R. A. THOMPSON, M.A. Crown 8vo, 6*s.*

BENSON, A. C.—**William Laud, sometime Archbishop of Canterbury.** A Study. With Portrait. Crown 8vo, 6*s.*

BEVAN, Theodore F., F.R.G.S.—**Toil, Travel, and Discovery in British New Guinea.** With Maps. Large crown 8vo, 7*s.* 6*d.*

BLACKET, W. S.—**Researches into the Lost Histories of America.** Illustrated by numerous Engravings. 8vo, 10*s.* 6*d.*

BLADES, W.—**The Biography and Typography of William Caxton, England's First Printer.** Demy 8vo, hand-made paper, imitation old bevelled binding, £1 1*s.* Cheap Edition. Crown 8vo, 5*s.*

BLEEK, W. H. I.—**Reynard the Fox in South Africa;** or, Hottentot Fables and Tales. From Original Manuscripts. Post 8vo, 3*s.* 6*d.*

A Brief Account of Bushman Folk-Lore, and Other Texts. Folio, 2*s.* 6*d.*

BOTTRELL, William.—**Stories and Folk-Lore of West Cornwall.** With Illustrations by JOSEPH BLIGHT. Second and Third Series. 8vo, 6*s.* each.

BRADLEY, F. H.—**The Principles of Logic.** Demy 8vo, 16*s.*

BRADSHAW.—**Dictionary of Bathing-Places and Climatic Health Resorts.** With Map. New Edition. Crown 8vo, 2*s.* 6*d.*

BRADSHAW—continued.

    A B C Dictionary of the United States, Canada, and Mexico. Showing the most important Towns and Points of Interest. With Maps, Routes, etc. New Edition, Revised. Fcap. 8vo, 2s. 6d.

Bradshaw, Henry: Memoir. By G. W. PROTHERO. With Portrait and Fac-simile. Demy 8vo, 16s.

BRENTANO, Lujo.—**On the History and Development of Gilds, and the Origin of Trade-Unions.** 8vo, 3s. 6d.

BRERETON, C. S. H.—**The Last Days of Olympus.** A Modern Myth. Crown 8vo, 3s. 6d.

BRIDGETT, Rev. T. E.—**Blunders and Forgeries.** Historical Essays. Crown 8vo, 6s.

BROWN, Horatio F.—**Life on the Lagoons.** With 2 Illustrations and Map. Crown 8vo, 6s.

    Venetian Studies. Crown 8vo, 7s. 6d.

BROWN, Marie A.—**The Icelandic Discoverers of America, or, Honour to whom Honour is due.** With 8 Plates. Crown 8vo, 7s. 6d.

BROWNE, Hugh Junor.—**The Grand Reality.** Being Experiences in Spirit-Life of a Celebrated Dramatist, received through a Trance Medium. Edited by HUGH JUNOR BROWNE. Large post 8vo, 7s. 6d.

Browning Society's Papers.—Demy 8vo, 1881-84. Part I., 10s. Part II., 10s. Part III., 10s. Part IV., 10s. Part V., 10s. Part VII., 10s. Part VIII., 10s. Part IX., 10s. Part X., 10s.

BROWNING. — **Bibliography of Robert Browning from 1833-81.** 12s.

    Poems of, Illustrations to. Parts I. and II. 4to, 10s. each.

BRUGMANN, Karl.—**Elements of a Comparative Grammar of the Indo-Germanic Languages.** Translated by JOSEPH WRIGHT. Vol. I. Introduction and Phonetics. 8vo, 18s.

BRYANT, Sophie, D.Sc.—**Celtic Ireland.** With 3 Maps. Crown 8vo, 5s.

BURKE, The Late Very Rev. T. N.—**His Life.** By W. J. FITZ-PATRICK. 2 vols. With Portrait. Demy 8vo, 30s.

Burma.—**The British Burma Gazetteer.** Compiled by Major H. R. SPEARMAN, under the direction of the Government of India. 2 vols. With 11 Photographs. 8vo, £2 10s.

BURTON, Lady.—**The Inner Life of Syria, Palestine, and the Holy Land.** Post 8vo, 6s.

BURY, Richard de.—Philobiblon. Edited by E. C. THOMAS. Crown 8vo, 10s. 6d.

CAMPBELL, Wm.—**An Account of Missionary Success in the Island of Formosa.** Published in London in 1650, and now reprinted with copious Appendices. 2 vols. With 6 Illustrations and Map of Formosa. Crown 8vo, 10s.

The Gospel of St. Matthew in Formosan (Sinkang Dialect). With Corresponding Versions in Dutch and English. Edited from Gravius's Edition of 1661. Fcap. 4to, 10s. 6d.

CATLIN, George.—**O-Kee-Pa.** A Religious Ceremony; and other Customs of the Mandans. With 13 Coloured Illustrations. Small 4to, 14s.

The Lifted and Subsided Rocks of America, with their Influence on the Oceanic, Atmospheric, and Land Currents, and the Distribution of Races. With 2 Maps. Crown 8vo, 6s. 6d.

Shut your Mouth and Save your Life. With 29 Illustrations. Eighth Edition. Crown 8vo, 2s. 6d.

CHAMBERS, John David.—**The Theological and Philosophical Works of Hermes Trismegistus, Christian Neoplatonist.** Translated from the Greek. Demy 8vo, 7s. 6d.

CHARNOCK, Richard Stephen.—**A Glossary of the Essex Dialect.** Fcap., 3s. 6d.

Nuces Etymologicæ. Crown 8vo, 10s.

Prœnomina; or, The Etymology of the Principal Christian Names of Great Britain and Ireland. Crown 8vo, 6s.

Chaucer Society.—Subscription, two guineas per annum. List of Publications on application.

CLAPPERTON, Jane Hume.—**Scientific Meliorism and the Evolution of Happiness.** Large crown 8vo, 8s. 6d.

CLARKE, Henry W.—**The History of Tithes, from Abraham to Queen Victoria.** Crown 8vo, 5s.

CLAUSEWITZ, General Carl von.—**On War.** Translated by Colonel J. J. GRAHAM. Fcap. 4to, 10s. 6d.

CLEMENT, C. E., and HUTTON, L.—**Artists of the Nineteenth Century and their Works.** Two Thousand and Fifty Biographical Sketches. Third, Revised Edition. Crown 8vo, 15s.

CLODD, Edward, F.R.A.S.—**The Childhood of the World:** a Simple Account of Man in Early Times. Eighth Edition. Crown 8vo, 3s.

A Special Edition for Schools. 1s.

The Childhood of Religions. Including a Simple Account of the Birth and Growth of Myths and Legends. Eighth Thousand. Crown 8vo, 5s.

A Special Edition for Schools. 1s. 6d.

CLODD, *Edward, F.R.A.S.—continued.*
> Jesus of Nazareth. With a brief sketch of Jewish History to the Time of His Birth. Second Edition. Small crown 8vo, 6s.
>> A Special Edition for Schools. In 2 parts. Each 1s. 6d.

COLEBROOKE, *Henry Thomas.*—Life and Miscellaneous Essays of. The Biography by his Son, Sir T. E. COLEBROOKE, Bart., M.P. 3 vols. Demy 8vo, 42s.

COLLETTE, *Charles Hastings.*—The Life, Times, and Writings of Thomas Cranmer, D.D., the First Reforming Archbishop of Canterbury. Demy 8vo, 7s. 6d.
> Pope Joan. An Historical Study. Translated from the Greek, with Preface. 12mo, 2s. 6d.

COLLINS, *Mabel.*—Through the Gates of Gold. A Fragment of Thought. Small 8vo, 4s. 6d.

CONWAY, *Moncure D.*—Travels in South Kensington. Illustrated. 8vo, 12s.

COOK, *Louisa S.*—Geometrical Psychology; or, The Science of Representation. An Abstract of the Theories and Diagrams of B. W. Betts. 16 Plates, coloured and plain. Demy 8vo, 7s. 6d.

COTTON, *H. J. S.*—New India, or India in Transition. Third Edition. Crown 8vo, 4s. 6d.; Cheap Edition, paper covers, 1s.

COTTON, *Louise.*—Palmistry and its Practical Uses. 12 Plates. Crown 8vo, 2s. 6d.

COX, *Rev. Sir George W., M.A., Bart.*—The Mythology of the Aryan Nations. New Edition. Demy 8vo, 16s.
> Tales of Ancient Greece. New Edition. Small crown 8vo, 6s.
> A Manual of Mythology in the form of Question and Answer. New Edition. Fcap. 8vo, 3s.
> An Introduction to the Science of Comparative Mythology and Folk-Lore. Second Edition. Crown 8vo, 7s. 6d.

COX, *Rev. Sir G. W., M.A., Bart., and* JONES, *Eustace Hinton.*—Popular Romances of the Middle Ages. Third Edition, in 1 vol. Crown 8vo, 6s.

CURR, *Edward M.*—The Australian Race: Its Origin, Languages, Customs, Place of Landing in Australia, and the Routes by which it spread itself over that Continent. In 4 vols. With Map and Illustrations. £2 2s.

CUST, *R. N.*—The Shrines of Lourdes, Zaragossa, the Holy Stairs at Rome, the Holy House of Loretto and Nazareth, and St. Ann at Jerusalem. With 4 Autotypes. Fcap. 8vo, 2s.

Davis, Thomas: The Memoirs of an Irish Patriot, 1840-46. By Sir CHARLES GAVAN DUFFY, K.C.M.G. Demy 8vo, 12s.

DAVITT, Michael.—Speech before the Special Commission. Crown 8vo, 5s.

DAWSON, Geo.—Biographical Lectures. Edited by GEORGE ST. CLAIR, F.G.S. Third Edition. Large crown 8vo, 7s. 6d.

Shakespeare, and other Lectures. Edited by GEORGE ST. CLAIR, F.G.S. Large crown 8vo, 7s. 6d.

DEAN, Teresa H.—How to be Beautiful. Nature Unmasked. A Book for Every Woman. Fcap. 8vo, 2s. 6d.

DEATH, J.—The Beer of the Bible: one of the hitherto Unknown Leavens of Exodus. With a Visit to an Arab Brewery, and Map of the Routes of the Exodus, etc. Crown 8vo, 6s.

DE JONCOURT, Madame Marie.—Wholesome Cookery. Fifth Edition. Crown 8vo, cloth, 1s. 6d.; paper covers, 1s.

DENMAN, Hon. G.—The Story of the Kings of Rome. In Verse. 16mo, parchment, 1s. 6d.

DONOVAN, J.—Music and Action; or, The Elective Affinity between Rhythm and Pitch. Crown 8vo, 3s. 6d.

DOWDEN, Edward, LL.D.—Shakspere: a Critical Study of his Mind and Art. Ninth Edition. Post 8vo, 12s.

Shakspere's Sonnets. With Introduction and Notes. Large post 8vo, 7s. 6d.

Studies in Literature, 1789-1877. Fourth Edition. Large post 8vo, 6s.

Transcripts and Studies. Large post 8vo, 12s.

DOWSETT, F. C.—Striking Events in Irish History. Crown 8vo, 2s. 6d.

Dreamland and Ghostland. An Original Collection of Tales and Warnings from the Borderland of Substance and Shadow. 3 vols. 6s. per vol., sold separately.

Drummond, Thomas, Under Secretary in Ireland, 1835-40. Life and Letters. By R. BARRY O'BRIEN. Demy 8vo, 14s.

DU PREL, Carl.—The Philosophy of Mysticism. Translated from the German by C. C. MASSEY. 2 vols. Demy 8vo, cloth, 25s.

Early English Text Society.—Subscription, one guinea per annum. *Extra Series.* Subscriptions—Small paper, one guinea per annum. List of Publications on application.

EDMUNDSON, George.—Milton and Vondel. A Curiosity of Literature. Crown 8vo, 6s.

EDWARDS, *Edward.*—Memoirs of Libraries, together with a Practical Handbook of Library Economy. Numerous Illustrations. 2 vols. Royal 8vo, £2 8s. Large paper Edition. Imperial 8vo, £4 4s.

 Libraries and Founders of Libraries. 8vo, 18s. Large paper Edition. Imperial 8vo, £1 10s.

 Free Town Libraries, their Formation, Management, and History in Britain, France, Germany, and America. Together with Brief Notices of Book Collectors, and of the respective Places of Deposit of their Surviving Collections. 8vo, 21s.

Eighteenth Century Essays. Selected and Edited by AUSTIN DOBSON. Cheap Edition. Cloth, 1s. 6d.

Ellis, William (Founder of the Birkbeck Schools). Life, with Account of his Writings. By E. KELL BLYTH. Demy 8vo, 14s.

Emerson's (Ralph Waldo) Life. By OLIVER WENDELL HOLMES. English Copyright Edition. With Portrait. Crown 8vo, 6s.

Emerson (Ralph Waldo), Talks with. By CHARLES J. WOODBURY. Crown 8vo, 5s.

English Dialect Society.—Subscription, 10s. 6d. per annum. List of Publications on application.

FIELD, *David Dudley.*—Outlines of an International Code. Second Edition. Royal 8vo, £2 2s.

Five o'clock Tea. Containing Receipts for Cakes, Savoury Sandwiches, etc. Eighth Thousand. Fcap. 8vo, cloth, 1s. 6d.; paper covers, 1s.

Forbes, Bishop. A Memoir. By the Rev. DONALD J. MACKAY. With Portrait and Map. Crown 8vo, 7s. 6d.

FOTHERINGHAM, *James.*—Studies in the Poetry of Robert Browning. Second Edition. Crown 8vo, 6s.

FOX, *Charles.*—The Pilgrims. An Allegory of the Soul's Progress from the Earthly to the Heavenly State. Crown 8vo, 5s.

FOX, *J. A.*—A Key to the Irish Question. Crown 8vo, 7s. 6d.

FRANKLYN, *Henry Bowles.*—The Great Battles of 1870, and Blockade of Metz. With Large Map, Sketch Map, and Frontispiece. 8vo, 15s.

FREEBOROUGH, *E., and RANKEN, C. E.*—Chess Openings, Ancient and Modern. Revised and Corrected up to the Present Time from the best Authorities. Large post 8vo, 7s. 6d.; interleaved, 9s.

FREEMAN, *E. A.*—Lectures to American Audiences. I. The English People in its Three Homes. II. Practical Bearings of General European History. Post 8vo, 8s. 6d

FRITH, I.—**Life of Giordano Bruno, the Nolan.** Revised by Prof. MORIZ CARRIERE. With Portrait. Post 8vo, 14s.

Froebel's Ethical Teaching. Two Essays by M. J. LYSCHINSKA and THERESE G. MONTEFIORE. Fcap., 2s. 6d.

From World to Cloister; or, My Novitiate. By BERNARD. Crown 8vo, 5s.

Garfield, The Life and Public Service of James A., Twentieth President of the United States. A Biographical Sketch. By Captain F. H. MASON. With a Preface by BRET HARTE. With Portrait. Crown 8vo, 2s. 6d.

GASTER, M.—**Greeko-Slavonic Literature and its Relation to the Folk-Lore of Europe during the Middle Ages.** Large post 8vo, 7s. 6d.

GEORGE, Henry.—**Progress and Poverty.** An Inquiry into the Causes of Industrial Depressions, and of Increase of Want with Increase of Wealth. The Remedy. Fifth Library Edition. Post 8vo, 7s. 6d. Cabinet Edition. Crown 8vo, 2s. 6d. Also a Cheap Edition. Limp cloth, 1s. 6d.; paper covers, 1s.

Protection, or Free Trade. An Examination of the Tariff Question, with especial regard to the Interests of Labour. Second Edition. Crown 8vo, 5s. Cheap Edition. Limp cloth, 1s. 6d.; paper covers, 1s.

Social Problems. Fourth Thousand. Crown 8vo, 5s. Cheap Edition. Limp cloth, 1s. 6d.; paper covers, 1s.

GIBB, E. J. W.—**The History of the Forty Vezirs**; or, The Story of the Forty Morns and Eves. Translated from the Turkish. Crown 8vo, 10s. 6d.

GILBERT, Mrs.—**Autobiography, and other Memorials.** Edited by JOSIAH GILBERT. Fifth Edition. Crown 8vo, 7s. 6d.

Glossary of Terms and Phrases. Edited by the Rev. H. PERCY SMITH and others. Second and Cheaper Edition. Medium 8vo, 3s. 6d.

Goethe's Faust. Translated from the German by JOHN ANSTER, LL.D. With an Introduction by BURDETT MASON. Illustrated by FRANK M. GREGORY. Folio, £3 3s.

GORDON, Major-General C. G.—**His Journals at Kartoum.** Printed from the original MS. With Introduction and Notes by A. EGMONT HAKE. Portrait, 2 Maps, and 30 Illustrations. Two vols., demy 8vo, 21s. Also a Cheap Edition in 1 vol., 6s.

Gordon's (General) Last Journal. A Facsimile of the last Journal received in England from GENERAL GORDON. Reproduced by Photo-lithography. Imperial 4to, £3 3s.

GORDON, *Major-General C. G.—continued.*
    Events in his Life. From the Day of his Birth to the Day of his Death. By Sir H. W. GORDON. With Maps and Illustrations. Second Edition. Demy 8vo, 7s. 6d.

GOSSE, *Edmund.*—Seventeenth Century Studies. A Contribution to the History of English Poetry. Demy 8vo, 10s. 6d.

GOSSIP, *G. H. D.*—The Chess-Player's Text-Book. An Elementary Treatise on the Game of Chess. Illustrated by numerous Diagrams for Beginners and Advanced Students. Medium 16mo, 2s.

GOULD, *Rev. S. Baring, M.A.*—Germany, Present and Past. New and Cheaper Edition. Large crown 8vo, 7s. 6d.

GOWER, *Lord Ronald.*—My Reminiscences. MINIATURE EDITION, printed on hand-made paper, limp parchment antique, 10s. 6d.
    Bric-à-Brac. Being some Photoprints illustrating art objects at Gower Lodge, Windsor. With descriptions. Super royal 8vo, 15s.; extra binding, 21s.
    Last Days of Mary Antoinette. An Historical Sketch. With Portrait and Facsimiles. Fcap. 4to, 10s. 6d.
    Notes of a Tour from Brindisi to Yokohama, 1883-1884. Fcap. 8vo, 2s. 6d.
    Rupert of the Rhine: A Biographical Sketch of the Life of Prince Rupert. With 3 Portraits. Crown 8vo, buckram, 6s.

GRAHAM, *William, M.A.*—The Creed of Science, Religious, Moral, and Social. Second Edition, Revised. Crown 8vo, 6s.
    The Social Problem, in its Economic, Moral, and Political Aspects. Demy 8vo, 14s.

GUBERNATIS, *Angelo de.*—Zoological Mythology; or, The Legends of Animals. 2 vols. 8vo, £1 8s.

GURNEY, *Rev. Alfred.*—Wagner's Parsifal. A Study. Fcap. 8vo, 1s. 6d.

HADDON, *Caroline.*—The Larger Life: Studies in Hinton's Ethics. Crown 8vo, 5s.

HAGGARD, *H. Rider.*—Cetywayo and his White Neighbours; or, Remarks on Recent Events in Zululand, Natal, and the Transvaal. Third Edition. Crown 8vo, 6s.

HALDEMAN, *S. S.*—Pennsylvania Dutch: A Dialect of South Germany with an Infusion of English. 8vo, 3s. 6d.

HALL, *F. T.*—The Pedigree of the Devil. With 7 Autotype Illustrations from Designs by the Author. Demy 8vo, 7s. 6d.

HALLOCK, *Charles.*—The Sportsman's Gazetteer and General Guide. The Game Animals, Birds, and Fishes of North America. Maps and Portrait. Crown 8vo, 15s.

Hamilton, Memoirs of Arthur, B.A., of Trinity College, Cambridge. Crown 8vo, 6s.

Handbook of Home Rule, being Articles on the Irish Question by Various Writers. Edited by JAMES BRYCE, M.P. Second Edition. Crown 8vo, 1s. sewed, or 1s. 6d. cloth.

HARRIS, *Emily Marion.*—The Narrative of the Holy Bible. Crown 8vo, 5s.

HARTMANN, *Franz.*—Magic, White and Black; or, The Science of Finite and Infinite Life. Crown 8vo, 7s. 6d.

The Life of Paracelsus, and the Substance of his Teachings. Post 8vo, 10s. 6d.

Life and Doctrines of Jacob Behmen. Post 8vo, 10s. 6d.

HAWTHORNE, *Nathaniel.*—Works. Complete in Twelve Volumes. Large post 8vo, 7s. 6d. each volume.

HECKER, *J. F. C.*—The Epidemics of the Middle Ages. Translated by G. B. BABINGTON, M.D., F.R.S. Third Edition. 8vo, 9s. 6d.

HENDRIK, *Hans.*—Memoirs of Hans Hendrik, the Arctic Traveller; serving under Kane, Hayes, Hall, and Nares, 1853-76. Translated from the Eskimo Language by Dr. HENRY RINK. Crown 8vo, 3s. 6d.

HENDRIKS, *Dom Lawrence.*—The London Charterhouse: its Monks and its Martyrs. Illustrated. Demy 8vo, 14s.

HERZEN, *Alexander.*—Du Developpement des Idées Revolutionnaires en Russie. 12mo, 2s. 6d.

A separate list of A. Herzen's works in Russian may be had on application.

HILL, *Alfred.*—The History of the Reform Movement in the Dental Profession in Great Britain during the last twenty years. Crown 8vo, 10s. 6d.

HILLEBRAND, *Karl.*—France and the French in the Second Half of the Nineteenth Century. Translated from the Third German Edition. Post 8vo, 10s. 6d.

HINTON, *J.*—Life and Letters. With an Introduction by Sir W. W. GULL, Bart., and Portrait engraved on Steel by C. H. Jeens. Sixth Edition. Crown 8vo, 8s. 6d.

Philosophy and Religion. Selections from the Manuscripts of the late James Hinton. Edited by CAROLINE HADDON. Second Edition. Crown 8vo, 5s.

The Law Breaker, and The Coming of the Law. Edited by MARGARET HINTON. Crown 8vo, 6s.

The Mystery of Pain. New Edition. Fcap. 8vo, 1s.

HODGSON, *J. E.*—Academy Lectures. Crown 8vo, 7s. 6d.

Holbein Society.—Subscription, one guinea per annum. List of Publications on application.

HOLMES-FORBES, *Avary W.*—**The Science of Beauty.** An Analytical Inquiry into the Laws of Æsthetics. Second Edition. Post 8vo, 3s. 6d.

HOLYOAKE, *G. J.*—**The History of Co-operation in England**: Its Literature and its Advocates. 2 vols. Crown 8vo, 14s.

Self-Help by the People. Thirty-three Years of Co-operation in Rochdale. Ninth Edition. Crown 8vo, 2s. 6d.

HOME, *Mme. Dunglas.*—**D. D. Home: His Life and Mission.** With Portrait. Demy 8vo, 12s. 6d.

Gift of D. D. Home. Demy 8vo, 10s.

Homer's Iliad. Greek Text with Translation. By J. G. CORDERY, C.S.I. Two vols. Demy 8vo, 14s. Cheap Edition, Translation only. One vol. Crown 8vo, 5s.

HOOLE, *Henry.*—**The Science and Art of Training.** A Handbook for Athletes. Demy 8vo, 3s. 6d.

HOOPER, *Mary.*—**Little Dinners: How to Serve them with Elegance and Economy.** Twenty-first Edition. Crown 8vo, 2s. 6d.

Cookery for Invalids, Persons of Delicate Digestion, and Children. Fifth Edition. Crown 8vo, 2s. 6d.

Every-day Meals. Being Economical and Wholesome Recipes for Breakfast, Luncheon, and Supper. Seventh Edition. Crown 8vo, 2s. 6d.

HOPKINS, *Ellice.*—**Work amongst Working Men.** Sixth Edition. Crown 8vo, 3s. 6d.

HORNADAY, *W. T.*—**Two Years in a Jungle.** With Illustrations. Demy 8vo, 21s.

HOWELLS, *W. D.*—**A Little Girl among the Old Masters.** With Introduction and Comment. 54 Plates. Oblong crown 8vo, 10s.

HUMBOLDT, *Baron Wilhelm Von.*—**The Sphere and Duties of Government.** Translated from the German by JOSEPH COULTHARD, Jun. Post 8vo, 5s.

HYNDMAN, *H. M.*—**The Historical Basis of Socialism in England.** Large crown 8vo, 8s. 6d.

IM THURN, *Everard F.*—**Among the Indians of Guiana.** Being Sketches, chiefly anthropologic, from the Interior of British Guiana. With 53 Illustrations and a Map. Demy 8vo, 18s.

INGLEBY, *the late Clement M.*—**Essays.** Edited by his Son. Crown 8vo, 7s. 6d.

Irresponsibility and its Recognition. By a Graduate of Oxford. Crown 8vo, 3s. 6d.

JAGIELSKI, V.—Modern Massage Treatment in Combination with the Electric Bath. 8vo, 1s. 6d.

JAPP, Alexander H.—Days with Industrials. Adventures and Experiences among Curious Industries. With Illustrations. Crown 8vo, 6s.

JENKINS, E., and RAYMOND, J.—The Architect's Legal Handbook. Fourth Edition, Revised. Crown 8vo, 6s.

JENKINS, E.—A Modern Paladin. Contemporary Manners. Crown 8vo, 5s.

JENKINS, Jabez.—Vest-Pocket Lexicon. An English Dictionary of all except familiar Words, including the principal Scientific and Technical Terms, and Foreign Moneys, Weights, and Measures. 64mo, 1s.

JENKINS, Rev. Canon R. C.—Heraldry: English and Foreign. With a Dictionary of Heraldic Terms and 156 Illustrations. Small crown 8vo, 3s. 6d.

Jesus the Carpenter of Nazareth. By a Layman. Crown 8vo, 7s. 6d.

JOHNSON, C. P.—Hints to Collectors of Original Editions of the Works of Charles Dickens. Crown 8vo, vellum, 6s.

    Hints to Collectors of Original Editions of the Works of William Makepeace Thackeray. Crown 8vo, vellum, 6s.

JOHNSTON, H. H., F.Z.S.—The Kilima-njaro Expedition. A Record of Scientific Exploration in Eastern Equatorial Africa, and a General Description of the Natural History, Languages, and Commerce of the Kilima-njaro District. With 6 Maps, and over 80 Illustrations by the Author. Demy 8vo, 21s.

    The History of a Slave. With 47 Illustrations. Square 8vo, 6s.

Juvenalis Sátiræ. With a Literal English Prose Translation and Notes. By J. D. Lewis. Second Edition. 2 vols. 8vo, 12s.

KARDEC, Allen.—The Spirit's Book. The Principles of Spiritist Doctrine on the Immortality of the Soul, etc. Transmitted through various mediums. Translated by Anna Blackwell. Crown 8vo, 7s. 6d.

    The Medium's Book; or, Guide for Mediums and for Evocations. Translated by Anna Blackwell. Crown 8vo, 7s. 6d.

    Heaven and Hell; or, The Divine Justice Vindicated in the Plurality of Existences. Translated by Anna Blackwell. Crown 8vo, 7s. 6d.

KAUFMANN, *Rev. M., M.A.*—Socialism : its Nature, its Dangers, and its Remedies considered. Crown 8vo, 7s. 6d.

Utopias ; or, Schemes of Social Improvement, from Sir Thomas More to Karl Marx. Crown 8vo, 5s.

Christian Socialism. Crown 8vo, 4s. 6d.

KERRISON, *Lady Caroline.*—A Commonplace Book of the Fifteenth Century. Containing a Religious Play and Poetry, Legal Forms, and Local Accounts. From the Original MS. at Brome Hall, Suffolk. Edited by LUCY TOULMIN SMITH. With 2 Facsimiles. Demy 8vo, 7s. 6d.

KINGSFORD, *Anna, M.D.*—The Perfect Way in Diet. A Treatise advocating a Return to the Natural and Ancient Food of our Race. Third Edition. Small crown 8vo, 2s.

The Spiritual Hermeneutics of Astrology and Holy Writ. Illustrated. 4to, parchment, 10s. 6d.

KINGSFORD, *Anna, and MAITLAND, Edward.*—The Virgin of the World of Hermes Mercurius Trismegistus. Rendered into English. 4to, parchment, 10s. 6d.

The Perfect Way ; or, The Finding of Christ. Third Edition, Revised. Square 16mo, 7s. 6d.

KINGSFORD, *William.*—History of Canada. 3 vols. 8vo, £2 5s.

KITTON, *Fred. G.*—John Leech, Artist and Humourist. A Biographical Sketch. Demy 18mo, 1s.

KRAUS, *J.*—Carlsbad and its Natural Healing Agents. With Notes, Introductory, by the Rev. JOHN T. WALLERS. Third Edition. Crown 8vo, 6s. 6d.

LAMB, *Charles.*—Beauty and the Beast ; or, A Rough Outside with a Gentle Heart. A Poem. Fcap. 8vo, vellum, 10s. 6d.

LANG, *Andrew.*—Lost Leaders. Crown 8vo, 5s.

Lathe (The) and its Uses ; or, Instruction in the Art of Turning Wood and Metal. Sixth Edition. Illustrated. 8vo, 10s. 6d.

LEE, *Frederick Geo.*—A Manual of Politics. In three Chapters. With Footnotes and Appendices. Small crown 8vo, 2s. 6d.

LEFEVRE, *Right Hon. G. Shaw.*—Peel and O'Connell. Demy 8vo, 10s. 6d.

Incidents of Coercion. A Journal of Visits to Ireland. Third Edition. Crown 8vo, limp cloth, 1s. 6d. ; paper covers, 1s.

Irish Members and English Gaolers. Crown 8vo, limp cloth, 1s. 6d. ; paper covers, 1s.

Combination and Coercion in Ireland. A Sequel to "Incidents of Coercion." Crown 8vo, cloth, 1s. 6d. ; paper covers, 1s.

LELAND, *Charles G.*—**The Breitmann Ballads.** The only authorized Edition. Complete in 1 vol., including Nineteen Ballads, illustrating his Travels in Europe (never before printed). Crown 8vo, 6s.

Gaudeamus. Humorous Poems translated from the German of JOSEPH VICTOR SCHEFFEL and others. 16mo, 3s. 6d.

The English Gipsies and their Language. Second Edition. Crown 8vo, 7s. 6d.

Fu-Sang; or, The Discovery of America by Chinese Buddhist Priests in the Fifth Century. Crown 8vo, 7s. 6d.

Pidgin-English Sing-Song; or, Songs and Stories in the China-English Dialect. With a Vocabulary. Second Edition. Crown 8vo, 5s.

The Gypsies. Crown 8vo, 10s. 6d.

Light on the Path. For the Personal Use of those who are Ignorant of the Eastern Wisdom. Written down by M. C. Fcap. 8vo, 1s. 6d.

LOCHER, Carl.—**An Explanation of Organ Stops**, with Hints for Effective Combinations. Demy 8vo, 5s.

LONGFELLOW, H. Wadsworth.—**Life.** By his Brother, SAMUEL LONGFELLOW. With Portraits and Illustrations. 3 vols. Demy 8vo, 42s.

LONSDALE, Margaret.—**Sister Dora : a Biography.** With Portrait. Thirtieth Edition. Small crown 8vo, 2s. 6d.

George Eliot : Thoughts upon her Life, her Books, and Herself. Second Edition. Small crown 8vo, 1s. 6d.

Lotos Series (The). Pot 8vo, bound in two styles: (1) cloth, gilt back and edges; (2) half-parchment, cloth sides, gilt top, uncut, 3s. 6d. each.

The Original Travels and Surprising Adventures of Baron Munchausen. Illustrated by ALFRED CROWQUILL.

The Breitmann Ballads. By CHARLES G. LELAND. Author's Copyright Edition, with a New Preface and Additional Poems.

Essays on Men and Books Selected from the Earlier Writings of Lord Macaulay. Vol. I. Introductory—Lord Clive—Milton—Earl Chatham—Lord Byron. With Critical Introduction and Notes by ALEXANDER H. JAPP, LL.D. With Portraits.

The Light of Asia; or, The Great Renunciation. Being the Life and Teaching of Gautama, Prince of India and Founder of Buddhism. Told in Verse by an Indian Buddhist. By Sir EDWIN ARNOLD, K.C.I.E., C.S.I. With Illustrations and a Portrait of the Author.

Lotos Series (The)—*continued.*

The Marvellous and Rare Conceits of Master Tyll Owlglass. Newly Collected, Chronicled, and set forth in an English Tongue. By KENNETH H. R. MACKENZIE. Adorned with many most Diverting and Cunning Devices by ALFRED CROWQUILL.

A Lover's Litanies, and other Poems. By ERIC MACKAY. With Portrait of the Author.

The Large Paper Edition of these Volumes will be limited to 101 numbered copies for sale in England, price 12s. 6d. each, net.

Lowder, Charles: A Biography. By the Author of "St. Teresa." Twelfth Edition. With Portrait. Crown 8vo, 3s. 6d.

LOWELL, James Russell.—**The Biglow Papers.** Edited by THOMAS HUGHES, Q.C. First and Second Series in 1 vol. Fcap., 2s. 6d.

LOWSLEY, Major B.—**A Glossary of Berkshire Words and Phrases.** Crown 8vo, half-calf, gilt edges, interleaved, 12s. 6d.

LÜCKES, Eva C. E.—**Lectures on General Nursing,** delivered to the Probationers of the London Hospital Training School for Nurses. Third Edition. Crown 8vo, 2s. 6d.

LUDEWIG, Hermann E.—**The Literature of American Aboriginal Languages.** Edited by NICOLAS TRÜBNER. 8vo, 10s. 6d.

LUKIN, J.—**Amongst Machines.** A Description of Various Mechanical Appliances used in the Manufacture of Wood, Metal, etc. A Book for Boys. Second Edition. 64 Engravings. Crown 8vo, 3s. 6d.

The Young Mechanic. Containing Directions for the Use of all Kinds of Tools, and for the Construction of Steam-Engines, etc. A Book for Boys. Second Edition. With 70 Engravings. Crown 8vo, 3s. 6d.

The Boy Engineers: What they Did, and How they Did it. A Book for Boys. 30 Engravings. Imperial 16mo, 3s. 6d.

LUMLEY, E.—**The Art of Judging the Character of Individuals from their Handwriting and Style.** With 35 Plates. Square 16mo, 5s.

LYTTON, Edward Bulwer, Lord.—**Life, Letters and Literary Remains.** By his Son, the EARL OF LYTTON. With Portraits, Illustrations and Facsimiles. Demy 8vo. Vols. I. and II., 32s.

MACDONALD, W. A.—**Humanitism:** The Scientific Solution of the Social Problem. Large post 8vo, 7s. 6d.

C

MACHIAVELLI, Niccolò.
> Discourses on the First Decade of Titus Livius. Translated from the Italian by NINIAN HILL THOMSON, M.A. Large crown 8vo, 12s.
>
> The Prince. Translated from the Italian by N. H. T. Small crown 8vo, printed on hand-made paper, bevelled boards, 6s.

MAIDEN, J. H.—The Useful Native Plants of Australia (including Tasmania). Demy 8vo, 12s. 6d.

Maintenon, Madame de. By EMILY BOWLES. With Portrait. Large crown 8vo, 7s. 6d.

MARCHANT, W. T.—In Praise of Ale. Songs, Ballads, Epigrams, and Anecdotes. Crown 8vo, 10s. 6d.

MARKHAM, Capt. Albert Hastings, R.N.—The Great Frozen Sea: A Personal Narrative of the Voyage of the *Alert* during the Arctic Expedition of 1875-6. With 6 full-page Illustrations, 2 Maps, and 27 Woodcuts. Sixth and Cheaper Edition. Crown 8vo, 6s.

Marriage and Divorce. Including Religious, Practical, and Political Aspects of the Question. By AP RICHARD. Crown 8vo, 5s.

MARTIN, G. A.—The Family Horse: Its Stabling, Care, and Feeding. Crown 8vo, 3s. 6d.

MATHERS, S. L. M.—The Key of Solomon the King. Translated from Ancient MSS. in the British Museum. With Plates. Crown 4to, 25s.

> The Kabbalah Unveiled. Containing the Three Books of the Zohar. Translated into English. With Plates. Post 8vo, 10s. 6d.
>
> The Tarot: its Occult Signification, Use in Fortune-Telling, and Method of Play. 32mo, 1s. 6d.; with pack of 78 Tarot Cards, 5s.

MAUDSLEY, H., M.D.—Body and Will. Being an Essay concerning Will, in its Metaphysical, Physiological, and Pathological Aspects. 8vo, 12s.

> Natural Causes and Supernatural Seemings. Second Edition. Crown 8vo, 6s.

Mechanic, The Young. A Book for Boys. Containing Directions for the Use of all Kinds of Tools, and for the Construction of Steam-Engines and Mechanical Models. By the Rev. J. LUKIN. Sixth Edition. With 70 Engravings. Crown 8vo, 3s. 6d.

Mechanic's Workshop, Amateur. Plain and Concise Directions for the Manipulation of Wood and Metals. By the Author of "The Lathe and its Uses." Sixth Edition. Illustrated. Demy 8vo, 6s.

Mendelssohn's Letters to Ignaz and Charlotte Moscheles. Translated by FELIX MOSCHELLES. Numerous Illustrations and Facsimiles. 8vo, 12s.

METCALFE, Frederick.—**The Englishman and the Scandinavian.** Post 8vo, 18s.

MINTON, Rev. Francis.—**Capital and Wages.** 8vo, 15s.

The Welfare of the Millions. Crown 8vo, limp cloth, 1s. 6d.; paper covers, 1s.

Mitchel, John, Life. By WILLIAM DILLON. 2 vols. With Portrait. 8vo, 21s.

MITCHELL, Lucy M.—**A History of Ancient Sculpture.** With numerous Illustrations, including 6 Plates in Phototype. Super-royal 8vo, 42s.

Mohl, Julius and Mary, Letters and Recollections of. By M. C. M. SIMPSON. With Portraits and 2 Illustrations. Demy 8vo, 15s.

MOODIE, D. C. F.—**The History of the Battles and Adventures of the British, the Boers, the Zulus, etc., in Southern Africa,** from the Time of Pharaoh Necho to 1880. With Illustrations and Coloured Maps. 2 vols. Crown 8vo, 36s.

MORFIT, Campbell.—**A Practical Treatise on the Manufacture of Soaps.** With Illustrations. Demy 8vo, £2 12s. 6d.

A Practical Treatise on Pure Fertilizers, and the Chemical Conversion of Rock Guanos, etc., into various valuable Products, With 28 Plates. 8vo, £4 4s.

MOORE, Aubrey L.—**Science and the Faith:** Essays on Apologetic Subjects. Crown 8vo, 6s.

MORISON, J. Cotter.—**The Service of Man:** an Essay towards the Religion of the Future. Crown 8vo, 5s.

MORRIS, Charles.—**Aryan Sun-Myths the Origin of Religions.** With an Introduction by CHARLES MORRIS. Crown 8vo, 6s.

MORRIS, Gouverneur, U.S. Minister to France.—**Diary and Letters.** 2 vols. Demy 8vo, 30s.

MOSENTHAL, J. de, and HARTING, James E.—**Ostriches and Ostrich Farming.** Second Edition. With 8 full-page Illustrations and 20 Woodcuts. Royal 8vo, 10s. 6d.

Motley, John Lothrop. A Memoir. By OLIVER WENDELL HOLMES. Crown 8vo, 6s.

MULHALL, M. G. and E. T.—**Handbook of the River Plate,** comprising the Argentine Republic, Uruguay, and Paraguay. With Six Maps. Fifth Edition. Crown 8vo, 7s. 6d.

Munro, Major-Gen. Sir Thomas. A Memoir. By Sir A. J. ARBUTHNOT. Crown 8vo, 3s. 6d.

Natural History. "Riverside" Edition. Edited by J. S. KINGSLEY. 6 vols. 2200 Illustrations. 4to, £6 6s.

NEVILL, J. H. N.—**The Biology of Daily Life.** Post 8vo, 3s. 6d.

NEWMAN, Cardinal.—**Characteristics from the Writings of.** Being Selections from his various Works. Arranged with the Author's personal Approval. Eighth Edition. With Portrait. Crown 8vo, 6s.

⁎⁎⁎ A Portrait of Cardinal Newman, mounted for framing, can be had, 2s. 6d.

NEWMAN, Francis William.—**Essays on Diet.** Small crown 8vo, cloth limp, 2s.

Miscellanies. Vol. II., III., and IV. Essays, Tracts, and Addresses, Moral and Religious. Demy 8vo. Vols. II. and III., 12s. Vol. IV., 10s. 6d.

Reminiscences of Two Exiles and Two Wars. Crown 8vo, 3s. 6d.

Phases of Faith; or, Passages from the History of my Creed. Crown 8vo, 3s. 6d.

The Soul: Her Sorrows and her Aspirations. Tenth Edition. Post 8vo, 3s. 6d.

Hebrew Theism. Royal 8vo, 4s. 6d.

Anglo-Saxon Abolition of Negro Slavery. Demy 8vo, 5s.

New South Wales, Journal and Proceedings of the Royal Society of. Published annually. Price 10s. 6d.

New South Wales, Publications of the Government of. List on application.

New Zealand Institute Publications:—

I. **Transactions and Proceedings of** the New Zealand Institute. Vols. I. to XX., 1868 to 1887. Demy 8vo, stitched, £1 1s. each.

II. **An Index to the Transactions and Proceedings of** the New Zealand Institute. Edited by JAMES HECTOR, M.D., F.R.S. Vols. I. to VIII. Demy 8vo, 2s. 6d.

New Zealand: Geological Survey. List of Publications on application.

OATES, Frank, F.R.G.S.—**Matabele Land and the Victoria Falls.** A Naturalist's Wanderings in the Interior of South Africa. Edited by C. G. OATES, B.A. With numerous Illustrations and 4 Maps. Demy 8vo, 21s.

O'BRIEN, R. Barry.—**Irish Wrongs and English Remedies,** with other Essays. Crown 8vo, 5s.

Kegan Paul, Trench, Trübner & Co.'s Publications. 21

O'BRIEN, *R. Barry.—continued.*
 The Home Ruler's Manual. Crown 8vo, cloth, 1*s*. 6*d*.; paper covers, 1*s*.

OLCOTT, *Henry S.*—Theosophy, Religion, and Occult Science. With Glossary of Eastern Words. Crown 8vo, 7*s*. 6*d*.

 Posthumous Humanity. A Study of Phantoms. By ADOLPHE D'ASSIER. Translated and Annotated by HENRY S. OLCOTT. Crown 8vo, 7*s*. 6*d*.

Our Public Schools—Eton, Harrow, Winchester, Rugby, Westminster, Marlborough, The Charterhouse. Crown 8vo, 6*s*.

OWEN, *Robert Dale.*—Footfalls on the Boundary of Another World. With Narrative Illustrations. Post 8vo, 7*s*. 6*d*.

 The Debatable Land between this World and the Next. With Illustrative Narrations. Second Edition. Crown 8vo, 7*s*. 6*d*.

 Threading my Way. Twenty-Seven Years of Autobiography. Crown 8vo, 7*s*. 6*d*.

OXLEY, *William.*—Modern Messiahs and Wonder-Workers. A History of the Various Messianic Claimants to Special Divine Prerogatives. Post 8vo, 5*s*.

Parchment Library. Choicely Printed on hand-made paper, limp parchment antique or cloth, 6*s*. ; vellum, 7*s*. 6*d*. each volume.

 Selected Poems of Matthew Prior. With an Introduction and Notes by AUSTIN DOBSON.

 Sartor Resartus. By THOMAS CARLYLE.

 The Poetical Works of John Milton. 2 vols.

 Chaucer's Canterbury Tales. Edited by A. W. POLLARD, 2 vols.

 Letters and Journals of Jonathan Swift. Selected and edited, with a Commentary and Notes, by STANLEY LANE-POOLE.

 De Quincey's Confessions of an English Opium Eater. Reprinted from the First Edition. Edited by RICHARD GARNETT.

 The Gospel according to Matthew, Mark, and Luke.

 Selections from the Prose Writings of Jonathan Swift. With a Preface and Notes by STANLEY LANE-POOLE and Portrait.

 English Sacred Lyrics.

 Sir Joshua Reynolds's Discourses. Edited by EDMUND GOSSE.

Parchment Library—*continued.*

Selections from Milton's Prose Writings. Edited by ERNEST MYERS.

The Book of Psalms. Translated by the Rev. Canon T. K. CHEYNE, M.A., D.D.

The Vicar of Wakefield. With Preface and Notes by AUSTIN DOBSON.

English Comic Dramatists. Edited by OSWALD CRAWFURD.

English Lyrics.

The Sonnets of John Milton. Edited by MARK PATTISON. With Portrait after Vertue.

French Lyrics. Selected and Annotated by GEORGE SAINTSBURY. With a Miniature Frontispiece designed and etched by H. G. Glindoni.

Fables by Mr. John Gay. With Memoir by AUSTIN DOBSON, and an Etched Portrait from an unfinished Oil Sketch by Sir Godfrey Kneller.

Select Letters of Percy Bysshe Shelley. Edited, with an Introduction, by RICHARD GARNETT.

The Christian Year. Thoughts in Verse for the Sundays and Holy Days throughout the Year. With Miniature Portrait of the Rev. J. Keble, after a Drawing by G. Richmond, R.A.

Shakspere's Works. Complete in Twelve Volumes.

Eighteenth Century Essays. Selected and Edited by AUSTIN DOBSON. With a Miniature Frontispiece by R. Caldecott.

Q. Horati Flacci Opera. Edited by F. A. CORNISH, Assistant Master at Eton. With a Frontispiece after a design by L. Alma Tadema, etched by Leopold Lowenstam.

Edgar Allan Poe's Poems. With an Essay on his Poetry by ANDREW LANG, and a Frontispiece by Linley Sambourne.

Shakspere's Sonnets. Edited by EDWARD DOWDEN. With a Frontispiece etched by Leopold Lowenstam, after the Death Mask.

English Odes. Selected by EDMUND GOSSE. With Frontispiece on India paper by Hamo Thornycroft, A.R.A.

Of the Imitation of Christ. By THOMAS À KEMPIS. A revised Translation. With Frontispiece on India paper, from a Design by W. B. Richmond.

Poems: Selected from PERCY BYSSHE SHELLEY. Dedicated to Lady Shelley. With a Preface by RICHARD GARNETT and a Miniature Frontispiece.

PARSLOE, Joseph.—**Our Railways.** Sketches, Historical and Descriptive. With Practical Information as to Fares and Rates, etc., and a Chapter on Railway Reform. Crown 8vo, 6s.

PATON, A. A.—**A History of the Egyptian Revolution**, from the Period of the Mamelukes to the Death of Mohammed Ali. Second Edition. 2 vols. Demy 8vo, 7s. 6d.

PAULI, Reinhold.—**Simon de Montfort, Earl of Leicester**, the Creator of the House of Commons. Crown 8vo, 6s.

Paul of Tarsus. By the Author of "Rabbi Jeshua." Crown 8vo, 4s. 6d.

PEMBERTON, T. Edgar.—**Charles Dickens and the Stage.** A Record of his Connection with the Drama. Crown 8vo, 6s.

PEZZI, Domenico.—**Aryan Philology**, according to the most recent researches (Glottologia Aria Recentissima). Translated by E. S. ROBERTS. Crown 8vo, 6s.

PFEIFFER, Emily.—**Women and Work.** An Essay on the Relation to Health and Physical Development of the Higher Education of Girls. Crown 8vo, 6s.

Phantasms of the Living. By EDMUND GURNEY, FREDERIC W. H. MYERS, M.A., and FRANK PODMORE, M.A. 2 vols. Demy 8vo, 21s.

Philological Society, Transactions of. Published irregularly. List of Publications on application.

PICCIOTTO, James.—**Sketches of Anglo-Jewish History.** Demy 8vo, 12s.

Pierce Gambit: Chess Papers and Problems. By JAMES PIERCE, M.A., and W. TIMBRELL PIERCE. Crown 8vo, 6s. 6d.

PIESSE, Charles H.—**Chemistry in the Brewing-Room.** Being the substance of a Course of Lessons to Practical Brewers. Fcap., 5s.

PLINY.—**The Letters of Pliny the Younger.** Translated by J. D. LEWIS. Post 8vo, 5s.

PLUMPTRE, Charles John.—**King's College Lectures on Elocution.** Fourth Edition. Post 8vo, 15s.

POOLE, W. F.—**An Index to Periodical Literature.** Third Edition. Royal 8vo, £3 13s. 6d.

POOLE, W. F., and FLETCHER, W. I.—**Index to Periodical Literature.** First Supplement. 1882 to 1887. Royal 8vo, £1 16s.

Practical Guides.—France, Belgium, Holland, and the Rhine. 1s. Italian Lakes. 1s. Wintering Places of the South. 2s. Switzerland, Savoy, and North Italy. 2s. 6d. General Continental Guide. 5s. Geneva. 1s. Paris. 1s. Bernese Oberland. 1s. Italy. 4s.

Psychical Research, Proceedings of the Society for. Published irregularly. Post 8vo. Vol. I. to III. 10s. each. Vol. IV. 8s. Vol. V. 10s.

PURITZ, Ludwig.—**Code-Book of Gymnastic Exercises.** Translated by O. KNOFE and J. W. MACQUEEN. 32mo, 1s. 6d.

RAPSON, Edward J.—**The Struggle between England and France for Supremacy in India.** Crown 8vo, 4s. 6d.

RAVENSTEIN, E. G., and HULLEY, John.—**The Gymnasium and its Fittings.** With 14 Plates of Illustrations. 8vo, 2s. 6d.

READE, Winwood.—**The Martyrdom of Man.** Thirteenth Edition. 8vo, 7s. 6d.

RENDELL, J. M.—**Concise Handbook of the Island of Madeira.** With Plan of Funchal and Map of the Island. Second Edition. Fcap. 8vo, 1s. 6d.

RHYS, John.—**Lectures on Welsh Philology.** Second Edition. Crown 8vo, 15s.

RIDEAL, C. F.—**Wellerisms, from "Pickwick" and "Master Humphrey's Clock."** 18mo, 2s.

RIPPER, William.—**Machine Drawing and Design,** for Engineering Students and Practical Engineers. Illustrated by 55 Plates and numerous Explanatory Notes. Royal 4to, 25s.

ROBINSON, A. Mary F.—**The Fortunate Lovers.** Twenty-seven Novels of the Queen of Navarre. Large crown 8vo, 10s. 6d.

ROLFE, Eustace Neville, and INGLEBY, Holcombe.—**Naples in 1888.** With Illustrations. Crown 8vo, 6s.

ROSMINI SERBATI, Antonio.—**Life.** By the Rev. W. LOCKHART. 2 vols. With Portraits. Crown 8vo, 12s.

ROSS, Percy.—**A Professor of Alchemy.** Crown 8vo, 3s. 6d.

ROUTLEDGE, James.—**English Rule and Native Opinion in India.** 8vo, 10s. 6d.

RULE, Martin, M.A.—**The Life and Times of St. Anselm, Archbishop of Canterbury and Primate of the Britains.** 2 vols. Demy 8vo, 32s.

RUTHERFORD, Mark.—**The Autobiography of Mark Rutherford and Mark Rutherford's Deliverance.** Edited by REUBEN SHAPCOTT. Third Edition. Crown 8vo, 7s. 6d.

> **The Revolution in Tanner's Lane.** Edited by REUBEN SHAPCOTT. Crown 8vo, 7s. 6d.

> **Miriam's Schooling: and other Papers.** Edited by REUBEN SHAPCOTT. Crown 8vo, 6s.

SAMUELSON, James.—**India, Past and Present:** Historical, Social, and Political. With a Map, Explanatory Woodcuts and Collotype Views, Portraits, etc., from 36 Photographs. 8vo, 21s.

SAMUELSON, *James—continued.*
>History of Drink. A Review, Social, Scientific, and Political. Second Edition. 8vo, 6*s.*
>Bulgaria, Past and Present: Historical, Political, and Descriptive. With Map and numerous Illustrations. Demy 8vo, 10*s.* 6*d.*

SANDWITH, *F. M.*—Egypt as a Winter Resort. Crown 8vo, 3*s.* 6*d.*

SANTIAGOE, *Daniel.*—The Curry Cook's Assistant. Fcap. 8vo, cloth. 1*s.* 6*d.*; paper covers, 1*s.*

SAYCE, *Rev. Archibald Henry.*—Introduction to the Science of Language. New and Cheaper Edition. 2 vols. Crown 8vo, 9*s.*

SAYWELL, *J. L.*—New Popular Handbook of County Dialects. Crown 8vo, 5*s.*

SCHAIBLE, *C. H.*—An Essay on the Systematic Training of the Body. Crown 8vo, 5*s.*

SCHLEICHER, *August.*—A Compendium of the Comparative Grammar of the Indo-European, Sanskrit, Greek, and Latin Languages. Translated from the Third German Edition by HERBERT BENDALL. 2 parts. 8vo, 13*s.* 6*d.*

SCOONES, *W. Baptiste.*—Four Centuries of English Letters: A Selection of 350 Letters by 150 Writers, from the Period of the Paston Letters to the Present Time. Third Edition. Large crown 8vo, 6*s.*

SCOTT, *Benjamin.*—A State Iniquity: Its Rise, Extension, and Overthrow. Demy 8vo, plain cloth, 3*s.* 6*d.*; gilt, 5*s.*

SELBY, *H. M.*—The Shakespeare Classical Dictionary; or, Mythological Allusions in the Plays of Shakespeare Explained. Fcap. 8vo, 1*s.*

Selwyn, Bishop, *of New Zealand and of Lichfield.* A Sketch of his Life and Work, with Further Gleanings from his Letters, Sermons, and Speeches. By the Rev. Canon CURTEIS. Large crown 8vo, 7*s.* 6*d.*

SERJEANT, *W. C. Eldon.*—The Astrologer's Guide (Anima Astrologiæ). Demy 8vo, 7*s.* 6*d.*

Shakspere's Works. The Avon Edition, 12 vols., fcap. 8vo, cloth, 18*s.*; in cloth box, 21*s.*; bound in 6 vols., cloth, 15*s.*

Shakspere's Works, an Index to. By EVANGELINE O'CONNOR. Crown 8vo, 5*s.*

SHAKESPEARE.—The Bankside Shakespeare. The Comedies, Histories, and Tragedies of Mr. William Shakespeare, as presented at the Globe and Blackfriars Theatres, *circa* 1591-1623. Being the Text furnished the Players, in parallel pages with the first revised folio text, with Critical Introductions. 8vo.
[*In preparation.*

SHAKESPEARE—*continued.*

A **New Study of Shakespeare.** An Inquiry into the Connection of the Plays and Poems, with the Origins of the Classical Drama, and with the Platonic Philosophy, through the Mysteries. Demy 8vo, 10s. 6d.

Shakespeare's Cymbeline. Edited, with Notes, by C. M. INGLEBY. Crown 8vo, 1s. 6d.

A **New Variorum Edition of Shakespeare.** Edited by HORACE HOWARD FURNESS. Royal 8vo. Vol. I. Romeo and Juliet. 18s. Vol. II. Macbeth. 18s. Vols. III. and IV. Hamlet. 2 vols. 36s. Vol. V. King Lear. 18s. Vol. VI. Othello. 18s.

Shakspere Society (The New).—Subscription, one guinea per annum. List of Publications on application.

SHELLEY, Percy Bysshe.—Life. By EDWARD DOWDEN, LL.D. 2 vols. With Portraits. Demy 8vo, 36s.

SIBREE, James, Jun.—**The Great African Island.** Chapters on Madagascar. A Popular Account of the Physical Geography, etc., of the Country. With Physical and Ethnological Maps and 4 Illustrations. 8vo, 10s. 6d.

SIGERSON, George, M.D.—**Political Prisoners at Home and Abroad.** With Appendix on Dietaries. Crown 8vo, 2s. 6d.

SIMCOX, Edith.—**Episodes in the Lives of Men, Women, and Lovers.** Crown 8vo, 7s. 6d.

SINCLAIR, Thomas.—**Essays: in Three Kinds.** Crown 8vo, 1s. 6d.; wrappers, 1s.

Sinclairs of England (The). Crown 8vo, 12s.

SINNETT, A. P.—**The Occult World.** Fourth Edition. Crown 8vo, 3s. 6d.

Incidents in the Life of Madame Blavatsky. Demy 8vo, 10s. 6d.

Skinner, James: A Memoir. By the Author of "Charles Lowder." With a Preface by the Rev. Canon CARTER, and Portrait. Large crown, 7s. 6d.

*** Also a cheap Edition. With Portrait. Fourth Edition. Crown 8vo, 3s. 6d.

SMITH, Huntington.—**A Century of American Literature:** Benjamin Franklin to James Russell Lowell. Crown 8vo, 6s.

SMITH, S.—**The Divine Government.** Fifth Edition. Crown 8vo, 6s.

SMYTH, *R. Brough.*—The Aborigines of Victoria. Compiled for the Government of Victoria. With Maps, Plates, and Woodcuts. 2 vols. Royal 8vo, £3 3s.

Sophocles: The Seven Plays in English Verse. Translated by LEWIS CAMPBELL. Crown 8vo, 7s. 6d.

Specimens of English Prose Style from Malory to Macaulay. Selected and Annotated, with an Introductory Essay, by GEORGE SAINTSBURY. Large crown 8vo, printed on handmade paper, parchment antique or cloth, 12s.; vellum, 15s.

SPEDDING, *James.*—The Life and Times of Francis Bacon. 2 vols. Post 8vo, 21s.

Spinoza, Benedict de: His Life, Correspondence, and Ethics. By R. WILLIS, M.D. 8vo, 21s.

SPRAGUE, *Charles E.*—Handbook of Volapük: The International Language. Second Edition. Crown 8vo, 5s.

ST. HILL, *Katharine.*—The Grammar of Palmistry. With 18 Illustrations. 12mo, 1s.

STOKES, *Whitley.*—Goidelica: Old and Early-Middle Irish Glosses. Prose and Verse. Second Edition. Med. 8vo, 18s.

STRACHEY, *Sir John, G.C.S.I.*—India. With Map. Demy 8vo, 15s.

STREET, *J. C.*—The Hidden Way across the Threshold; or, The Mystery which hath been hidden for Ages and from Generations. With Plates. Large 8vo, 15s.

SUMNER, *W. G.*—What Social Classes owe to Each Other. 18mo, 3s. 6d.

SWINBURNE, *Algernon Charles.*—A Word for the Navy. Imperial 16mo, 5s.

The Bibliography of Swinburne, 1857-1887. Crown 8vo, vellum gilt, 6s.

Sylva, Carmen (Queen of Roumania), The Life of. Translated by Baroness DEICHMANN. With 4 Portraits and 1 Illustration. 8vo, 12s.

TAYLER, *J. J.*—A Retrospect of the Religious Life of England; or, Church, Puritanism, and Free Inquiry. Second Edition. Post 8vo, 7s. 6d.

TAYLOR, *Rev. Canon Isaac, LL.D.*—The Alphabet. An Account of the Origin and Development of Letters. With numerous Tables and Facsimiles. 2 vols. Demy 8vo, 36s.

Leaves from an Egyptian Note-book. Crown 8vo, 5s.

TAYLOR, *Sir Henry.*—The Statesman. Fcap. 8vo, 3s. 6d.

Taylor, Reynell, C.B., C.S.I.: A Biography. By E. GAMBIER PARRY. With Portait and Map. Demy 8vo, 14s.

Technological Dictionary of the Terms employed in the Arts and Sciences; Architecture; Engineering; Mechanics; Shipbuilding and Navigation; Metallurgy; Mathematics, etc. Second Edition. 3 vols. 8vo.
Vol. I. German-English-French. 12*s.*
Vol. II. English-German-French. 12*s.*
Vol. III. French-German-English. 15*s.*

THACKERAY, Rev. S. W., LL.D—**The Land and the Community.** Crown 8vo, 3*s.* 6*d.*

THACKERAY, William Makepeace.—**An Essay on the Genius of George Cruikshank.** Reprinted verbatim from the *Westminster Review*. 40 Illustrations. Large paper Edition. Royal 8vo, 7*s.* 6*d.*

Sultan Stork; and other Stories and Sketches. 1829-1844. Now First Collected. To which is added the Bibliography of Thackeray, Revised and Considerably Enlarged. Large demy 8vo, 10*s.* 6*d.*

THOMPSON, Sir H.—**Diet in Relation to Age and Activity.** Fcap. 8vo, cloth, 1*s.* 6*d.*; paper covers, 1*s.*

Modern Cremation. Crown 8vo, 2*s.* 6*d.*

Tobacco Talk and Smokers' Gossip. 16mo, 2*s.*

TRANT, William.—**Trade Unions: Their Origin, Objects, and Efficacy.** Small crown 8vo, 1*s.* 6*d.*; paper covers, 1*s.*

TRENCH, The late R. C., Archbishop.—**Letters and Memorials.** By the Author of "Charles Lowder." With two Portraits. 2 vols. 8vo, 21*s.*

A Household Book of English Poetry. Selected and Arranged, with Notes. Fourth Edition, Revised. Extra fcap. 8vo, 5*s.*

An Essay on the Life and Genius of Calderon. With Translations from his "Life's a Dream" and "Great Theatre of the World." Second Edition, Revised and Improved. Extra fcap. 8vo, 5*s.* 6*d.*

Gustavus Adolphus in Germany, and other Lectures on the Thirty Years' War. Third Edition, Enlarged. Fcap. 8vo, 4*s.*

Plutarch: his Life, his Lives, and his Morals. Second Edition, Enlarged. Fcap. 8vo, 3*s.* 6*d.*

Remains of the late Mrs. Richard Trench. Being Selections from her Journals, Letters, and other Papers. New and Cheaper Issue. With Portrait. 8vo, 6*s.*

Lectures on Mediæval Church History. Being the Substance of Lectures delivered at Queen's College, London. Second Edition. 8vo, 12*s.*

TRENCH, *The late R. C., Archbishop—continued.*
  English, Past and Present. Thirteenth Edition, Revised and Improved. Fcap. 8vo, 5s.
  On the Study of Words. Twentieth Edition, Revised. Fcap. 8vo, 5s.
  Select Glossary of English Words used Formerly in Senses Different from the Present. Seventh Edition, Revised and Enlarged. Fcap. 8vo, 5s.
  Proverbs and Their Lessons. Seventh Edition, Enlarged. Fcap. 8vo, 4s.

TRIMEN, *Roland.*—**South-African Butterflies.** A Monograph of the Extra-Tropical Species. With 12 Coloured Plates. 3 vols. Demy 8vo, £2 12s. 6d.

Trübner's Bibliographical Guide to American Literature. A Classed List of Books published in the United States of America, from 1817 to 1857. Edited by NICOLAS TRÜBNER. 8vo, half-bound, 18s.

TRUMBULL, *H. Clay.*—**The Blood-Covenant, a Primitive Rite, and its Bearings on Scripture.** Post 8vo, 7s. 6d.

TURNER, *Charles Edward.*—**Count Tolstoï, as Novelist and Thinker.** Lectures delivered at the Royal Institution. Crown 8vo, 3s. 6d.
  The Modern Novelists of Russia. Lectures delivered at the Taylor Institution, Oxford. Crown 8vo, 3s. 6d.

TWEEDIE, *Mrs. Alec.*—**The Ober-Ammergau Passion Play, 1890.** Small crown 8vo, 2s. 6d.

VAUGHAN, *H. H.*—**British Reason in English Rhyme.** Crown 8vo, 6s.

VESCELIUS-SHELDON, *Louise.*—**An I. D. B. in South Africa.** Illustrated by G. E. GRAVES and AL. HENCKE. Crown 8vo, 7s. 6d.
  Yankee Girls in Zulu-Land. Illustrated by G. E. GRAVES. Crown 8vo, 5s.

Victoria Government, Publications of the. [*List in preparation.*]

VINCENT, *Frank.*—**Around and about South America.** Twenty Months of Quest and Query. With Maps, Plans, and 54 Illustrations. Medium 8vo, 21s.

WAITE, *A. E.*—**Lives of Alchemystical Philosophers.** Demy 8vo, 10s. 6d.
  The Magical Writings of Thomas Vaughan. Small 4to, 10s. 6d.
  The Real History of the Rosicrucians. With Illustrations. Crown 8vo, 7s. 6d.

WAITE, A. E.—continued.
   The Mysteries of Magic. A Digest of the Writings of Éliphas Lévi. With Illustrations. Demy 8vo, 10s. 6d.

WAKE, C. Staniland.—Serpent-Worship, and other Essays, with a Chapter on Totemism. Demy 8vo, 10s. 6d.
   The Development of Marriage and Kinship. Demy 8vo, 18s.

Wales.—Through North Wales with a Knapsack. By Four Schoolmistresses. With a Sketch Map. Small crown 8vo, 2s. 6d.

WALL, George.—The Natural History of Thought in its Practical Aspect, from its Origin in Infancy. Demy 8vo, 12s. 6d.

WALLACE, Alfred Russel.—On Miracles and Modern Spiritualism. Second Edition. Crown 8vo, 5s.

WALPOLE, Chas. George.—A Short History of Ireland from the Earliest Times to the Union with Great Britain. With 5 Maps and Appendices. Third Edition. Crown 8vo, 6s.

WALTERS, J. Cuming.—In Tennyson Land. Being a Brief Account of the Home and Early Surroundings of the Poet-Laureate. With Illustrations. Demy 8vo, 5s.

WARTER, J. W.—An Old Shropshire Oak. 2 vols. Demy 8vo, 28s.

WATSON, R. G.—Spanish and Portuguese South America during the Colonial Period. 2 vols. Post 8vo, 21s.

WEDGWOOD, H.—A Dictionary of English Etymology. Fourth Edition, Revised and Enlarged. With Introduction on the Origin of Language. 8vo, £1 1s.
   Contested Etymologies in the Dictionary of the Rev. W. W. Skeat. Crown 8vo, 5s.

WEDGWOOD, Julia.—The Moral Ideal. An Historic Study. Second Edition. Demy 8vo, 9s.

WEISBACH, Julius.—Theoretical Mechanics. A Manual of the Mechanics of Engineering. Designed as a Text-book for Technical Schools, and for the Use of Engineers. Translated from the German by ECKLEY B. COXE. With 902 Woodcuts. Demy 8vo, 31s. 6d.

WESTROPP, Hodder M.—Primitive Symbolism as Illustrated in Phallic Worship; or, The Reproductive Principle. With an Introduction by Major-Gen. FORLONG. Demy 8vo, parchment, 7s. 6d.

WHEELDON, J. P.—Angling Resorts near London. The Thames and the Lea. Crown 8vo, paper, 1s. 6d.

WHIBLEY, Chas.—**In Cap and Gown**: Three Centuries of Cambridge Wit. Crown 8vo, 7s. 6d.

WHITMAN, Sidney.—**Imperial Germany.** A Critical Study of Fact and Character. Crown 8vo, 7s. 6d.

WIGSTON, W. F. C.—**Hermes Stella**; or, Notes and Jottings on the Bacon Cipher. 8vo, 6s.

Wilberforce, Bishop, *of Oxford and Winchester*, **Life.** By his Son REGINALD WILBERFORCE. Crown 8vo, 6s.

WILDRIDGE, T. Tyndall.—**The Dance of Death, in Painting and in Print.** With Woodcuts. 4to, 3s. 6d; the Woodcuts coloured by hand, 5s.

WOLTMANN, Dr. Alfred, and WOERMANN, Dr. Karl.—**History of Painting.** With numerous Illustrations. Medium 8vo. Vol. I. Painting in Antiquity and the Middle Ages. 28s.; bevelled boards, gilt leaves, 30s. Vol. II. The Painting of the Renascence. 42s.; bevelled boards, gilt leaves, 45s.

HOOD, M. W.—**Dictionary of Volapük.** Volapük-English and English-Volapük. Volapükatidel e cif. Crown 8vo, 10s. 6d.

WORTHY, Charles.—**Practical Heraldry**; or, An Epitome of English Armory. 124 Illustrations. Crown 8vo, 7s. 6d.

WRIGHT, Thomas.—**The Homes of Other Days.** A History of Domestic Manners and Sentiments during the Middle Ages. With Illustrations from the Illuminations in Contemporary Manuscripts and other Sources. Drawn and Engraved by F. W. FAIRHOLT, F.S.A. 350 Woodcuts. Medium 8vo, 21s.

Anglo-Saxon and Old English Vocabularies. Second Edition. Edited by RICHARD PAUL WULCKER. 2 vols. Demy 8vo, 28s.

The Celt, the Roman, and the Saxon. A History of the Early Inhabitants of Britain down to the Conversion of the Anglo-Saxons to Christianity. Illustrated by the Ancient Remains brought to light by Recent Research. Corrected and Enlarged Edition. With nearly 300 Engravings. Crown 8vo, 9s.

YELVERTON, Christopher.—**Oneiros**; or, Some Questions of the Day. Crown 8vo, 5s.

THEOLOGY AND PHILOSOPHY.

ALEXANDER, William, D.D., Bishop of Derry.—**The Great Question, and other Sermons.** Crown 8vo, 6s.

AMBERLEY, Viscount.—**An Analysis of Religious Belief.** 2 vols. Demy 8vo, 30s.

Antiqua Mater: A Study of Christian Origins. Crown 8vo, 7s. 6d.

BELANY, Rev. R.—**The Bible and the Papacy.** Crown 8vo, 2s.

BENTHAM, Jeremy.—**Theory of Legislation.** Translated from the French of Etienne Dumont by R. HILDRETH. Fifth Edition. Post 8vo, 7s. 6d.

BEST, George Payne.—**Morality and Utility.** A Natural Science of Ethics. Crown 8vo, 5s.

BROOKE, Rev. Stopford A.—**The Fight of Faith.** Sermons preached on various occasions. Fifth Edition. Crown 8vo, 7s. 6d.

The Spirit of the Christian Life. Third Edition. Crown 8vo, 5s.

Theology in the English Poets. Cowper, Coleridge, Wordsworth, and Burns. Sixth Edition. Post 8vo, 5s.

Christ in Modern Life. Seventeenth Edition. Crown 8vo, 5s.

Sermons. First Series. Thirteenth Edition. Crown 8vo, 5s.

Sermons. Second Series. Sixth Edition. Crown 8vo, 5s.

BROWN, Rev. J. Baldwin.—**The Higher Life.** Its Reality, Experience, and Destiny. Seventh Edition. Crown 8vo, 5s.

Doctrine of Annihilation in the Light of the Gospel of Love. Five Discourses. Fourth Edition. Crown 8vo, 2s. 6d.

The Christian Policy of Life. A Book for Young Men of Business. Third Edition. Crown 8vo, 3s. 6d.

BUNSEN, Ernest de.—**Islam**; or, True Christianity. Crown 8vo, 5s.

Catholic Dictionary. Containing some Account of the Doctrine, Discipline, Rites, Ceremonies, Councils, and Religious Orders of the Catholic Church. Edited by THOMAS ARNOLD, M.A. Third Edition. Demy 8vo, 21s.

CHEYNE, Canon.—**The Prophecies of Isaiah.** Translated with Critical Notes and Dissertations. 2 vols. Fifth Edition. Demy 8vo, 25s.

Job and Solomon; or, The Wisdom of the Old Testament. Demy 8vo, 12s. 6d.

The Psalms; or, Book of The Praises of Israel. Translated with Commentary. Demy 8vo, 16s.

CLARKE, James Freeman.—**Ten Great Religions.** An Essay in Comparative Theology. Demy 8vo, 10s. 6d.

Ten Great Religions. Part II. A Comparison of all Religions. Demy 8vo, 10s. 6d.

COKE, Henry.—**Creeds of the Day**; or, Collated Opinions of Reputable Thinkers. 2 vols. Demy 8vo, 21s.

COMTE, *Auguste.*—The Catechism of Positive Religion. Translated from the French by RICHARD CONGREVE. Second Edition. Crown 8vo, 2s. 6d.

The Eight Circulars of Auguste Comte. Translated from the French. Fcap. 8vo, 1s. 6d.

Appeal to Conservatives. Crown 8vo, 2s. 6d.

The Positive Philosophy of Auguste Comte. Translated and condensed by HARRIET MARTINEAU. 2 vols. Second Edition. 8vo, 25s.

CONWAY, *Moncure D.*—The Sacred Anthology. A Book of Ethnical Scriptures. Edited by MONCURE D. CONWAY. New Edition. Crown 8vo, 5s.

Idols and Ideals. With an Essay on Christianity. Crown 8vo, 4s.

COX, *Rev. Samuel, D.D.*—A Commentary on the Book of Job. With a Translation. Second Edition. Demy 8vo, 15s.

Salvator Mundi; or, Is Christ the Saviour of all Men? Twelfth Edition. Crown 8vo, 2s. 6d.

The Larger Hope. A Sequel to "Salvator Mundi." Second Edition. 16mo, 1s.

The Genesis of Evil, and other Sermons, mainly expository. Third Edition. Crown 8vo, 6s.

Balaam. An Exposition and a Study. Crown 8vo, 5s.

Miracles. An Argument and a Challenge. Crown 8vo, 2s. 6d.

CRANBROOK, *James.*—Credibilia; or, Discourses on Questions of Christian Faith. Post 8vo, 3s. 6d.

The Founders of Christianity; or, Discourses upon the Origin of the Christian Religion. Post 8vo, 6s.

DAWSON, *Geo., M.A.*—Prayers, with a Discourse on Prayer. Edited by his Wife. First Series. Tenth Edition. Small Crown 8vo, 3s. 6d.

Prayers, with a Discourse on Prayer. Edited by GEORGE ST. CLAIR, F.G.S. Second Series. Small Crown 8vo, 3s. 6d.

Sermons on Disputed Points and Special Occasions. Edited by his Wife. Fourth Edition. Crown 8vo, 3s. 6d.

Sermons on Daily Life and Duty. Edited by his Wife. Fifth Edition. Small crown 8vo, 3s. 6d.

The Authentic Gospel, and other Sermons. Edited by GEORGE ST. CLAIR, F.G.S. Third Edition. Crown 8vo, 6s.

Every-day Counsels. Edited by GEORGE ST. CLAIR, F.G.S. Crown 8vo, 6s.

DELEPIERRE, Octave.—L'Enfer : Essai Philosophique et Historique sur les Légendes de la Vie Future. Only 250 copies printed. Crown 8vo, 6s.

Doubter's Doubt about Science and Religion. Crown 8vo, 3s. 6d.

FICHTE, Johann Gottlieb.—Characteristics of the Present Age. Translated by WILLIAM SMITH. Post 8vo, 6s.

Memoir of Johann Gottlieb Fichte. By WILLIAM SMITH. Second Edition. Post 8vo, 4s.

On the Nature of the Scholar, and its Manifestations. Translated by WILLIAM SMITH. Second Edition. Post 8vo, 3s.

New Exposition of the Science of Knowledge. Translated by A. E. KROEGER. 8vo, 6s.

FITZ-GERALD, Mrs. P. F.—A Protest against Agnosticism: Introduction to a New Theory of Idealism. Demy 8vo.

An Essay on the Philosophy of Self-Consciousness. Comprising an Analysis of Reason and the Rationale of Love. Demy 8vo, 5s.

A Treatise on the Principle of Sufficient Reason. A Psychological Theory of Reasoning, showing the Relativity of Thought to the Thinker, of Recognition to Cognition, the Identity of Presentation and Representation, of Perception and Apperception. Demy 8vo, 6s.

GALLWEY, Rev. P.—Apostolic Succession. A Handbook. Demy 8vo, 1s.

GOUGH, Edward.—The Bible True from the Beginning. A Commentary on all those Portions of Scripture that are most Questioned and Assailed. Vols. I., II., and III. Demy 8vo, 16s. each.

GREG, W. R.—Literary and Social Judgments. Fourth Edition. 2 vols. Crown 8vo, 15s.

The Creed of Christendom. Eighth Edition. 2 vols. Post 8vo, 15s.

Enigmas of Life. Seventeenth Edition. Post 8vo, 10s. 6d.

Political Problems for our Age and Country. Demy 8vo, 10s. 6d.

Miscellaneous Essays. 2 Series. Crown 8vo, 7s. 6d. each.

GRIMLEY, Rev. H. N., M.A.—Tremadoc Sermons, chiefly on the Spiritual Body, the Unseen World, and the Divine Humanity. Fourth Edition. Crown 8vo, 6s.

The Temple of Humanity, and other Sermons. Crown 8vo, 6s.

GURNEY, Alfred.—**Our Catholic Inheritance in the Larger Hope.** Crown 8vo, 1s. 6d.

HAINES, C. R.—**Christianity and Islam in Spain, A.D. 756-1031.** Crown 8vo, 2s. 6d.

HAWEIS, Rev. H. R., M.A.—**Current Coin.** Materialism—The Devil—Crime—Drunkenness—Pauperism—Emotion—Recreation—The Sabbath. Fifth Edition. Crown 8vo, 5s.

Arrows in the Air. Fifth Edition. Crown 8vo, 5s.

Speech in Season. Sixth Edition. Crown 8vo, 5s.

Thoughts for the Times. Fourteenth Edition. Crown 8vo, 5s.

Unsectarian Family Prayers. New Edition. Fcap. 8vo, 1s. 6d.

HUGHES, Rev. H., M.A.—**Principles of Natural and Supernatural Morals.** Vol. I. Natural Morals. Demy 8vo, 12s.

JOSEPH, N. S.—**Religion, Natural and Revealed.** A Series of Progressive Lessons for Jewish Youth. Crown 8vo, 3s.

KEMPIS, Thomas à.—**Of the Imitation of Christ.** Parchment Library Edition.—Parchment or cloth, 6s.; vellum, 7s. 6d. The Red Line Edition, fcap. 8vo, cloth extra, 2s. 6d. The Cabinet Edition, small 8vo, cloth limp, 1s.; cloth boards, 1s. 6d. The Miniature Edition, cloth limp, 32mo, 1s.; or with red lines, 1s. 6d.

Of the Imitation of Christ. A Metrical Version. By HENRY CARRINGTON. Crown 8vo, 5s.

Notes of a Visit to the Scenes in which his Life was spent. With numerous Illustrations. By F. R. CRUISE, M.D. Demy 8vo, 12s.

Keys of the Creeds (The). Third Revised Edition. Crown 8vo, 2s. 6d.

LEWES, George Henry.—**Problems of Life and Mind.** Demy 8vo. First Series: The Foundations of a Creed. 2 vols. 28s. Second Series: The Physical Basis of Mind. With Illustrations. 16s. Third Series. 2 vols. 22s. 6d.

LEWIS, Harry S.—**Targum on Isaiah i.-v.** With Commentary. Demy 8vo, 5s.

MANNING, Cardinal.—**Towards Evening.** Selections from his Writings. Third Edition. 16mo, 2s.

MARTINEAU, James.—**Essays, Philosophical and Theological.** 2 vols. Crown 8vo, £1 4s.

MEAD, C. M., D.D.—**Supernatural Revelation.** An Essay concerning the Basis of the Christian Faith. Royal 8vo, 14s.

Meditations on Death and Eternity. Translated from the German by FREDERICA ROWAN. Published by Her Majesty's gracious permission. Crown 8vo, 6s.

Meditations on Life and its Religious Duties. Translated from the German by FREDERICA ROWAN. Published by Her Majesty's gracious permission. Being the Companion Volume to "Meditations on Death and Eternity." Crown 8vo, 6s.

NEVILL, F.—Retrogression or Development. Crown 8vo, 3s. 6d.

NICHOLS, J. Broadhurst, and DYMOND, Charles William.—Practical Value of Christianity. Two Prize Essays. Crown 8vo, 3s. 6d.

PARKER, Theodore. — Discourse on Matters pertaining to Religion. People's Edition. Crown 8vo, 1s. 6d.; cloth, 2s.

The Collected Works of Theodore Parker, Minister of the Twenty-eighth Congregational Society at Boston, U.S. In 14 vols. 8vo, 6s. each.

Vol. I. Discourse on Matters pertaining to Religion. II. Ten Sermons and Prayers. III. Discourses on Theology. IV. Discourses on Politics. V. and VI. Discourses on Slavery. VII. Discourses on Social Science. VIII. Miscellaneous Discourses. IX. and X. Critical Writings. XI. Sermons on Theism, Atheism, and Popular Theology. XII. Autobiographical and Miscellaneous Pieces. XIII. Historic Americans. XIV. Lessons from the World of Matter and the World of Man.

Plea for Truth in Religion. Crown 8vo, 2s. 6d

Psalms of the West. Small crown 8vo, 5s.

Pulpit Commentary, The. (*Old Testament Series.*) Edited by the Rev. J. S. EXELL, M.A., and the Very Rev. Dean H. D. M. SPENCE, M.A., D.D.

Genesis. By the Rev. T. WHITELAW, D.D. With Homilies by the Very Rev. J. F. MONTGOMERY, D.D., Rev. Prof. R. A. REDFORD, M.A., LL.B., Rev. F. HASTINGS, Rev. W. ROBERTS, M.A. An Introduction to the Study of the Old Testament by the Venerable Archdeacon FARRAR, D.D., F.R.S.; and Introductions to the Pentateuch by the Right Rev. H. COTTERILL, D.D., and Rev. T. WHITELAW, D.D. Ninth Edition. 1 vol., 15s.

Exodus. By the Rev. Canon RAWLINSON. With Homilies by the Rev. J. ORR, D.D., Rev. D. YOUNG, B.A., Rev. C. A. GOODHART, Rev. J. URQUHART, and the Rev. H. T. ROBJOHNS. Fourth Edition. 2 vols., 9s. each.

Leviticus. By the Rev. Prebendary MEYRICK, M.A. With Introductions by the Rev. R. COLLINS, Rev. Professor A. CAVE, and Homilies by the Rev. Prof. REDFORD, LL.B., Rev. J. A. MACDONALD, Rev. W. CLARKSON, B.A., Rev. S. R. ALDRIDGE, LL.B., and Rev. MCCHEYNE EDGAR. Fourth Edition. 15s.

Pulpit Commentary, The—*continued.*

Numbers. By the Rev. R. WINTERBOTHAM, LL.B. With Homilies by the Rev. Professor W. BINNIE, D.D., Rev. E. S. PROUT, M.A., Rev. D. YOUNG, B.A., Rev. J. WAITE, B.A., and an Introduction by the Rev. THOMAS WHITELAW, D.D. Fifth Edition. 15s.

Deuteronomy. By the Rev. W. L. ALEXANDER, D.D. With Homilies by the Rev. C. CLEMANCE, D.D., Rev. J. ORR, D.D., Rev. R. M. EDGAR, M.A., Rev. D. DAVIES, M.A. Fourth edition. 15s.

Joshua. By the Rev. J. J. LIAS, M.A. With Homilies by the Rev. S. R. ALDRIDGE, LL.B., Rev. R. GLOVER, Rev. E. DE PRESSENSÉ, D.D., Rev. J. WAITE, B.A., Rev. W. F. ADENEY, M.A.; and an Introduction by the Rev. A. PLUMMER, D.D. Fifth Edition. 12s. 6d.

Judges and Ruth. By the Bishop of BATH and WELLS, and Rev. J. MORISON, D.D. With Homilies by the Rev. A. F. MUIR, M.A., Rev. W. F. ADENEY, M.A., Rev. W. M. STATHAM, and Rev. Professor J. THOMSON, M.A. Fifth Edition. 10s. 6d.

1 and 2 Samuel. By the Very Rev. R. P. SMITH, D.D. With Homilies by the Rev. DONALD FRASER, D.D., Rev. Prof. CHAPMAN, Rev. B. DALE, and Rev. G. WOOD, B.A. Seventh Edition. 15s. each.

1 Kings. By the Rev. JOSEPH HAMMOND, LL.B. With Homilies by the Rev. E. DE PRESSENSÉ, D.D., Rev. J. WAITE, B.A., Rev. A. ROWLAND, LL.B., Rev. J. A. MACDONALD, and Rev. J. URQUHART. Fifth Edition. 15s.

2 Kings. By the Rev. Canon RAWLINSON. With Homilies by the Rev. J. ORR, D.D., Rev. D. THOMAS, D.D., and Rev. C. H. IRWIN, M.A. 15s.

1 Chronicles. By the Rev. Prof. P. C. BARKER, M.A., LL.B. With Homilies by the Rev. Prof. J. R. THOMSON, M.A., Rev. R. TUCK, B.A., Rev. W. CLARKSON, B.A., Rev. F. WHITFIELD, M.A., and Rev. RICHARD GLOVER. 15s.

Ezra, Nehemiah, and Esther. By the Rev. Canon G. RAWLINSON, M.A. With Homilies by the Rev. Prof. J. R. THOMSON, M.A., Rev. Prof. R. A. REDFORD, LL.B., M.A., Rev. W. S. LEWIS, M.A., Rev. J. A. MACDONALD, Rev. A. MACKENNAL, B.A., Rev. W. CLARKSON, B.A., Rev. F. HASTINGS, Rev. W. DINWIDDIE, LL.B., Rev. Prof. ROWLANDS, B.A., Rev. G. WOOD, B.A., Rev. Prof. P. C. BARKER, M.A., LL.B., and the Rev. J. S. EXELL, M.A. Seventh Edition. 1 vol., 12s. 6d.

Isaiah. By the Rev. Canon G. RAWLINSON, M.A. With Homilies by the Rev. Prof. E. JOHNSON, M.A., Rev. W. CLARKSON, B.A., Rev. W. M. STATHAM, and Rev. R. TUCK, B.A. **Second Edition.** 2 vols., 15s. each.

Pulpit Commentary, The—*continued*.

    Jeremiah. (Vol. I.) By the Rev. Canon T. K. CHEYNE, D.D. With Homilies by the Rev. W. F. ADENEY, M.A., Rev. A. F. MUIR, M.A., Rev. S. CONWAY, B.A., Rev. J. WAITE, B.A., and Rev. D. YOUNG, B.A. Third Edition. 15s.

    Jeremiah (Vol. II.) and Lamentations. By the Rev. Canon T. K. CHEYNE, D.D. With Homilies by the Rev. Prof. J. R. THOMSON, M.A., Rev. W. F. ADENEY, M.A., Rev. A. F. MUIR, M.A., Rev. S. CONWAY, B.A., Rev. D. YOUNG, B.A. 15s.

    Hosea and Joel. By the Rev. Prof. J. J. GIVEN, Ph.D., D.D. With Homilies by the Rev. Prof. J. R. THOMSON, M.A., Rev. A. ROWLAND, B.A., LL.B., Rev. C. JERDAN, M.A., LL.B., Rev. J. ORR, D.D., and Rev. D. THOMAS, D.D. 15s.

Pulpit Commentary, The. (*New Testament Series.*)

    St. Mark. By the Very Rev. E. BICKERSTETH, D.D., Dean of Lichfield. With Homilies by the Rev. Prof. THOMSON, M.A., Rev. Prof. J. J. GIVEN, Ph.D., D.D., Rev. Prof. JOHNSON, M.A., Rev. A. ROWLAND, B.A., LL.B., Rev. A. MUIR, and Rev. R. GREEN. Fifth Edition. 2 vols., 10s. 6d. each.

    St. Luke. By the Very Rev. H. D. M. SPENCE. With Homilies by the Rev. J. MARSHALL LANG, D.D., Rev. W. CLARKSON, B.A., and Rev. R. M. EDGAR, M.A. 2 vols., 10s. 6d. each.

    St. John. By the Rev. Prof. H. R. REYNOLDS, D.D. With Homilies by the Rev. Prof. T. CROSKERY, D.D., Rev. Prof. J. R. THOMSON, M.A., Rev. D. YOUNG, B.A., Rev. B. THOMAS, Rev. G. BROWN. Second Edition. 2 vols., 15s. each.

    The Acts of the Apostles. By the Bishop of BATH and WELLS. With Homilies by the Rev. Prof. P. C. BARKER, M.A., LL.B., Rev. Prof. E. JOHNSON, M.A., Rev. Prof. R. A. REDFORD, LL.B., Rev. R. TUCK, B.A., Rev. W. CLARKSON, B.A. Fourth Edition. 2 vols., 10s. 6d. each.

    1 Corinthians. By the Ven. Archdeacon FARRAR, D.D. With Homilies by the Rev. Ex-Chancellor LIPSCOMB, LL.D., Rev. DAVID THOMAS, D.D., Rev. D. FRASER, D.D., Rev. Prof. J. R. THOMSON, M.A., Rev. J. WAITE, B.A., Rev. R. TUCK, B.A., Rev. E. HURNDALL, M.A., and Rev. H. BREMNER, B.D. Fourth Edition. 15s.

    2 Corinthians and Galatians. By the Ven. Archdeacon FARRAR, D.D., and Rev. Prebendary E. HUXTABLE. With Homilies by the Rev. Ex-Chancellor LIPSCOMB, LL.D., Rev. DAVID THOMAS, D.D., Rev. DONALD FRASER, D.D., Rev. R. TUCK, B.A., Rev. E. HURNDALL, M.A., Rev. Prof. J. R. THOMSON, M.A., Rev. R. FINLAYSON, B.A., Rev. W. F. ADENEY, M.A., Rev. R. M. EDGAR, M.A., and Rev. T. CROSKERY, D.D. Second Edition. 21s.

Pulpit Commentary, The—*continued.*

Ephesians, Philippians, and Colossians. By the Rev. Prof. W. G. BLAIKIE, D.D., Rev. B. C. CAFFIN, M.A., and Rev. G. G. FINDLAY, B.A. With Homilies by the Rev. D. THOMAS, D.D., Rev. R. M. EDGAR, M.A., Rev. R. FINLAYSON, B.A., Rev. W. F. ADENEY, M.A., Rev. Prof. T. CROSKERY, D.D., Rev. E. S. PROUT, M.A., Rev. Canon VERNON HUTTON, and Rev. U. R. THOMAS, D.D. Second Edition. 21s.

Thessalonians, Timothy, Titus, and Philemon. By the Bishop of BATH and WELLS, Rev. Dr. GLOAG, and Rev. Dr. EALES. With Homilies by the Rev. B. C. CAFFIN, M.A., Rev. R. FINLAYSON, B.A., Rev. Prof. T. CROSKERY, D.D., Rev. W. F. ADENEY, M.A., Rev. W. M. STATHAM, and Rev. D. THOMAS, D.D. 15s.

Hebrews and James. By the Rev. J. BARMBY, D.D., and Rev. Prebendary E. C. S. GIBSON, M.A. With Homiletics by the Rev. C. JERDAN, M.A., LL.B., and Rev. Prebendary E. C. S. GIBSON. And Homilies by the Rev. W. JONES, Rev. C. NEW, Rev. D. YOUNG, B.A., Rev. J. S. BRIGHT, Rev. T. F. LOCKYER, B.A., and Rev. C. JERDAN, M.A., LL.B. Second Edition. 15s.

Peter, John, and Jude. By the Rev. B. C. CAFFIN, M.A., Rev. A. PLUMMER, D.D., and Rev. S. D. F. SALMOND, D.D. With Homilies by the Rev. A. MACLAREN, D.D., Rev. C. CLEMANCE, D.D., Rev. Prof. J. R. THOMSON, M.A., Rev. C. NEW, Rev. U. R. THOMAS, Rev. R. FINLAYSON, B.A., Rev. W. JONES, Rev. Prof. T. CROSKERY, D.D., and Rev. J. S. BRIGHT, D.D. 15s.

Revelation. Introduction by the Rev. T. RANDELL, B.D., Principal of Bede College, Durham; and Exposition by the Rev. T. RANDELL, assisted by the Rev. A. PLUMMER, M.A., D.D., Principal of University College, Durham, and A. T. BOTT, M.A. With Homilies by the Rev. C. CLEMANCE, D.D., Rev. S. CONWAY, B.A., Rev. R. GREEN, and Rev. D. THOMAS, D.D.

PUSEY, Dr.—**Sermons for the Church's Seasons from Advent to Trinity.** Selected from the Published Sermons of the late EDWARD BOUVERIE PUSEY, D.D. Crown 8vo, 5s.

RENAN, Ernest.—**Philosophical Dialogues and Fragments.** From the French. Post 8vo, 7s. 6d.

An Essay on the Age and Antiquity of the Book of Nabathæan Agriculture. Crown 8vo, 3s. 6d.

The Life of Jesus. Crown 8vo, cloth, 1s. 6d.; paper covers, 1s.

The Apostles. Crown 8vo, cloth, 1s. 6d.; paper covers, 1s.

REYNOLDS, Rev. J. W.—**The Supernatural in Nature.** A Verification by Free Use of Science. Third Edition, Revised and Enlarged. Demy 8vo, 14s.

REYNOLDS, Rev. J. W.—continued.
> The Mystery of Miracles. Third and Enlarged Edition. Crown 8vo, 6s.
>
> The Mystery of the Universe our Common Faith. Demy 8vo, 14s.
>
> The World to Come: Immortality a Physical Fact. Crown 8vo, 6s.

RICHARDSON, Austin.—"What are the Catholic Claims?" With Introduction by Rev. LUKE RIVINGTON. Crown 8vo, 3s. 6d.

RIVINGTON, Luke.—Authority, or a Plain Reason for joining the Church of Rome. Fifth Edition. Crown 8vo, 3s. 6d.
> Dependence; or, The Insecurity of the Anglican Position. Crown 8vo, 5s.

ROBERTSON, The late Rev. F. W., M.A.—Life and Letters of. Edited by the Rev. STOPFORD BROOKE, M.A.
> I. Two vols., uniform with the Sermons. With Steel Portrait. Crown 8vo, 7s. 6d.
> II. Library Edition, in Demy 8vo, with Portrait. 12s.
> III. A Popular Edition, in 1 vol. Crown 8vo, 6s.
>
> Sermons. Five Series. Small crown 8vo, 3s. 6d. each.
>
> Notes on Genesis. New and Cheaper Edition. Small crown 8vo, 3s. 6d.
>
> Expository Lectures on St. Paul's Epistles to the Corinthians. A New Edition. Small crown 8vo, 5s.
>
> Lectures and Addresses, with other Literary Remains. A New Edition. Small crown 8vo, 5s.
>
> An Analysis of Tennyson's "In Memoriam." (Dedicated by Permission to the Poet-Laureate.) Fcap. 8vo, 2s.
>
> The Education of the Human Race. Translated from the German of GOTTHOLD EPHRAIM LESSING. Fcap. 8vo, 2s. 6d.
>
> *⁎* A Portrait of the late Rev. F. W. Robertson, mounted for framing, can be had, 2s. 6d.

SCANNELL, Thomas B., B.D., and WILHELM, Joseph, D.D.—A Manual of Catholic Theology. Based on SCHEEBEN'S "Dogmatik." 2 vols. Demy 8vo. Vol. I., 15s.

SHEEPSHANKS, Rev. J.—Confirmation and Unction of the Sick. Small crown 8vo, 3s. 6d.

STEPHEN, Caroline E.—Quaker Strongholds. Crown 8vo, 5s.

Theology and Piety alike Free; from the Point of View of Manchester New College, Oxford. A Contribution to its effort offered by an old Student. Demy 8vo, 9s.

TRENCH, *Archbishop.*—**Notes on the Parables of Our Lord.** 8vo, 12*s.* Cheap Edition. Fifty-sixth Thousand. 7*s.* 6*d.*

 Notes on the Miracles of Our Lord. 8vo, 12*s.* Cheap Edition. Forty-eighth Thousand. 7*s.* 6*d.*

 Studies in the Gospels. Fifth Edition, Revised. 8vo, 10*s.* 6*d.*

 Brief Thoughts and Meditations on Some Passages in Holy Scripture. Third Edition. Crown 8vo, 3*s.* 6*d.*

 Synonyms of the New Testament. Tenth Edition, Enlarged. 8vo, 12*s.*

 Sermons New and Old. Crown 8vo, 6*s.*

 Westminster and other Sermons. Crown 8vo, 6*s.*

 On the Authorized Version of the New Testament. Second Edition. 8vo, 7*s.*

 Commentary on the Epistles to the Seven Churches in Asia. Fourth Edition, Revised. 8vo, 8*s.* 6*d.*

 The Sermon on the Mount. An Exposition drawn from the Writings of St. Augustine, with an Essay on his Merits as an Interpreter of Holy Scripture. Fourth Edition, Enlarged. 8vo, 10*s.* 6*d.*

 Shipwrecks of Faith. Three Sermons preached before the University of Cambridge in May, 1867. Fcap. 8vo, 2*s.* 6*d.*

TRINDER, *Rev. D.*—**The Worship of Heaven, and other Sermons.** Crown 8vo, 5*s.*

WARD, *Wilfrid.*—**The Wish to Believe.** A Discussion Concerning the Temper of Mind in which a reasonable Man should undertake Religious Inquiry. Small crown 8vo, 5*s.*

WARD, *William George, Ph.D.*—**Essays on the Philosophy of Theism.** Edited, with an Introduction, by WILFRID WARD. 2 vols. Demy 8vo, 21*s.*

What is Truth? A Consideration of the Doubts as to the Efficacy of Prayer, raised by Evolutionists, Materialists, and others. By "Nemo."

WILHELM, *Joseph, D.D., and* SCANNELL, *Thomas B., B.D.*—**A Manual of Catholic Theology.** Based on SCHEEBEN'S "Dogmatik." 2 vols. Demy 8vo. Vol. I., 15*s.*

WYNELL-MAYOW, *S. S.*—**The Light of Reason.** Crown 8vo, 5*s.*

ENGLISH AND FOREIGN PHILOSOPHICAL LIBRARY.

Auguste Comte and Positivism. By the late JOHN STUART MILL. Third Edition. 3s. 6d.

Candid Examination of Theism (A). By PHYSICUS. Second Edition. 7s. 6d.

Colour-Sense (The): Its Origin and Development. An Essay in Comparative Psychology. By GRANT ALLEN. 10s. 6d.

Contributions to the History of the Development of the Human Race. Lectures and Dissertations. By LAZARUS GEIGER. Translated from the German by D. ASHER. 6s.

Creed of Christendom (The). Its Foundations contrasted with its Superstructure. By W. R. GREG. Eighth Edition. 2 vols. 15s.

Dr. Appleton: His Life and Literary Relics. By J. H. APPLETON and A. H. SAYCE. 10s. 6d.

Edgar Quinet: His Early Life and Writings. By RICHARD HEATH. With Portraits, Illustrations, and an Autograph Letter. 12s. 6d.

Emerson at Home and Abroad. By M. D. CONWAY. With Portrait. 10s. 6d.

Enigmas of Life. By W. R. GREG. Seventeenth Edition. 10s. 6d.

Essays and Dialogues of Giacomo Leopardi. Translated by CHARLES EDWARDES. With Biographical Sketch. 7s. 6d.

Essence of Christianity (The). By L. FEUERBACH. Translated from the German by MARIAN EVANS. Second Edition. 7s. 6d.

Ethic Demonstrated in Geometrical Order and Divided into Five Parts, which treat (1) Of God, (2) Of the Nature and Origin of the Mind, (3) Of the Origin and Nature of the Affects, (4) Of Human Bondage, or of the Strength of the Affects, (5) Of the Power of the Intellect, or of Human Liberty. By BENEDICT DE SPINOZA. Translated from the Latin by WILLIAM HALE WHITE. 10s. 6d.

Guide of the Perplexed of Maimonides (The). Translated from the Original Text and Annotated by M. FRIEDLANDER. 3 vols. 31s. 6d.

History of Materialism (A), and Criticism of its present Importance. By Prof. F. A. LANGE. Authorized Translation from the German by ERNEST C. THOMAS. In 3 vols. 10s. 6d. each.

Johann Gottlieb Fichte's Popular Works. The Nature of the Scholar; The Vocation of the Scholar; The Vocation of Man; The Doctrine of Religion; Characteristics of the Present Age; Outlines of the Doctrine of Knowledge. With a Memoir by WILLIAM SMITH, LL.D. 2 vols. 21s.

Moral Order and Progress. An Analysis of Ethical Conceptions. By S. ALEXANDER. 14s.

Natural Law. An Essay in Ethics. By EDITH SIMCOX. Second Edition. 10s. 6d.

Outlines of the History of Religion to the Spread of the Universal Religions. By Prof. C. P. TIELE. Translated from the Dutch by J. ESTLIN CARPENTER. Fourth Edition. 7s. 6d.

Philosophy of Law (The). By Prof. DIODATO LIOY. Translated by W. HASTIE.

Philosophy of Music (The). Lectures delivered at the Royal Institution of Great Britain. By WILLIAM POLE, F.R.S. Second Edition. 7s. 6d.

Philosophy of the Unconscious (The). By EDUARD VON HARTMANN. Translated by WILLIAM C. COUPLAND. 3 vols. 31s. 6d.

Religion and Philosophy in Germany. A Fragment. By HEINRICH HEINE. Translated by J. SNODGRASS. 6s.

Religion in China. Containing a brief Account of the Three Religions of the Chinese; with Observations on the Prospects of Christian Conversion amongst that People. By JOSEPH EDKINS, D.D. Third Edition. 7s. 6d.

Science of Knowledge (The). By J. G. FICHTE. Translated from the German by A. E. KROEGER. With an Introduction by Prof. W. T. HARRIS. 10s. 6d.

Science of Rights (The). By J. G. FICHTE. Translated from the German by A. E. KROEGER. With an Introduction by Prof. W. T. HARRIS. 12s. 6d.

World as Will and Idea (The). By ARTHUR SCHOPENHAUER. Translated from the German by R. B. HALDANE and JOHN KEMP. 3 vols. £2 10s.

Extra Series.

An Account of the Polynesian Race: Its Origin and Migrations, and the Ancient History of the Hawaiian People. By ABRAHAM FORNANDER. 3 vols. 27s.

Lessing: His Life and Writings. By JAMES SIME. Second Edition. 2 vols. With Portraits. 21s.

Oriental Religions, and their Relation to Universal Religion—India. By SAMUEL JOHNSON. 2 vols. 21s.

SCIENCE.

BADER, C.—**The Natural and Morbid Changes of the Human Eye, and their Treatment.** Medium 8vo, 16s.

Plates illustrating the Natural and Morbid Changes of the Human Eye. With Explanatory Text. Medium 8vo, in a portfolio, 21s. Price for Text and Atlas taken together, £1 12s.

BICKNELL, C.—**Flowering Plants and Ferns of the Riviera and Neighbouring Mountains.** Drawn and described by C. BICKNELL. With 82 full-page Plates, containing Illustrations of 350 Specimens. Imperial 8vo, half-roan, gilt edges, £3 3s.

BLATER, Joseph.—**Table of Quarter-Squares of all Whole Numbers from 1 to 200,000.** For Simplifying Multiplication, Squaring, and Extraction of the Square Root. Royal 4to, half-bound, 21s.

Table of Napier. Giving the Nine Multiples of all Numbers. Cloth case, 1s. 3d.

BROWNE, Edgar A.—**How to use the Ophthalmoscope.** Being Elementary Instruction in Ophthalmoscopy. Third Edition. Crown 8vo, 3s. 6d.

BUNGE, G.—**Text-Book of Physiological and Pathological Chemistry.** For Physicians and Students. Translated from the German by L. C. WOODBRIDGE, M.D. Demy 8vo, 16s.

CALLEJA, Camilo, M.D.—**Principles of Universal Physiology.** Crown 8vo, 3s. 6d.

CANDLER, C.—**The Prevention of Consumption:** A New Theory of the Nature of the Tubercle-Bacillus. Demy 8vo, 10s. 6d.

The Prevention of Measles. Crown 8vo, 5s.

CARPENTER, W. B.—**The Principles of Mental Physiology.** With their Applications to the Training and Discipline of the Mind, and the Study of its Morbid Conditions. Illustrated. Sixth Edition. 8vo, 12s.

Nature and Man. With a Memorial Sketch by the Rev. J. ESTLIN CARPENTER. Portrait. Large crown 8vo, 8s. 6d.

COTTA, B. von.—**Geology and History.** A Popular Exposition of all that is known of the Earth and its Inhabitants in Pre-historic Times. 12mo, 2s.

DANA, James D.—**A Text-Book of Geology,** designed for Schools and Academies. Illustrated. Crown 8vo, 10s.

Manual of Geology. Illustrated by a Chart of the World, and over 1000 Figures. 8vo, 21s.

DANA, *James D.—continued.*
> The Geological Story Briefly Told. Illustrated. 12mo, 7s. 6d.
>
> A System of Mineralogy. By J. D. DANA, aided by G. J. BRUSH. Fifth Edition. Royal 8vo, £2 2s.
>
> Manual of Mineralogy and Petrography. Fourth Edition. Numerous Woodcuts. Crown 8vo, 8s. 6d.

DANA, *E. S.*—A Text-Book of Mineralogy. With Treatise on Crystallography and Physical Mineralogy. Third Edition. 800 Woodcuts and 1 Coloured Plate. 8vo, 15s.

DU MONCEL, *Count.*—The Telephone, the Microphone, and the Phonograph. With 74 Illustrations. Third Edition. Small crown 8vo, 5s.

DYMOCK, *W.*—The Vegetable Materia Medica of Western India. 4 Parts. 8vo, 5s. each.

FEATHERMAN, *A.*—The Social History of the Races of Mankind. Demy 8vo. Div. I. The Nigritians. £1 11s. 6d. Div. II.-I. Papuo and Malayo Melanesians. £1 5s. Div. II.-II. Oceano-Melanesians. £1 5s. Div. III.-I. Aoneo-Maranonians. 25s. Div. III.-II. Chiapo and Guazano Maranonians. 28s. Div. V. The Aramæans. £1 1s.

FITZGERALD, *R. D.*—Australian Orchids. Folio. Part I. 7 Plates. Part II. 10 Plates. Part III. 10 Plates. Part IV. 10 Plates. Part V. 10 Plates. Part VI. 10 Plates. Each Part, coloured, 21s.; plain, 10s. 6d. Part VII. 10 Plates. Vol. II., Part I. 10 Plates. Each, coloured, 25s.

GALLOWAY, *Robert.*—A Treatise on Fuel. Scientific and Practical. With Illustrations. Post 8vo, 6s.
> Education: Scientific and Technical; or, How the Inductive Sciences are Taught, and How they Ought to be Taught. 8vo, 10s. 6d.

HAECKEL, *Prof. Ernst.*—The History of Creation. Translation revised by Professor E. RAY LANKESTER, M.A., F.R.S. With Coloured Plates and Genealogical Trees of the various groups of both Plants and Animals. 2 vols. Third Edition. Post 8vo, 32s.
> The History of the Evolution of Man. With numerous Illustrations. 2 vols. Post 8vo, 32s
>
> A Visit to Ceylon. Post 8vo, 7s. 6d.
>
> Freedom in Science and Teaching. With a Prefatory Note by T. H. HUXLEY, F.R.S. Crown 8vo, 5s.

HEIDENHAIN, *Rudolph, M.D.*—Hypnotism, or Animal Magnetism. With Preface by G. J. ROMANES. Second Edition. Small crown 8vo, 2s. 6d.

HENWOOD, *William Jory.*—**The Metalliferous Deposits of Cornwall and Devon.** With Appendices on Subterranean Temperature; the Electricity of Rocks and Veins; the Quantities of Water in the Cornish Mines; and Mining Statistics. With 113 Tables, and 12 Plates, half-bound. 8vo, £2 2s.

Observations on Metalliferous Deposits, and on Subterranean Temperature. In 2 Parts. With 38 Tables, 31 Engravings on Wood, and 6 Plates. 8vo, £1 16s.

HOSPITALIER, *E.*—**The Modern Applications of Electricity.** Translated and Enlarged by JULIUS MAIER, Ph.D. 2 vols. Second Edition, Revised, with many additions and numerous Illustrations. Demy 8vo, 25s.

HULME, *F. Edward.*—**Mathematical Drawing Instruments, and How to Use Them.** With Illustrations. Third Edition. Imperial 16mo, 3s. 6d.

INMAN, *James.*—**Nautical Tables.** Designed for the Use of British Seamen. New Edition, Revised and Enlarged. Demy 8vo, 16s.

KINAHAN, *G. H.*—**Valleys and their Relation to Fissures, Fractures, and Faults.** Crown 8vo, 7s. 6d.

KLEIN, *Felix.*—**Lectures on the Ikosahedron, and the Solution of Equations of the Fifth Degree.** Translated by G. G. MORRICE. Demy 8vo, 10s. 6d.

LENDENFELD, *R. von.*—**Monograph of the Horny Sponges.** With 50 Plates. Issued by direction of the Royal Society. 4to, £3.

LESLEY, *J. P.*—**Man's Origin and Destiny.** Sketched from the Platform of the Physical Sciences. Second Edition. Crown 8vo, 7s. 6d.

LIVERSIDGE, *A.*—**The Minerals of New South Wales, etc.** With large Coloured Map. Royal 8vo, 18s.

MIVART, *St. George.*—**On Truth.** Demy 8vo, 16s.

The Origin of Human Reason. Demy 8vo, 10s. 6d.

NICOLS, *Arthur, F.G.S., F.R.G.S.*—**Chapters from the Physical History of the Earth.** An Introduction to Geology and Palæontology. With numerous Illustrations. Crown 8vo, 5s.

PYE, *Walter.*—**Surgical Handicraft.** A Manual of Surgical Manipulations. With 233 Illustrations on Wood. Second Edition. Crown 8vo, 10s. 6d.

Elementary Bandaging and Surgical Dressing. For the Use of Dressers and Nurses. 18mo, 2s.

RAMSAY, *E. P.*—**Tabular List of all the Australian Birds at present known to the Author.** Crown 4to, 12s. 6d.

RIBOT, Prof. Th.—Heredity: A Psychological Study of its Phenomena, its Laws, its Causes, and its Consequences. Second Edition. Large crown 8vo, 9s.

English Psychology. Crown 8vo, 7s. 6d.

RODD, Edward Hearle.—The Birds of Cornwall and the Scilly Islands. Edited by J. E. HARTING. With Portrait and Map. 8vo, 14s.

ROMANES, G. J.—Mental Evolution in Animals. With a Posthumous Essay on Instinct by CHARLES DARWIN, F.R.S. Demy 8vo, 12s.

Mental Evolution in Man: Origin of Human Faculty. Demy 8vo, 14s.

ROSS, Lieut.-Colonel W. A.—Alphabetical Manual of Blow-pipe Analysis. Crown 8vo, 5s.

Pyrology, or Fire Chemistry. Small 4to, 36s.

SCHWENDLER, Louis.—Instructions for Testing Telegraph Lines, and the Technical Arrangements in Offices. 2 vols. Demy 8vo, 21s.

SMITH, Hamilton, Jun.—Hydraulics. The Flow of Water through Orifices, over Weirs, and through Open Conduits and Pipes. With 17 Plates. Royal 4to, 30s.

STRECKER-WISLICENUS.—Organic Chemistry. Translated and Edited, with Extensive Additions, by W. R. HODGKINSON, Ph.D., and A. J. GREENAWAY, F.I.C. Second and cheaper Edition. Demy 8vo, 12s. 6d.

SYMONS, G. J.—The Eruption of Krakatoa, and Subsequent Phenomena. Report of the Krakatoa Committee of the Royal Society. Edited by G. J. SYMONS, F.R.S. With 6 Chromolithographs of the Remarkable Sunsets of 1883, and 40 Maps and Diagrams. 4to, £1 10s.

WANKLYN, J. A.—Milk Analysis. A Practical Treatise on the Examination of Milk and its Derivatives, Cream, Butter, and Cheese. Second Edition. Crown 8vo, 5s.

Tea, Coffee, and Cocoa. A Practical Treatise on the Analysis of Tea, Coffee, Cocoa, Chocolate, Maté (Paraguay Tea). Crown 8vo, 5s.

WANKLYN, J. A., and COOPER, W. J.—Bread Analysis. A Practical Treatise on the Examination of Flour and Bread. Crown 8vo, 5s.

WANKLYN, J. A., and CHAPMAN, E. T.—Water Analysis. A Treatise on the Examination of Potable Water. Seventh Edition. Entirely rewritten. Crown 8vo, 5s.

WRIGHT, G. Frederick, D.D.—**The Ice Age in North America, and its bearing upon the Antiquity of Man.** With Maps and Illustrations. 8vo, 21s.

THE INTERNATIONAL SCIENTIFIC SERIES.

I. **Forms of Water in Clouds and Rivers, Ice and Glaciers.** By J. Tyndall, LL.D., F.R.S. With 25 Illustrations. Ninth Edition. 5s.

II. **Physics and Politics;** or, Thoughts on the Application of the Principles of "Natural Selection" and "Inheritance" to Political Society. By Walter Bagehot. Eighth Edition. 5s.

III. **Foods.** By Edward Smith, M.D., LL.B., F.R.S. With numerous Illustrations. Ninth Edition. 5s.

IV. **Mind and Body: the Theories of their Relation.** By Alexander Bain, LL.D. With Four Illustrations. Eighth Edition. 5s.

V. **The Study of Sociology.** By Herbert Spencer. Fourteenth Edition. 5s.

VI. **The Conservation of Energy.** By Balfour Stewart, M.A., LL.D., F.R.S. With 14 Illustrations. Seventh Edition. 5s.

VII. **Animal Locomotion;** or, Walking, Swimming, and Flying. By J. B. Pettigrew, M.D., F.R.S., etc. With 130 Illustrations. Third Edition. 5s.

VIII. **Responsibility in Mental Disease.** By Henry Maudsley, M.D. Fourth Edition. 5s.

IX. **The New Chemistry.** By Professor J. P. Cooke. With 31 Illustrations. Ninth Edition. 5s.

X. **The Science of Law.** By Professor Sheldon Amos. Sixth Edition. 5s.

XI. **Animal Mechanism:** a Treatise on Terrestrial and Aerial Locomotion. By Professor E. J. Marey. With 117 Illustrations. Third Edition. 5s.

XII. **The Doctrine of Descent and Darwinism.** By Professor Oscar Schmidt. With 26 Illustrations. Seventh Edition. 5s.

XIII. **The History of the Conflict between Religion and Science.** By J. W. Draper, M.D., LL.D. Twentieth Edition. 5s.

XIV. **Fungi: their Nature, Influences, and Uses.** By M. C. Cooke, M.A., LL.D. Edited by the Rev. M. J. Berkeley, M.A., F.L.S. With numerous Illustrations. Fourth Edition. 5s.

XV. **The Chemistry of Light and Photography.** By Dr. Hermann Vogel. With 100 Illustrations. Fifth Edition. 5s.

XVI. **The Life and Growth of Language.** By Professor William Dwight Whitney. Fifth Edition. 5s.

XVII. **Money and the Mechanism of Exchange.** By W. Stanley Jevons, M.A., F.R.S. Eighth Edition. 5s.

XVIII. **The Nature of Light.** With a General Account of Physical Optics. By Dr. Eugene Lommel. With 188 Illustrations and a Table of Spectra in Chromo-lithography. Fifth Edition. 5s.

XIX. **Animal Parasites and Messmates.** By P. J. Van Beneden. With 83 Illustrations. Third Edition. 5s.

XX. **On Fermentation.** By Professor Schützenberger. With 28 Illustrations. Fourth Edition. 5s.

XXI. **The Five Senses of Man.** By Professor Bernstein. With 91 Illustrations. Fifth Edition. 5s.

XXII. **The Theory of Sound in its Relation to Music.** By Professor Pietro Blaserna. With numerous Illustrations. Third Edition. 5s.

XXIII. **Studies in Spectrum Analysis.** By J. Norman Lockyer, F.R.S. With 6 Photographic Illustrations of Spectra, and numerous engravings on Wood. Fourth Edition. 6s. 6d.

XXIV. **A History of the Growth of the Steam Engine.** By Professor R. H. Thurston. With numerous Illustrations. Fourth Edition. 5s.

XXV. **Education as a Science.** By Alexander Bain, LL.D. Seventh Edition. 5s.

XXVI. **The Human Species.** By Professor A. de Quatrefages. Fifth Edition. 5s.

XXVII. **Modern Chromatics.** With Applications to Art and Industry. By Ogden N. Rood. With 130 original Illustrations. Second Edition. 5s.

XXVIII. **The Crayfish: an Introduction to the Study of Zoology.** By Professor T. H. Huxley. With 82 Illustrations. Fifth Edition, 5s.

XXIX. **The Brain as an Organ of Mind.** By H. Charlton Bastian, M.D. With numerous Illustrations. Third Edition. 5s.

XXX. **The Atomic Theory.** By Professor Wurtz. Translated by E. Cleminshaw, F.C.S. Fifth Edition. 5s.

XXXI. **The Natural Conditions of Existence as they affect Animal Life.** By Karl Semper. With 2 Maps and 106 Woodcuts. Third Edition. 5s.

XXXII. **General Physiology of Muscles and Nerves.** By Professor J. Rosenthal. Third Edition. With 75 Illustrations. 5s.

E

XXXIII. **Sight:** an Exposition of the Principles of Monocular and Binocular Vision. By Joseph le Conte, LL.D. Second Edition. With 132 Illustrations. 5*s*.

XXXIV. **Illusions:** a Psychological Study. By James Sully. Third Edition. 5*s*.

XXXV. **Volcanoes: what they are and what they teach.** By Professor J. W. Judd, F.R.S. With 96 Illustrations on Wood. Fourth Edition. 5*s*.

XXXVI. **Suicide:** an Essay on Comparative Moral Statistics. By Professor H. Morselli. Second Edition. With Diagrams. 5*s*.

XXXVII. **The Brain and its Functions.** By J. Luys. With Illustrations. Second Edition. 5*s*.

XXXVIII. **Myth and Science:** an Essay. By Tito Vignoli. Third Edition. With Supplementary Note. 5*s*.

XXXIX. **The Sun.** By Professor Young. With Illustrations. Third Edition. 5*s*.

XL. **Ants, Bees, and Wasps:** a Record of Observations on the Habits of the Social Hymenoptera. By Sir John Lubbock, Bart., M.P. With 5 Chromo-lithographic Illustrations. Ninth Edition. 5*s*.

XLI. **Animal Intelligence.** By G. J. Romanes, LL.D., F.R.S. Fourth Edition. 5*s*.

XLII. **The Concepts and Theories of Modern Physics.** By J. B. Stallo. Third Edition. 5*s*.

XLIII. **Diseases of Memory:** an Essay in the Positive Psychology. By Professor Th. Ribot. Third Edition. 5*s*.

XLIV. **Man before Metals.** By N. Joly. With 148 Illustrations. Fourth Edition. 5*s*.

XLV. **The Science of Politics.** By Professor Sheldon Amos. Third Edition. 5*s*.

XLVI. **Elementary Meteorology.** By Robert H. Scott. Fourth Edition. With numerous Illustrations. 5*s*.

XLVII. **The Organs of Speech and their Application in the Formation of Articulate Sounds.** By Georg Hermann Von Meyer. With 47 Woodcuts. 5*s*.

XLVIII. **Fallacies.** A View of Logic from the Practical Side. By Alfred Sidgwick. Second Edition. 5*s*.

XLIX. **Origin of Cultivated Plants.** By Alphonse de Candolle. Second Edition. 5*s*.

L. **Jelly-Fish, Star-Fish, and Sea-Urchins.** Being a Research on Primitive Nervous Systems. By G. J. Romanes. With Illustrations. 5*s*.

LI. **The Common Sense of the Exact Sciences.** By the late William Kingdon Clifford. Second Edition. With 100 Figures. 5s.

LII. **Physical Expression : Its Modes and Principles.** By Francis Warner, M.D., F.R.C.P., Hunterian Professor of Comparative Anatomy and Physiology, R.C.S.E. With 50 Illustrations. 5s.

LIII. **Anthropoid Apes.** By Robert Hartmann. With 63 Illustrations. 5s.

LIV. **The Mammalia in their Relation to Primeval Times.** By Oscar Schmidt. With 51 Woodcuts. 5s.

LV. **Comparative Literature.** By H. Macaulay Posnett, LL.D. 5s.

LVI. **Earthquakes and other Earth Movements.** By Professor John Milne. With 38 Figures. Second Edition. 5s.

LVII. **Microbes, Ferments, and Moulds.** By E. L. Trouessart. With 107 Illustrations. 5s.

LVIII. **Geographical and Geological Distribution of Animals.** By Professor A. Heilprin. With Frontispiece. 5s.

LIX. **Weather.** A Popular Exposition of the Nature of Weather Changes from Day to Day. By the Hon. Ralph Abercromby. Second Edition. With 96 Illustrations. 5s.

LX. **Animal Magnetism.** By Alfred Binet and Charles Féré. Second Edition. 5s.

LXI. **Manual of British Discomycetes,** with descriptions of all the Species of Fungi hitherto found in Britain included in the Family, and Illustrations of the Genera. By William Phillips, F.L.S. 5s.

LXII. **International Law.** With Materials for a Code of International Law. By Professor Leone Levi. 5s.

LXIII. **The Geological History of Plants.** By Sir J. William Dawson. With 80 Figures. 5s.

LXIV. **The Origin of Floral Structures through Insect and other Agencies.** By Rev. Professor G. Henslow. With 88 Illustrations. 5s.

LXV. **On the Senses, Instincts, and Intelligence of Animals.** With special Reference to Insects. By Sir John Lubbock, Bart., M.P. 100 Illustrations. Second Edition. 5s.

LXVI. **The Primitive Family : Its Origin and Development.** By C. N. Starcke. 5s.

LXVII. **Physiology of Bodily Exercise.** By Fernand Lagrange, M.D. 5s.

LXVIII. The Colours of Animals: their Meaning and Use, especially considered in the Case of Insects. By E. B. Poulton, F.R.S. With Coloured Frontispiece and 66 Illustrations in Text. 5*s.*

LXIX. Introduction to Fresh-Water Algæ. With an Enumeration of all the British Species. By M. C. Cooke. 13 Plates. 5*s.*

ORIENTAL, EGYPTIAN, ETC.

AHLWARDT, W.—The Divans of the Six Ancient Arabic Poets, Ennābiga, 'Antara, Tharafa, Zuhair, 'Alquama, and Imruulquais. Edited by W. AHLWARDT. Demy 8vo, 12*s.*

ALABASTER, Henry.—The Wheel of the Law: Buddhism illustrated from Siamese Sources. Demy 8vo, 14*s.*

ALI, Moulavî Cherâgh.—The Proposed Political, Legal, and Social Reforms in the Ottoman Empire and other Mohammedan States. Demy 8vo, 8*s.*

ARNOLD, Sir Edwin, C.S.I.—With Sa'di in the Garden; or, The Book of Love. Being the "Ishk," or Third Chapter of the "Bostân" of the Persian Poet Sa'di. Embodied in a Dialogue held in the Garden of the Taj Mahal, at Agra. Crown 8vo, 7*s.* 6*d.*

 Lotus and Jewel. Containing "In an Indian Temple," "A Casket of Gems," "A Queen's Revenge," with Other Poems. Second Edition. Crown 8vo, 7*s.* 6*d.*

 Death—and Afterwards. Reprinted from the *Fortnightly Review* of August, 1885. With a Supplement. Ninth Edition. Crown 8vo, 1*s.* 6*d.*; paper, 1*s.*

 India Revisited. With 32 Full-page Illustrations. From Photographs selected by the Author. Crown 8vo, 7*s.* 6*d.*

 The Light of Asia; or, The Great Renunciation. Being the Life and Teaching of Gautama, Prince of India, and Founder of Buddhism. With Illustrations and a Portrait of the Author. Post 8vo, cloth, gilt back and edges; or half-parchment, cloth sides, 3*s.* 6*d.* Library Edition. Crown 8vo, 7*s.* 6*d.* Illustrated Edition. Small 4to, 21*s.*

 Indian Poetry. Containing "The Indian Song of Songs," from the Sanskrit of the Gîta Govinda of Jayadeva; Two Books from "The Iliad of India;" and other Oriental Poems. Fifth Edition. 7*s.* 6*d*

ARNOLD, Sir Edwin, C.S.I.—continued.

> **Pearls of the Faith**; or, Islam's Rosary: being the Ninety-nine beautiful names of Allah. With Comments in Verse from various Oriental sources. Fourth Edition. Crown 8vo, 7s. 6d.
>
> **Indian Idylls.** From the Sanskrit of the Mahâbhârata. Crown 8vo, 7s. 6d.
>
> **The Secret of Death.** Being a Version of the Katha Upanishad, from the Sanskrit. Third Edition. Crown 8vo, 7s. 6d.
>
> **The Song Celestial**; or, Bhagavad-Gitâ. Translated from the Sanskrit Text. Second Edition. Crown 8vo, 5s.
>
> **Poetical Works.** Uniform Edition, comprising "The Light of Asia," "Indian Poetry," "Pearls of the Faith," "Indian Idylls," "The Secret of Death," "The Song Celestial," and "With Sa'di in the Garden." In 8 vols. Crown 8vo, cloth, 48s.
>
> **The Iliad and Odyssey of India.** Fcap. 8vo, 1s.
>
> **A Simple Transliteral Grammar of the Turkish Language.** Post 8vo, 2s. 6d.

Asiatic Society.—Journal of the Royal Asiatic Society of Great Britain and Ireland, from the Commencement to 1863. First Series, complete in 20 vols. 8vo, with many Plates, £10, or in parts from 4s. to 6s. each.

> **Journal of the Royal Asiatic Society of Great Britain and Ireland.** New Series. 8vo. Stitched in wrapper. 1864-88.
>
> Vol. I., 2 Parts, pp. iv. and 490, 16s.—Vol. II., 2 Parts, pp. 522, 16s.—Vol. III., 2 Parts, pp. 516, with Photograph, 22s.—Vol. IV., 2 Parts, pp. 521, 16s.—Vol. V., 2 Parts, pp. 463, with 10 full-page and folding Plates, 18s. 6d.—Vol. VI., Part 1, pp. 212, with 2 Plates and a Map, 8s.—Vol. VI., Part 2, pp. 272, with Plate and a Map, 8s.—Vol. VII., Part 1, pp. 194, with a Plate, 8s.—Vol. VII., Part 2, pp. 204, with 7 Plates and a Map, 8s.—Vol. VIII., Part 1, pp. 156, with 3 Plates and a Plan, 8s.—Vol. VIII., Part 2, pp. 152, 8s.—Vol. IX., Part 1, pp. 154, with a Plate, 8s.—Vol. IX., Part 2, pp. 292, with 3 Plates, 10s. 6d.—Vol. X., Part 1, pp. 156, with 2 Plates and a Map, 8s.—Vol. X., Part 2, pp. 146, 6s.—Vol. X., Part 3, pp. 204, 8s.—Vol. XI., Part 1, pp. 128, 5s.—Vol. XI., Part 2, pp. 158, with 2 Plates, 7s. 6d.—Vol. XI., Part 3, pp. 250, 8s.—Vol. XII., Part 1, pp. 152, 5s.—Vol. XII., Part 2, pp. 182, with 2 Plates and a Map, 6s.—Vol. XII., Part 3, pp. 100, 4s.—Vol. XII., Part 4, pp. x., 152, cxx., 16, 8s.—Vol. XIII., Part 1, pp. 120, 5s.—Vol. XIII., Part 2, pp. 170, with a Map, 8s.—Vol. XIII., Part 3, pp. 178, with a Table, 7s. 6d.—Vol. XIII., Part 4, pp. 282, with a Plate and Table, 10s. 6d.—Vol. XIV., Part 1, pp. 124, with a Table and 2 Plates, 5s.—Vol. XIV., Part 2, pp. 164, with 1 Table, 7s. 6d.—Vol. XIV., Part 3, pp. 206, with 6 Plates, 8s.—Vol. XIV., Part 4, pp. 492, with 1 Plate, 14s.—Vol. XV., Part 1, pp. 136, 6s.—Vol. XV., Part 2, pp. 158, with 3 Tables, 5s.—Vol. XV., Part 3, pp. 192, 6s.—Vol. XV., Part 4, pp.

Asiatic Society—*continued.*

140, 5*s*.—Vol. XVI., Part 1, pp. 138, with 2 Plates, 7*s*.—Vol. XVI., Part 2, pp. 184, with 1 Plate, 9*s*.—Vol. XVI., Part 3, July, 1884, pp. 74-clx., 10*s*. 6*d*.—Vol. XVI., Part 4, pp. 132, 8*s*.—Vol. XVII., Part 1, pp. 144, with 6 Plates, 10*s*. 6*d*.—Vol. XVII., Part 2, pp. 194, with a Map, 9*s*.—Vol. XVII., Part 3, pp. 342, with 3 Plates, 10*s*. 6*d*.—Vol. XVIII., Part 1, pp. 126, with 2 Plates, 5*s*.—Vol. XVIII., Part 2, pp. 196, with 2 Plates, 6*s*.—Vol. XVIII., Part 3, pp. 130, with 11 Plates, 10*s*. 6*d*.—Vol. XVIII., Part 4, pp. 314, with 8 Plates, 7*s*. 6*d*.—Vol. XIX., Part 1, pp. 100, with 3 Plates, 10*s*.—Vol. XIX., Part 2, pp. 156, with 6 Plates, 10*s*.—Vol. XIX., Part 3, pp. 216, with 6 Plates, 10*s*.—Vol. XIX., Part 4, pp. 216, with 1 Plate, 10*s*.—Vol. XX., Part 1, pp. 163, 10*s*.—Vol. XX., Part 2, pp. 155, 10*s*.—Vol. XX., Part 3, pp. 143, with 3 Plates and a Map, 10*s*.—Vol. XX., Part 4, pp. 318, 10*s*.

ASTON, *W. G.*—**A Short Grammar of the Japanese Spoken Language.** Fourth Edition. Crown 8vo, 12*s*.

A Grammar of the Japanese Written Language. Second Edition. 8vo, 28*s*.

Auctores Sanscriti :—

Vol. I. **The Jaiminîya-Nyâya-Mâlâ-Vistara.** Edited under the supervision of THEODOR GOLDSTÜCKER. Large 4to, £3 13*s*. 6*d*.

Vol. II. **The Institutes of Gautama.** Edited, with an Index of Words, by A. F. STENZLER, Ph.D., Prof. of Oriental Languages in the University of Breslau. 8vo, cloth, 4*s*. 6*d*. ; stitched, 3*s*. 6*d*.

Vol. III. **Vaitâna Sutra : The Ritual of the Atharva Veda.** Edited, with Critical Notes and Indices, by Dr. R. GARBE. 8vo, 5*s*.

Vols. IV. and V. **Vardhamana's Ganaratnamahodadhi,** with the Author's Commentary. Edited, with Critical Notes and Indices, by JULIUS EGGELING. Part I. 8vo, 6*s*. Part II. 8vo, 6*s*.

BABA, *Tatui.*—**An Elementary Grammar of the Japanese Language.** With Easy Progressive Exercises. Second Edition. Crown 8vo, 5*s*.

BADGER, *George Percy, D.C.L.*—**An English-Arabic Lexicon.** In which the equivalent for English Words and Idiomatic Sentences are rendered into literary and colloquial Arabic. Royal 4to, 80*s*.

BALFOUR, *F. H.*—**The Divine Classic of Nan-Hua.** Being the Works of Chuang Tsze, Taoist Philosopher. 8vo, 14*s*.

Taoist Texts, Ethical, Political, and Speculative. Imperial 8vo, 10*s*. 6*d*.

Leaves from my Chinese Scrap-Book. Post 8vo, 7*s*. 6*d*.

BALLANTYNE, J. R.—Elements of Hindi and Braj Bhakha Grammar. Compiled for the use of the East India College at Haileybury. Second Edition. Crown 8vo, 5s.

First Lessons in Sanskrit Grammar; together with an Introduction to the Hitopadeśa. Fourth Edition. 8vo, 3s. 6d.

BEAL, S.—A Catena of Buddhist Scriptures from the Chinese. 8vo, 15s.

The Romantic Legend of Sakya Buddha. From the Chinese-Sanskrit. Crown 8vo, 12s.

Buddhist Literature in China. Four Lectures. Demy 8vo, 10s. 6d.

BEAMES, John.—Outlines of Indian Philology. With a Map showing the Distribution of Indian Languages. Second enlarged Edition. Crown 8vo, 5s.

A Comparative Grammar of the Modern Aryan Languages of India: Hindi, Panjabi, Sindhi, Gujarati, Marathi, Oriya, and Bengali. 3 vols. 16s. each.

BELLEW, Deputy-Surgeon-General H. W.—The History of Cholera in India from 1862 to 1881. With Maps and Diagrams. Demy 8vo, £2 2s.

A Short Practical Treatise on the Nature, Causes, and Treatment of Cholera. Demy 8vo, 7s. 6d.

From the Indus to the Tigris. A Narrative of a Journey through Balochistan, Afghanistan, Khorassan, and Iran, in 1872. 8vo, 10s. 6d.

Kashmir and Kashghar. A Narrative of the Journey of the Embassy to Kashghar in 1873-74. Demy 8vo, 10s. 6d.

The Races of Afghanistan. Being a Brief Account of the Principal Nations inhabiting that Country. 8vo, 7s. 6d.

BELLOWS, John.—English Outline Vocabulary, for the Use of Students of the Chinese, Japanese, and other Languages. Crown 8vo, 6s.

BENFEY, Theodor.—A Practical Grammar of the Sanskrit Language, for the Use of Early Students. Second Edition. Royal 8vo, 10s. 6d.

BENTLEY, W. Holman.—Dictionary and Grammar of the Kongo Language, as spoken at San Salvador, the Ancient Capital of the Old Kongo Empire, West Africa. Demy 8vo, 21s.

BEVERIDGE, H.—The District of Bakarganj: Its History and Statistics. 8vo, 21s.

Buddhist Catechism (A); or, Outline of the Doctrine of the Buddha Gotama. By SUBHADRA BHIKSHU. 12mo, 2s.

BUDGE, *Ernest A.*—**Archaic Classics.** Assyrian Texts; being Extracts from the Annals of Shalmaneser II., Sennacherib, and Assur-Bani-Pal. With Philological Notes. Small 4to, 7s. 6d.

BURGESS, *James.*—ARCHÆOLOGICAL SURVEY OF WESTERN INDIA :—

Reports—

The Belgâm and Kaladi Districts. With 56 Photographs and Lithographic Plates. Royal 4to, half-bound, £2 2s.

The Antiquities of Kâthiâwâd and Kachh. Royal 4to, with 74 Plates. Half-bound, £3 3s.

The Antiquities in the Bidar and Aurangabad Districts, in the Territories of His Highness the Nizam of Haiderabad. With 63 Photographic Plates. Royal 4to, half-bound, £2 2s.

The Buddhist Cave-Temples and their Inscriptions. Containing Views, Plans, Sections, and Elevation of Façades of Cave-Temples; Drawings of Architectural and Mythological Sculptures; Facsimiles of Inscriptions, etc.; with Descriptive and Explanatory Text, and Translations of Inscriptions. With 86 Plates and Woodcuts. Royal 4to, half-bound, £3 3s.

Elura Cave-Temples, and the Brahmanical and Jaina Caves in Western India. With 66 Plates and Woodcuts. Royal 4to, half-bound, £3 3s.

ARCHÆOLOGICAL SURVEY OF SOUTHERN INDIA :—

Reports of the Amaravati and Jaggaypyaeta Buddhist Stupas. Containing numerous Collotype and other Illustrations of Buddhist Sculpture and Architecture, etc., in South-Eastern India; Facsimiles of Inscriptions, etc.; with Descriptive and Explanatory Text. Together with Transcriptions, Translations, and Elucidations of the Dhauli and Jaugada Inscriptions of Asoka, by Professor G. BUHLER, LL.D. Vol. I. With numerous Plates and Woodcuts. Royal 4to, half-bound, £4 4s.

BURGESS, *James.*—**Epigraphia Indica and Record of the Archæological Survey of India.** Edited by JAS. BURGESS, LL.D. Parts I., II., and III. Royal 4to, wrappers, 7s. each.

BURNELL, *A. C.*—**Elements of South Indian Palæography**, from the Fourth to the Seventeenth Century A.D. Being an Introduction to the Study of South Indian Inscriptions and MSS. Second enlarged and improved Edition. Map and 35 Plates. 4to, £2 12s. 6d.

A Classified Index to the Sanskrit MSS. in the Palace at Tanjore. Prepared for the Madras Government. 3 Parts. 4to, 10s. each.

CALDWELL, *Bishop R.*—A Comparative Grammar of the Dravidian or South Indian Family of Languages. A second, corrected, and enlarged Edition. Demy 8vo, 28*s.*

CAPPELLER, *Carl.*—A Sanskrit-English Dictionary. Based upon the St. Petersburg Lexicons. Royal 8vo. [*In preparation.*

CHALMERS, *J.*—Structure of Chinese Characters, under 300 Primary Forms, after the Shwoh-wan, 100 A.D. Demy 8vo, 12*s.* 6*d.*

CHAMBERLAIN, *B. H.*—A Romanised Japanese Reader. Consisting of Japanese Anecdotes, Maxims, with English Translation and Notes. 12mo, 6*s.*

The Classical Poetry of the Japanese. Post 8vo, 7*s.* 6*d.*

Handbook of Colloquial Japanese. 8vo, 12*s.* 6*d.*

CHATTERJI, *Mohini M.*—The Bhagavad Gîtâ ; or, The Lord's Lay. With Commentary and Notes. Translated from the Sanskrit. Second Edition. Royal 8vo, 10*s.* 6*d.*

CHILDERS, *R. C.*—A Pali-English Dictionary, with Sanskrit Equivalents. Imperial 8vo, £3 3*s.*

The Mahaparinibbanasutta of the Sutta Pitaka. The Pali Text. Edited by R. C. CHILDERS. 8vo, 5*s.*

CHINTAMON, *H.*—A Commentary on the Text of the Bhagavad-Gîtâ ; or, The Discourse between Khrishna and Arjuna of Divine Matters. Post 8vo, 6*s.*

COOMARA SWAMY, *Mutu.*—The Dathavansa ; or, The History of the Tooth Relic of Gotama Buddha, in Pali Verse. Edited by MUTU COOMARA SWAMY. Demy 8vo, 10*s.* 6*d.* English Translation. With Notes. 6*s.*

Sutta Nipata ; or, Dialogues and Discourses of Gotama Buddha. Translated from the original Pali. Crown 8vo, 6*s.*

COWELL, *E. B.*—A Short Introduction to the Ordinary Prakrit of the Sanskrit Dramas. Crown 8vo, 3*s.* 6*d.*

Prakrita-Prakasa ; or, The Prakrit Grammar of Vararuchi, with the Commentary (Manorama) of Bhamaha. 8vo, 14*s.*

CRAVEN, *T.*—English-Hindustani and Hindustani-English Dictionary. 18mo, 3*s.* 6*d.*

CUNNINGHAM, *Major-General Alexander.*—The Ancient Geography of India. I. The Buddhist Period, including the Campaigns of Alexander and the Travels of Hwen-Thsang. With 13 Maps. 8vo, £1 8*s.*

Archæological Survey of India, Reports. With numerous Plates. Vols. I. to XXIII. Royal 8vo, 10*s.* and 12*s.* each. General Index to Vols. I. to XXIII. Royal 8vo, 12*s.*

CUST, R. N.—**Pictures of Indian Life,** Sketched with the Pen from 1852 to 1881. With Maps. Crown 8vo, 7s. 6d.

DENNYS, N. B.—**The Folk-Lore of China, and its Affinities with that of the Aryan and Semitic Races.** 8vo, 10s. 6d.

DOUGLAS, R. K.—**Chinese Language and Literature.** Two Lectures. Crown 8vo, 5s.

The Life of Jenghiz Khan. Translated from the Chinese. Crown 8vo, 5s.

DOWSON, John.—**A Grammar of the Urdū or Hindūstānī Language.** Second Edition. Crown 8vo, 10s. 6d.

A Hindūstānī Exercise Book. Containing a Series of Passages and Extracts adapted for Translation into Hindūstānī. Crown 8vo, 2s. 6d.

DUKA, Theodore.—**An Essay on the Brāhūī Grammar.** Demy 8vo, 3s. 6d.

DUTT, Romesh Chunder.—**A History of Civilization in Ancient India.** Based on Sanscrit Literature. 3 vols. Crown 8vo. Vol. I. Vedic and Epic Ages. 8s. Vol. II. Rationalistic Age. 8s. Vol. III. [*In preparation.*

EDKINS, Joseph.—**China's Place in Philology.** An Attempt to show that the Languages of Europe and Asia have a common origin. Crown 8vo, 10s. 6d.

The Evolution of the Chinese Language. As Exemplifying the Origin and Growth of Human Speech. Demy 8vo, 4s. 6d.

The Evolution of the Hebrew Language. Demy 8vo, 5s.

Introduction to the Study of the Chinese Characters. Royal 8vo, 18s.

Egypt Exploration Fund :—

The Store-City of Pithom, and the Route of the Exodus. By EDOUARD NAVILLE. Third Edition. With 13 Plates and 2 Maps. Royal 4to, 25s.

Tanis. Part I., 1883-84. By W. M. FLINDERS PETRIE. With 19 Plates and Plans. Royal 4to, 25s.

Tanis. Part II. Nebesha, Daphnæ (Tahpenes). By W. M. FLINDERS PETRIE and F. LL. GRIFFITH. 64 Plates. Royal 4to, 25s.

Naukratis. Part I. By W. M. FLINDERS PETRIE, CECIL SMITH, E. A. GARDNER, and B. V. HEAD. With 45 Plates. Royal 4to, 25s.

Naukratis. Part II. By ERNEST A. GARDNER. With an Appendix by F. LL. GRIFFITH. With 24 Plates. Royal 4to, 25s.

Goshen. By E. NAVILLE. With 11 Plates. Royal 4to, 25s.

EITEL, E. J.—**Buddhism :** Its Historical, Theoretical, and Popular Aspects. Third, Revised Edition. Demy 8vo, 5s.

Handbook for the Student of Chinese Buddhism. Second Edition. Crown 8vo, 18s.

ELLIOT, Sir H. M.—**Memoirs on the History, Folk-Lore, and Distribution of the Races of the North-Western Provinces of India.** Edited by J. BEAMES. 2 vols. With 3 Coloured Maps. Demy 8vo, £1 16s.

The History of India, as told by its own Historians. The Muhammadan Period. Edited from the Posthumous Papers of the late Sir H. M. ELLIOT. Revised and continued by Professor JOHN DOWSON. 8 vols. 8vo, £8 8s.

EMERSON, Ellen Russell.—**Indian Myths;** or, Legends, Traditions, and Symbols of the Aborigines of America. Illustrated. Post 8vo, £1 1s.

FERGUSSON, T.—**Chinese Researches.** First Part. Chinese Chronology and Cycles. Crown 8vo, 10s. 6d.

FINN, Alexander.—**Persian for Travellers.** Oblong 32mo, 5s.

FRYER, Major G. E.—**The Khyeng People of the Sandoway District, Arakan.** With 2 Plates. 8vo, 3s. 6d.

Páli Studies. No. I. Analysis, and Páli Text of the Subodhálankara, or Easy Rhetoric, by Sangharakkhita Thera. 8vo, 3s. 6d.

GHOSE, Loke N.—**The Modern History of the Indian Chiefs, Rajas,** etc. 2 vols. Post 8vo, 21s.

GILES, Herbert A.—**Chinese Sketches.** 8vo, 10s. 6d.

A Dictionary of Colloquial Idioms in the Mandarin Dialect. 4to, 28s.

Synoptical Studies in Chinese Character. 8vo, 15s.

Chinese without a Teacher. Being a Collection of Easy and Useful Sentences in the Mandarin Dialect. With a Vocabulary. 12mo, 5s.

The San Tzu Ching; or, Three Character Classic; and the Ch'Jen Tsu Wen; or, Thousand Character Essay. Metrically translated by HERBERT A. GILES. 12mo, 2s. 6d.

GOVER, C. E.—**The Folk-Songs of Southern India.** Containing Canarese, Badaga, Coorg, Tamil, Malayalam, and Telugu Songs. The Cural. 8vo, 10s. 6d.

GRIFFIN, L. H.—**The Rajas of the Punjab.** History of the Principal States in the Punjab, and their Political Relations with the British Government. Royal 8vo, 21s.

GRIFFITH, F. L.—**The Inscriptions of Siut and Der Rifeh.** With 21 Plates. 4to, 10s.

GRIFFIS, W. E.—The Mikado's Empire. Book I. History of Japan, from B.C. 660 to A.D. 1872. Book II. Personal Experiences, Observations, and Studies in Japan, 1870–1874. Second Edition. Illustrated. 8vo, 20*s.*

Japanese Fairy World. Stories from the Wonder-Lore of Japan. With 12 Plates. Square 16mo, 7*s.* 6*d.*

HAFIZ OF SHIRAZ.—Selections from his Poems. Translated from the Persian by HERMANN BICKNELL. With Oriental Bordering in gold and colour, and Illustrations by J. R. HERBERT, R.A. Demy 4to, £2 2*s.*

HAGGARD, W. H., and LE STRANGE, G.—The Vazir of Lankuran. A Persian Play. Edited, with a Grammatical Introduction, a Translation, Notes, and a Vocabulary, giving the Pronunciation. Crown 8vo, 10*s.* 6*d.*

HALL, John Carey.—A General View of Chinese Civilization, and of the Relations of the West with China. From the French of M. PIERRE LAFFITTE. Demy 8vo, 3*s.*

Hebrew Literature Society.—Lists on application.

HEPBURN, J. C.—A Japanese and English Dictionary. Second Edition. Imperial 8vo, 18*s.*

A Japanese-English and English-Japanese Dictionary. Abridged by the Author. Square 16mo, 14*s.*

A Japanese-English and English-Japanese Dictionary. Third Edition. Demy 8vo, half-morocco, cloth sides. 30*s.*

HILMY, H.H. Prince Ibrahim.—The Literature of Egypt and the Soudan. From the Earliest Times to the Year 1885 inclusive. A Bibliography; comprising Printed Books, Periodical Writings and Papers of Learned Societies, Maps and Charts, Ancient Papyri, Manuscripts, Drawings, etc. 2 vols. Demy 4to, £3 3*s.*

Hindoo Mythology Popularly Treated. An Epitomised Description of the various Heathen Deities illustrated on the Silver Swami Tea Service presented, as a memento of his visit to India, to H.R.H. the Prince of Wales, K.G., by His Highness the Gaekwar of Baroda. Small 4to, 3*s.* 6*d.*

HODGSON, B. H.—Essays on the Languages, Literature, and Religion of Nepal and Tibet. Together with further Papers on the Geography, Ethnology, and Commerce of those Countries. Royal 8vo, 14*s.*

HOPKINS, F. L.—Elementary Grammar of the Turkish Language. With a few Easy Exercises. Crown 8vo, 3*s.* 6*d.*

Kegan Paul, Trench, Trübner & Co.'s Publications. 61

HUNTER, *Sir William Wilson.*—The Imperial Gazetteer of India. New Edition. In 14 vols. With Maps. 1886–87. Half-morocco, £3 3s.

    The Indian Empire: Its People, History, and Products. Second and Revised Edition, incorporating the general results of the Census of 1881. With Map. Demy 8vo, £1 1s.

    A Brief History of the Indian People. Fourth Edition. With Map. Crown 8vo, 3s. 6d.

    The Indian Musalmans. Third Edition. 8vo, 10s. 6d.

    Famine Aspects of Bengal Districts. A System of Famine Warnings. Crown 8vo, 7s. 6d.

    A Statistical Account of Bengal. In 20 vols. 8vo, half-morocco, £5.

    A Statistical Account of Assam. 2 vols. With 2 Maps. 8vo, half-morocco, 10s.

    Catalogue of Sanskrit Manuscripts (Buddhist). Collected in Nepal by B. H. Hodgson. 8vo, 2s.

India.—Publications of the Geographical Department of the India Office, London. A separate list, also list of all the Government Maps, on application.

India.—Publications of the Geological Survey of India. A separate list on application.

India Office Publications:—

    Aden, Statistical Account of. 5s.

    Baden Powell. Land Revenues, etc., in India. 12s.

        Do.   Jurisprudence for Forest Officers. 12s.

    Beal's Buddhist Tripitaka. 4s.

    Bombay Code. 21s.

    Bombay Gazetteer. Vol. II. 14s. Vol. VIII. 9s. Vol. XIII. (2 parts) 16s. Vol. XV. (2 parts) 16s.

        Do.   do.   Vols. III. to VII., and X., XI., XII., XIV., XVI. 8s. each.

        Do.   do.   Vols. XXI., XXII., and XXIII. 9s. each.

    Burgess' Archæological Survey of Western India.
                                                        Vol. II. 63s.

        Do.   do.   do.   Vol. III. 42s.

        Do.   do.   Vols. IV. and V. 126s.

        Do.   do.   Southern India.
                                                       Vol. I. 84s.

    Burma (British) Gazetteer. 2 vols. 50s.

India Office Publications—*continued.*
 Corpus Inscriptionem Indicarum. Vol. I. 32*s.* Vol. III. 50*s.*
 Cunningham's Archæological Survey. Vols. I. to XXIII. 10*s.* and 12*s.* each.
  Do.   Index to Vols. I. to XXIII. 12*s.*
 Finance and Revenue Accounts of the Government of India for 1883-4. 2*s.* 6*d.*
 Gamble. Manual of Indian Timbers. 10*s.*
 Indian Education Commission, Report of the. 12*s.* Appendices. 10 vols. 10*s.*
 Jaschke's Tibetan-English Dictionary. 30*s.*
 Liotard's Silk in India. Part I. 2*s.*
 Loth. Catalogue of Arabic MSS. 10*s.* 6*d.*
 Markham's Abstract of Reports of Surveys. 1*s.* 6*d.*
 Mitra (Rajendralala), Buddha Gaya. 60*s.*
 Moir. Torrent Regions of the Alps. 1*s.*
 Mueller. Select Plants for Extra-Tropical Countries. 8*s.*
 Mysore and Coorg Gazetteer. Vols. I. and II. 10*s.* each.
  Do.   do.   Vol. III. 5*s.*
 N. W. P. Gazetteer. Vols. I. and II. 10*s.* each.
  Do.   do.   Vols. III. to XI., XIII. and XIV. 12*s.* each.
 Oudh : do.   Vols. I. to III. 10*s.* each.
 Rajputana Gazetteer. 3 vols. 15*s.*
 Saunders' Mountains and River Basins of India. 3*s.*
 Taylor. Indian Marine Surveys. 2*s.* 6*d.*
 Trigonometrical Survey, Synopsis of Great. Vols. I. to VI. 10*s.* 6*d.* each.
 Trumpp's Adi Granth. 52*s.* 6*d.*
 Waring. Pharmacopœia of India (The). 6*s.*
 Watson's Tobacco. 5*s.*
 Wilson. Madras Army. Vols. I. and II. 21*s.*
International Numismata Orientalia (The). Royal 4to, in paper wrapper. Part I. Ancient Indian Weights. By E. THOMAS, F.R.S. With a Plate and Map of the India of Manu. 9*s.* 6*d.* Part II. Coins of the Urtuki Turkumáns. By STANLEY LANE POOLE. With 6 Plates. 9*s.* Part III. The Coinage of Lydia

International Numismata Orientalia (The)—*continued.*
and Persia, from the Earliest Times to the Fall of the Dynasty of the Achæmenidæ. By BARCLAY V. HEAD. With 3 Autotype Plates. 10s. 6d. Part IV. The Coins of the Tuluni Dynasty. By EDWARD THOMAS ROGERS. 1 Plate. 5s. Part V. The Parthian Coinage. By PERCY GARDNER. 8 Autotype Plates. 18s. Part VI. The Ancient Coins and Measures of Ceylon. By T. W. RHYS DAVIDS. 1 Plate. 10s.

Vol. I. Containing the first six parts, as specified above. Royal 4to, half-bound, £3 13s. 6d.

Vol. II. **Coins of the Jews.** Being a History of the Jewish Coinage and Money in the Old and New Testaments. By F. W. MADDEN, M.R.A.S. With 279 Woodcuts and a Plate of Alphabets. Royal 4to, £2.

Vol. III. Part I. **The Coins of Arakan, of Pegu, and of Burma.** By Lieut.-General Sir ARTHUR PHAYRE, C.B. Also contains the Indian Balhara, and the Arabian Intercourse with India in the Ninth and following Centuries. By EDWARD THOMAS, F.R.S. With 5 Autotype Illustrations. Royal 4to, 8s. 6d.

Vol. III. Part II. **The Coins of Southern India.** By Sir W. ELLIOT. With Map and Plates. Royal 4to, 25s.

JASCHKE, H. A.—A **Tibetan-English Dictionary.** With special reference to the Prevailing Dialects. To which is added an English-Tibetan Vocabulary. Imperial 8vo, £1 10s.

Jataka (The), together with its **Commentary.** Being Tales of the Anterior Birth of Gotama Buddha. Now first published in Pali, by V. FAUSBOLL. Text. 8vo. Vol. I. 28s. Vol. II. 28s. Vol. III. 28s. Vol. IV. 28s. Vol. V., completing the work, is in preparation.

JENNINGS, Hargrave.—**The Indian Religions**; or, Results of the Mysterious Buddhism. Demy 8vo, 10s. 6d.

JOHNSON, Samuel.—**Oriental Religions and their Relation to Universal Religion.** Persia. Demy 8vo, 18s.

KISTNER, Otto.—**Buddha and his Doctrines.** A Bibliographical Essay. 4to, 2s. 6d.

KNOWLES, J. H.—**Folk-Tales of Kashmir.** Post 8vo, 16s.

KOLBE, F. W.—**A Language-Study based on Bantu**; or, An Inquiry into the Laws of Root-Formation. Demy 8vo, 6s.

KRAPF, L.—**Dictionary of the Suahili Language.** 8vo, 30s.

LEGGE, James.—**The Chinese Classics.** With a Translation, Critical and Exegetical. In 7 vols. Vols. I.-V. in 8 Parts, published. Royal 8vo, £2 2s. each part.

LEGGE, *James—continued.*
>The Chinese Classics, translated into English. With Preliminary Essays and Explanatory Notes. Popular Edition. Crown 8vo. Vol. I. Life and Teachings of Confucius. Sixth Edition. 10*s.* 6*d.* Vol. II. Works of Mencius. 12*s.* Vol. III. She-King; or, Book of Poetry. 12*s.*

LILLIE, *Arthur, M.R.A.S.*—**The Popular Life of Buddha.** Containing an Answer to the Hibbert Lectures of 1881. With Illustrations. Crown 8vo, 6*s.*
>Buddhism in Christendom; or, Jesus the Essene. With Illustrations. Demy 8vo, 15*s.*

LOBSCHEID, *W.*—Chinese and English Dictionary, arranged according to the Radicals. Imperial 8vo, £2 8*s.*
>English and Chinese Dictionary, with the Punti and Mandarin Pronunciation. Folio, £8 8*s.*

Maha-vira-Charita; or, The Adventures of the Great Hero Rama. An Indian Drama. Translated from the Sanskrit of BHAVABHŪTI. By JOHN PICKFORD. Crown 8vo, 5*s.*

MARIETTE-BEY, *Auguste.*—**The Monuments of Upper Egypt.** A Translation of the "Itinéraire de la Haute Egypt" of AUGUSTE MARIETTE-BEY. By ALPHONSE MARIETTE. Crown 8vo, 7*s.* 6*d.*

MARSDEN, *William.*—Numismata Orientalia Illustrata: The Plates of the Oriental Coins, Ancient and Modern, of the Collection of the late WILLIAM MARSDEN, F.R.S. Engraved from Drawings made under his Directions. 57 Plates. 4to, 31*s.* 6*d.*

MASON, *F.*—Burma: Its People and Productions; or, Notes on the Fauna, Flora, and Minerals of Tenasserim, Pegu, and Burma. Vol. I. Geology, Mineralogy, and Zoology. Vol. II. Botany. Rewritten by W. THEOBALD. 2 vols. Royal 8vo, £3.

MAXWELL, *W. E.*—A Manual of the Malay Language. Second Edition. Crown 8vo, 7*s.* 6*d.*

MAYERS, *Wm. Fred.*—The Chinese Government. A Manual of Chinese Titles. Second Edition. Royal 8vo, 15*s.*

Megha-Duta (The). (Cloud Messenger.) By KĀLIDĀSA. Translated from the Sanskrit into English Verse by the late H. H. WILSON, F.R.S. The Vocabulary by FRANCIS JOHNSON. New Edition. 4to, 10*s.* 6*d.*

MOCKLER, *E.*—A Grammar of the Baloochee Language, as it is spoken in Makran (Ancient Gedrosia), in the Persia-Arabic and Roman characters. Fcap. 8vo, 5*s.*

MUIR, *John.*—Original Sanskrit Texts, on the Origin and History of the People of India. Translated by JOHN MUIR, LL.D.

MUIR, *John—continued.*
> Vol. I. Mythical and Legendary Accounts of the Origin of Caste, with an Inquiry into its Existence in the Vedic Age. Third Edition. 8vo, £1 1s.
> Vol. II. The Trans-Himalayan Origin of the Hindus, and their Affinity with the Western Branches of the Aryan Race. Second Edition. 8vo, £1 1s.
> Vol. III. The Vedas: Opinions of their Authors, and of later Indian Writers, on their Origin, Inspiration, and Authority. Second Edition. 8vo, 16s.
> Vol. IV. Comparison of the Vedic with the Later Representation of the Principal Indian Deities. Second Edition. 8vo, £1 1s.
> Vol. V. Contributions to a Knowledge of the Cosmogony, Mythology, Religious Ideas, Life and Manners of the Indians in the Vedic Age. Third Edition. 8vo, £1 1s.

MÜLLER, *F. Max.*—Outline Dictionary, for the Use of Missionaries, Explorers, and Students of Language. 12mo, morocco, 7s. 6d.

> The Sacred Hymns of the Brahmins, as preserved in the Oldest Collection of Religious Poetry, the Rig-Veda-Sanhita. Translated by F. MAX MÜLLER. Vol. I. Hymns to the Maruts, or the Storm-Gods. 8vo, 12s. 6d.

> The Hymns of the Rig-Veda, in the Samhita and Pada Texts. 2 vols. Second Edition. 8vo, £1 12s.

Nágánanda; or, The Joy of the Snake World. A Buddhist Drama. Translated from the Sanskrit of Sri-Harsha-Deva, with Notes. By P. BOYD. Crown 8vo, 4s. 6d.

NEWMAN, *Francis William.*—A Handbook of Modern Arabic. Post 8vo, 6s.

> A Dictionary of Modern Arabic. Anglo-Arabic Dictionary and Arabo-English Dictionary. 2 vols. Crown 8vo, £1 1s.

Oriental Text Society's Publications. A list may be had on application.

PALMER, *the late E. H.*—A Concise English-Persian Dictionary. With a Simplified Grammar of the Persian Language. Royal 16mo, 10s. 6d.

> A Concise Persian-English Dictionary. Second Edition. Royal 16mo, 10s. 6d.

PRATT, *George.*—A Grammar and Dictionary of the Samoan Language. Second Edition. Crown 8vo, 18s.

REDHOUSE, *J. W.*—The Turkish Vade-Mecum of Ottoman Colloquial Language. English and Turkish, and Turkish and English. The whole in English Characters, the Pronunciation being fully indicated. Third Edition. 32mo, 6s.

REDHOUSE, J. W.—continued.
  On the History, System, and Varieties of Turkish Poetry. Illustrated by Selections in the Original and in English Paraphrase. 8vo, 2s. 6d.; wrapper, 1s. 6d.
  A Tentative Chronological Synopsis of the History of Arabia and its Neighbours, from B.C. 500,000 (?) to A.D. 679. Demy 8vo, 1s.
Rig-Veda-Sanhita. A Collection of Ancient Hindu Hymns. Translated from the Sanskrit by the late H. H. WILSON, F.R.S. Edited by E. B. COWELL and W. F. WEBSTER. In 6 vols. 8vo, cloth. Vols. I., II., III. 21s. each. Vol. IV. 14s. Vols. V. and VI. 21s. each.

SACHAU, Edward.—Albêrûnî's India. An Account of the Religion, Philosophy, Literature, Geography, Chronology, Astronomy, Customs, Laws, and Astrology of India, about A.D. 1030. Edited in the Arabic Original by Dr. EDWARD SACHAU. 4to, £3 3s.
  An English Edition. With Notes and Indices. 2 vols. Post 8vo, 36s.

SALMONÉ, H. A.—An Arabic-English Dictionary. Comprising about 120,000 Arabic Words, with an English Index of about 50,000 Words. 2 vols. Post 8vo, 36s.

SATOW, Ernest Mason.—An English-Japanese Dictionary of the Spoken Language. Second Edition. Imperial 32mo, 12s. 6d.

SCHLAGINTWEIT, Emil.—Buddhism in Tibet. Illustrated by Literary Documents and Objects of Religious Worship. With a Folio Atlas of 20 Plates, and 20 Tables of Native Print in the Text. Royal 8vo, £2 2s.

SCOTT, James George.—Burma as it was, as it is, and as it will be. Cheap Edition. Crown 8vo, 2s. 6d.

SHERRING, M. A.—The Sacred City of the Hindus. An Account of Benares in Ancient and Modern Times. With Illustrations. 8vo, 21s.

STEELE, Th.—An Eastern Love-Story. Kusa Játakaya. Crown 8vo, 6s.

SUYEMATZ, K.—Genji Monogatari. The Most Celebrated of the Classical Japanese Romances. Translated by K. SUYEMATZ. Crown 8vo, 7s. 6d.

TARRING, C. J.—A Practical Elementary Turkish Grammar. Crown 8vo, 6s.

Vazir of Lankuran. A Persian Play. A Text-Book of Modern Colloquial Persian. Edited by W. H. HAGGARD and G. LE STRANGE. Crown 8vo, 10s. 6d.

WATSON, *John Forbes.*—Index to the Native and Scientific Names of Indian and other Eastern Economic Plants and Products. Imperial 8vo, £1 11s. 6d.

WHEELER, *J. Talboys.*—The History of India from the Earliest Ages. Demy 8vo. Vol. I. Containing the Vedic Period and the Mahá Bhárata. With Map. Vol. II. The Ramayana, and the Brahmanic Period. With 2 Maps. 21s. Vol. III. Hindu, Buddhist, Brahmanical Revival. With 2 Maps. 8vo, 18s. This volume may be had as a complete work with the following title, "History of India: Hindu, Buddhist, and Brahmanical." Vol. IV. Part I. Mussulman Rule. 14s. Vol. IV. Part II. Completing the History of India down to the time of the Moghul Empire. 12s.

Early Records of British India. A History of the English Settlements in India, as told in the Government Records, and other Contemporary Documents, from the earliest period down to the rise of British Power in India. Royal 8vo, 15s.

WHITNEY, *W. D.*—A Sanskrit Grammar, including both the Classical Language and the older Dialects of Veda and Brahmana. Second Edition. 8vo, 12s.

WHITWORTH, *George Clifford.*—An Anglo-Indian Dictionary: a Glossary of Indian Terms used in English, and of such English or other Non-Indian Terms as have obtained special meanings in India. Demy 8vo, cloth, 12s.

WILLIAMS, *S. Wells.*—A Syllabic Dictionary of the Chinese Language; arranged according to the Wu-Fang Yuen Yin, with the Pronunciation of the Characters as heard in Pekin, Canton, Amoy, and Shanghai. 4to, £5 5s.

WILSON.—Works of the late Horace Hayman Wilson.

Vols. I. and II. Essays and Lectures chiefly on the Religion of the Hindus. Collected and Edited by Dr. REINHOLD ROST. 2 vols. Demy 8vo, 21s.

Vols. III., IV., and V. Essays Analytical, Critical, and Philological, on Subjects connected with Sanskrit Literature. Collected and Edited by Dr. REINHOLD ROST. 3 vols. Demy 8vo, 36s.

Vols. VI., VII., VIII., IX., and X. (2 parts). Vishnu Puráná, a System of Hindu Mythology and Tradition. From the original Sanskrit. Illustrated by Notes derived chiefly from other Puránás, Edited by FITZEDWARD HALL, D.C.L. Vols. I. to V. (2 parts). Demy 8vo, £3 4s. 6d.

Vols. XI. and XII. Select Specimens of the Theatre of the Hindus. From the original Sanskrit. Third Edition. 2 vols. Demy 8vo, 21s.

WRIGHT, *W.*—The Book of Kalilah and Dimnah. Translated from Arabic into Syriac. Demy 8vo, 21s.

TRUBNER'S ORIENTAL SERIES.

Essays on the Sacred Language, Writings, and Religion of the Parsis. By MARTIN HAUG, Ph.D. Third Edition, Edited and Enlarged by E. W. WEST. 16s.

Texts from the Buddhist Canon, commonly known as Dhammapada. Translated from the Chinese by S. BEAL. 7s. 6d.

The History of Indian Literature. By ALBRECHT WEBER. Translated from the German by J. MANN and Dr. T. ZACHARIAE. Second Edition. 10s. 6d.

A Sketch of the Modern Languages of the East Indies. With 2 Language Maps. By ROBERT CUST. 7s. 6d.

The Birth of the War-God. A Poem. By KÁLIDASÁ. Translated from the Sanskrit by RALPH T. H. GRIFFITHS. Second Edition. 5s.

A Classical Dictionary of Hindu Mythology and History, Geography and Literature. By JOHN DOWSON. 16s.

Metrical Translations from Sanskrit Writers. By J. MUIR. 14s.

Modern India and the Indians. Being a Series of Impressions, Notes, and Essays. By Sir MONIER MONIER-WILLIAMS. Fourth Edition. 14s.

The Life or Legend of Gaudama, the Buddha of the Burmese. By the Right Rev. P. BIGANDET. Third Edition. 2 vols. 21s.

Miscellaneous Essays, relating to Indian Subjects. By B. H. HODGSON. 2 vols. 28s.

Selections from the Koran. By EDWARD WILLIAM LANE. A New Edition. With an Introduction by STANLEY LANE POOLE. 9s.

Chinese Buddhism. A Volume of Sketches, Historical and Critical. By J. EDKINS, D.D. 18s.

The Gulistan; or, Rose Garden of Shekh Mushliu-'d-Din Sadi of Shiraz. Translated from the Atish Kadah, by E. B. EASTWICK, F.R.S. Second Edition. 10s. 6d.

A Talmudic Miscellany; or, 'One Thousand and One Extracts from the Talmud, the Midrashim, and the Kabbalah. Compiled and Translated by P. J. HERSHON. 14s.

The History of Esarhaddon (Son of Sennacherib), King of Assyria, B.C. 681–668. Translated from the Cuneiform Inscriptions in the British Museum. Together with Original Texts. By E. A. BUDGE. 10s. 6d.

Buddhist Birth-Stories; or, Jātaka Tales. The Oldest Collection of Folk-Lore extant : being the Jātakatthavannanā. Edited in the original Pali by V. FAUSBÖLL, and translated by T. W. RHYS DAVIDS. Translation. Vol. I. 18s.

The Classical Poetry of the Japanese. By BASIL CHAMBERLAIN. 7s. 6d.

Linguistic and Oriental Essays. By R. CUST, LL.D. First Series, 10s. 6d. ; Second Series, with 6 Maps, 21s.

Indian Poetry. Containing "The Indian Song of Songs," from the Sanskrit of the Gita Govinda of Jayadeva ; Two Books from "The Iliad of India " (Mahábhárata) ; and other Oriental Poems. By Sir EDWIN ARNOLD, K.C.I.E. Third Edition. 7s. 6d.

The Religions of India. By A. BARTH. Translated by Rev. J. WOOD. Second Edition. 16s.

Hindū Philosophy. The Sānkhya Kārikā of Iswara Krishna. An Exposition of the System of Kapila. By JOHN DAVIES. 6s.

A Manual of Hindu Pantheism. The Vedantasara. Translated by Major G. A. JACOB. Second Edition. 6s.

The Mesnevī (usually known as the Mesnevīyi Sherīf, or Holy Mesnevī) of Mevlānā (Our Lord) Jelālu-'d-Dīn Muhammed, Er-Rūmī. Book the First. Illustrated by a Selection of Characteristic Anecdotes as collected by their Historian Mevlānā Shemsu-'d-Dīn Ahmed, El Eflākī El Arifī. Translated by J. W. REDHOUSE. £1 1s.

Eastern Proverbs and Emblems illustrating Old Truths. By the Rev. J. LONG. 6s.

The Quatrains of Omar Khayyám. A New Translation. By E. H. WHINFIELD. 5s.

The Quatrains of Omar Khayyám. The Persian Text, with an English Verse Translation. By E. H. WHINFIELD. 10s. 6d.

The Mind of Mencius; or, Political Economy founded upon Moral Philosophy. A Systematic Digest of the Doctrines of the Chinese Philosopher Mencius. The Original Text Classified and Translated by the Rev. E. FABER. Translated from the German, with Additional Notes, by the Rev. A. B. HUTCHINSON. 10s. 6d.

Yúsuf and Zulaika. A Poem by JAMI. Translated from the Persian into English Verse by R. T. H. GRIFFITH. 8s. 6d.

Tsuni- || Goam, the Supreme Being of the Khoi-Khoi. By THEOPHILUS HAHN. 7s. 6d.

A Comprehensive Commentary to the Quran. With SALE's Preliminary Discourse, and Additional Notes. By Rev. E. M. WHERRY. Vols. I., II., and III. 12s. 6d. each. Vol. IV. 10s. 6d.

Hindu Philosophy: The Bhagavad Gîtâ; or, The Sacred Lay. A Sanskrit Philosophical Lay. Translated by JOHN DAVIES. 8s. 6d.

The Sarva-Darsana-Samgraha; or, Review of the Different Systems of Hindu Philosophy. By MADHAVA ACHARYA. Translated by E. B. COWELL and A. E. GOUGH. 10s. 6d.

Tibetan Tales. Derived from Indian Sources. Translated from the Tibetan of the Kay-Gyur by F. ANTON VON SCHIEFNER. Done into English from the German by W. R. S. RALSTON. 14s.

Linguistic Essays. By CARL ABEL. 9s.

The Indian Empire: Its History, People, and Products. By Sir WILLIAM WILSON HUNTER, K.C.S.I. 21s.

History of the Egyptian Religion. By Dr. C. P. TIELE, Leiden. Translated by J. BALLINGAL. 7s. 6d.

The Philosophy of the Upanishads. By A. E. GOUGH. 9s.

Udanavarga. A Collection of Verses from the Buddhist Canon. Compiled by DHARMATRÂTA. Translated from the Tibetan by W. WOODVILLE ROCKHILL. 9s.

A History of Burma, including Burma Proper, Pegu, Taungu, Tenasserim, and Arakan. From the Earliest Time to the End of the First War with British India. By Lieut.-General Sir ARTHUR P. PHAYRE, C.B. 14s.

A Sketch of the Modern Languages of Africa. Accompanied by a Language Map. By R. N. CUST. 2 vols. With 31 Autotype Portraits. 18s.

Religion in China. Containing a Brief Account of the Three Religions of the Chinese. By JOSEPH EDKINS, D.D. Third Edition. 7s. 6d.

Outlines of the History of Religion to the Spread of the Universal Religions. By Prof. C. P. TIELE. Translated from the Dutch by J. ESTLIN CARPENTER. Fourth Edition. 7s. 6d.

Si-Yu-Ki. Buddhist Records of the Western World. Translated from the Chinese of HIUEN TSAING (A.D. 629). By SAMUEL BEAL. 2 vols. With Map. 24s.

The Life of the Buddha, and the Early History of his Order. Derived from Tibetan Works in the Bkah-Hgyur and the Bstan-Hgyur. By W. W. ROCKHILL. 10s. 6d.

The Sankhya Aphorisms of Kapila. With Illustrative Extracts from the Commentaries. Translated by J. R. BALLANTYNE, LL.D. Third Edition. 16s.

The Ordinances of Manu. Translated from the Sanskrit. With an Introduction by the late A. C. BURNELL, C.I.E. Edited by EDWARD W. HOPKINS. 12s.

The Life and Works of Alexander Csoma De Körös between 1819 and 1842. With a Short Notice of all his Works and Essays, from Original Documents. By T. DUKA, M.D. 9s.

Ancient Proverbs and Maxims from Burmese Sources; or, The Niti Literature of Burma. By JAMES GRAY. 6s.

Manava-Dharma-Castra. The Code of Manu. Original Sanskrit Text, with Critical Notes. By Prof. J. JOLLY, Ph.D. 10s. 6d.

Masnavi I Ma'navi. The Spiritual Couplets of Mauláná Jalálu-'d-Dín Muhammad I Rúmí. Translated and Abridged. By E. H. WHINFIELD. 7s. 6d.

Leaves from my Chinese Scrap-Book. By F. H. BALFOUR. 7s. 6d.

Miscellaneous Papers relating to Indo-China. Reprinted from "Dalrymple's Oriental Repertory," "Asiatick Researches," and the "Journal of the Asiatic Society of Bengal." 2 vols. 21s.

Miscellaneous Essays on Subjects connected with the Malay Peninsula and the Indian Archipelago. From the "Journals" of the Royal Asiatic, Bengal Asiatic, and Royal Geographical Societies; the "Transactions" and "Journal" of the Asiatic Society of Batavia, and the "Malayan Miscellanies." Edited by R. ROST. Second Series. 2 vols. With 5 Plates and a Map. £1 5s.

The Satakas of Bhartrihari. Translated from the Sanskrit by the Rev. B. HALE WORTHAM. 5s.

Albêrûnî's India. An Account of the Religion of India: its Philosophy, Literature, Geography, Chronology, Astronomy, Customs, Law, and Astrology, about A.D. 1030. By EDWARD SACHAU. 2 vols. 36s.

The Folk-Tales of Kashmir. By the Rev. J. HINTON KNOWLES. 16s.

Mediæval Researches from Eastern Asiatic Sources. Fragments towards the Knowledge of the Geography and History of Central and Western Asia from the Thirteenth to the Seventeenth Century. By E. BRETSCHNEIDER, M.D. 2 vols. With 2 Maps. 21s.

The Life of Hiuen-Tsiang. By the Shamans HWUI LI and YEN-TSUNG. With an Account of the Works of I-Tsing. By Prof. SAMUEL BEAL. 10s.

English Intercourse with Siam in the Seventeenth Century. By J. ANDERSON, M.D., LL.D., F.R.S. 15s.

Bihar Proverbs. By JOHN CHRISTIAN. [*In preparation.*

Original Sanskrit Texts on the Origin and History of the People of India: Their Religion and Institutions. Collected, Translated, and Illustrated. By J. MUIR, LL.D. Vol. I. Mythical and Legendary Accounts of the Origin of Caste, with an inquiry into its existence in the Vedic Age. Third Edition. 21s.

MILITARY WORKS.

BRACKENBURY, Col. C. B., R.A.—Military Handbooks for Regimental Officers.

I. **Military Sketching and Reconnaissance.** By Col. F. J. Hutchison and Major H. G. MacGregor. Fifth Edition. With 16 Plates. Small crown 8vo, 4s.

II. **The Elements of Modern Tactics Practically applied to English Formations.** By Lieut.-Col. Wilkinson Shaw. Seventh Edition. With 25 Plates and Maps. Small crown 8vo, 9s.

III. **Field Artillery.** Its Equipment, Organization and Tactics. By Lieut.-Col. Sisson C. Pratt, R.A. Fourth Edition. Small crown 8vo, 6s.

IV. **The Elements of Military Administration.** First Part: Permanent System of Administration. By Major J. W. Buxton. Small crown 8vo, 7s. 6d.

V. **Military Law: Its Procedure and Practice.** By Lieut.-Col. Sisson C. Pratt, R.A. Fifth Edition. Revised. Small crown 8vo, 4s. 6d.

VI. **Cavalry in Modern War.** By Major-General F. Chenevix Trench, C.M.G. Small crown 8vo, 6s.

VII. **Field Works.** Their Technical Construction and Tactical Application. By the Editor, Col. C. B. Brackenbury, R.A. Small crown 8vo, in 2 parts, 12s.

BROOKE, Major, C. K.—**A System of Field Training.** Small crown 8vo, cloth limp, 2s.

Campaign of Fredericksburg, November—December, 1862. A Study for Officers of Volunteers. By a Line Officer. With 5 Maps and Plans. Second Edition. Crown 8vo, 5s.

CLERY, C. Francis, Col.—**Minor Tactics.** With 26 Maps and Plans. Eighth Edition, Revised. Crown 8vo, 9s.

COLVILE, Lieut.-Col. C. F.—**Military Tribunals.** Sewed, 2s. 6d.

CRAUFURD, Capt. H. J.—Suggestions for the Military Training of a Company of Infantry. Crown 8vo, 1s. 6d.

HAMILTON, Capt. Ian, A.D.C.—The Fighting of the Future. 1s.

HARRISON, Col. R.—The Officer's Memorandum Book for Peace and War. Fourth Edition, Revised throughout. Oblong 32mo, red basil, with pencil, 3s. 6d.

Notes on Cavalry Tactics, Organisation, etc. By a Cavalry Officer. With Diagrams. Demy 8vo, 12s.

PARR, Col. H. Hallam, C.M.G.—The Dress, Horses, and Equipment of Infantry and Staff Officers. Crown 8vo, 1s.

Further Training and Equipment of Mounted Infantry. Crown 8vo, 1s.

PATERSON, Lieut.-Colonel William.—Notes on Military Surveying and Reconnaissance. Sixth Edition. With 16 Plates. Demy 8vo, 7s. 6d.

SCHAW, Col. H.—The Defence and Attack of Positions and Localities. Fourth Edition. Crown 8vo, 3s. 6d.

STONE, Capt. F. Gleadowe, R.A.—Tactical Studies from the Franco-German War of 1870-71. With 22 Lithographic Sketches and Maps. Demy 8vo, 10s. 6d.

WILKINSON, H. Spenser, Capt. 20th Lancashire R.V.—Citizen Soldiers. Essays towards the Improvement of the Volunteer Force. Crown 8vo, 2s. 6d.

EDUCATIONAL.

ABEL, Carl, Ph.D.—Linguistic Essays. Post 8vo, 9s.

Slavic and Latin. Ilchester Lectures on Comparative Lexicography. Post 8vo, 5s.

ABRAHAMS, L. B.—A Manual of Scripture History for Use in Jewish Schools and Families. With Map and Appendices. Crown 8vo, 1s. 6d.

AHN, F.—A Concise Grammar of the Dutch Language, with Selections from the best Authors in Prose and Poetry. After Dr. F. Ahn's Method. 12mo, 3s. 6d.

Practical Grammar of the German Language. Crown 8vo, 3s. 6d.

AHN, F.—continued.

> New, Practical, and Easy Method of Learning the German Language. First and Second Courses in 1 vol. 12mo, 3s.
>
> Key to Ditto. 12mo, 8d.
>
> Manual of German and English Conversations, or Vade Mecum for English Travellers. 12mo, 1s. 6d.
>
> New, Practical, and Easy Method of Learning the French Language. First Course and Second Course. 12mo, each 1s. 6d. The Two Courses in 1 vol. 12mo, 3s.
>
> New, Practical, and Easy Method of Learning the French Language. Third Course, containing a French Reader, with Notes and Vocabulary. 12mo, 1s. 6d.
>
> New, Practical, and Easy Method of Learning the Italian Language. First and Second Courses. 12mo, 3s. 6d.
>
> Ahn's Course. Latin Grammar for Beginners. By W. IHNE, Ph.D. 12mo, 3s.

BARANOWSKI, J. J.—Anglo-Polish Lexicon. Fcap. 8vo, 12s.

> Slownik Polsko-Angielski. (Polish-English Lexicon.) Fcap. 8vo, 12s.

BELLOWS, John.—French and English Dictionary for the Pocket. Containing the French-English and English-French divisions on the same page; conjugating all the verbs; distinguishing the genders by different types; giving numerous aids to pronunciation; indicating the *liaison* or *non-liaison* of terminal consonants; and translating units of weight, measure, and value by a series of tables. Second Edition. 32mo, roan, 10s. 6d.; morocco tuck, 12s. 6d.

> Tous les Verbes. Conjugations of all the Verbs in the French and English Languages. 32mo, 6d.

BOJESEN, Maria.—A Guide to the Danish Language. Designed for English Students. 12mo, 5s.

BOLIA, C.—The German Caligraphist. Copies for German Handwriting. Oblong 4to, 1s.

BOWEN, H. C., M.A.—Studies in English. For the use of Modern Schools. Tenth Thousand. Small crown 8vo, 1s. 6d.

> English Grammar for Beginners. Fcap. 8vo, 1s.
>
> Simple English Poems. English Literature for Junior Classes. In four parts. Parts I., II., and III., 6d. each. Part IV., 1s. Complete, 3s.

BRETTE, P.H., and THOMAS, F.—**French Examination Papers** set at the University of London. Arranged and Edited by the Rev. P. H. Ernest Brette, B.D., and Ferdinand Thomas, B.A. Part I. Matriculation, and the General Examination for Women. Crown 8vo, 3s. 6d.

French Examination Papers set at the University of London. Key to Part I. Edited by the Rev. P. H. E. Brette and F. Thomas. Crown 8vo, 5s.

French Examination Papers set at the University of London. Edited by the Rev. P. H. Ernest Brette and Ferdinand Thomas. Part II. Crown 8vo, 7s.

BUTLER, F.—**The Spanish Teacher and Colloquial Phrase Book.** 18mo, half-roan, 2s. 6d.

BYRNE, James.—**General Principles of the Structure of Language.** 2 vols. Demy 8vo, 36s.

The Origin of Greek, Latin, and Gothic Roots. Demy 8vo, 18s.

CAMERINI, E.—**L'Eco Italiano.** A Practical Guide to Italian Conversation. With a Vocabulary. 12mo, 4s. 6d.

CONTOPOULOS, N.—**A Lexicon of Modern Greek-English and English-Modern Greek.** 2 vols. 8vo, 27s.

CONWAY, R. Seymour.—**Verner's Law in Italy.** An Essay in the History of the Indo-European Sibilants. Demy 8vo, 5s.

The Italic Dialects. I. The Text of the Inscriptions. II. An Italic Lexicon. Edited and arranged by R. Seymour Conway. 8vo. [*In preparation.*

DELBRÜCK, B.—**Introduction to the Study of Language.** The History and Methods of Comparative Philology of the Indo-European Languages. 8vo, 5s.

D'ORSEY, A. J. D.—**A Practical Grammar of Portuguese and English.** Adapted to Ollendorff's System. Fourth Edition. 12mo, 7s.

Colloquial Portuguese; or, The Words and Phrases of Everyday Life. Fourth Edition. Crown 8vo, 3s. 6d.

DUSAR, P. Friedrich.—**A Grammar of the German Language.** With Exercises. Second Edition. Crown 8vo, 4s. 6d.

A Grammatical Course of the German Language. Third Edition. Crown 8vo, 3s. 6d.

Education Library. Edited by Sir Philip Magnus :—

An Introduction to the History of Educational Theories. By Oscar Browning, M.A. Second Edition. 3s. 6d.

Education Library—*continued.*

Industrial Education. By Sir PHILIP MAGNUS. 6s.

Old Greek Education. By the Rev. Prof. MAHAFFY, M.A. Second Edition. 3s. 6d.

School Management. Including a general view of the work of Education, Organization, and Discipline. By JOSEPH LANDON. Seventh Edition. 6s.

EGER, Gustav.—**Technological Dictionary in the English and German Languages.** Edited by GUSTAV EGER. 2 vols. Royal 8vo, £1 7s.

ELLIS, Robert.—**Sources of the Etruscan and Basque Languages.** Demy 8vo, 7s. 6d.

FRIEDRICH, P.—**Progressive German Reader.** With Copious Notes to the First Part. Crown 8vo, 4s. 6d.

FRŒMBLING, Friedrich Otto.—**Graduated German Reader.** A Selection from the most Popular Writers; with a Vocabulary for the First Part. Tenth Edition. 12mo, 3s. 6d.

Graduated Exercises for Translation into German. Consisting of Extracts from the best English Authors; with Idiomatic Notes. Crown 8vo, 4s. 6d. Without Notes, 4s.

GARLANDA, Federico.—**The Fortunes of Words.** Letters to a Lady. Crown 8vo, 5s.

The Philosophy of Words. A Popular Introduction to the Science of Language. Crown 8vo, 5s.

GELDART, E. M.—**A Guide to Modern Greek.** Post 8vo, 7s. 6d. Key, 2s. 6d.

GOWAN, Major Walter E.—**A. Ivanoff's Russian Grammar.** (16th Edition.) Translated, enlarged, and arranged for use of Students of the Russian Language. Demy 8vo, 6s.

HODGSON, W. B.—**The Education of Girls; and the Employment of Women of the Upper Classes Educationally considered.** Second Edition. Crown 8vo, 3s. 6d.

KARCHER, Theodore.—**Questionnaire Francais.** Questions on French Grammar, Idiomatic Difficulties, and Military Expressions. Fourth Edition. Crown 8vo, 4s. 6d.; interleaved with writing-paper, 5s. 6d.

LANDON, Joseph.—**School Management**; Including a General View of the Work of Education, Organization, and Discipline. Seventh Edition. Crown 8vo, 6s.

LANGE, F. K. W.—**Germania.** A German Reading-Book Arranged Progressively. Part I. Anthology of German Prose and Poetry, with Vocabulary and Biographical Notes. 8vo, 3s. 6d. Part II. Essays on German History and Institutions, with Notes. 8vo, 3s. 6d. Parts I. and II. together, 5s. 6d.

LANGE, F. K. W.—*continued.*
  German Grammar Practice. Crown 8vo, 1s. 6d.
  Colloquial German Grammar. Crown 8vo, 4s. 6d.
LE-BRUN, L.—Materials for Translating from English into French. Seventh Edition. Post 8vo, 4s. 6d.
  Little French Reader (The). Extracted from "The Modern French Reader." Third Edition. Crown 8vo, 2s.
MAGNUS, Sir Philip.—Industrial Education. Crown 8vo, 6s.
MASON, Charlotte M.—Home Education; a Course of Lectures to Ladies. Crown 8vo, 3s. 6d.
MILLHOUSE, John.—Pronouncing and Explanatory English and Italian Dictionary. 2 vols. 8vo, 12s.
  Manual of Italian Conversation. 18mo, 2s.
  Modern French Reader (The). A Glossary of Idioms, Gallicisms, and other Difficulties contained in the Senior Course of the Modern French Reader. By CHARLES CASSAL. Crown 8vo, 2s. 6d.
  Modern French Reader (The). Prose. Junior Course. Tenth Edition. Edited by CH. CASSAL and THÉODORE KARCHER. Crown 8vo, 2s. 6d.
  Senior Course. Third Edition. Crown 8vo, 4s.
  Modern French Reader. Senior Course and Glossary combined. 6s.
NUGENT.—Improved French and English and English and French Pocket Dictionary. 24mo, 3s.
OLLENDORFF.—Metodo para aprender a Leer, escribir y hablar el Inglés segun el sistema de Ollendorff. Por RAMON PALENZUELA y JUAN DE LA CARREÑO. 8vo, 4s. 6d. Key to ditto. Crown 8vo, 3s.
  Metodo para aprender a Leer, escribir y hablar el Frances, segun el verdadero sistema de Ollendorff. Por TEODORO SIMONNÉ. Crown 8vo, 6s. Key to ditto. Crown 8vo, 3s. 6d.
OTTÉ, E. C.—Dano-Norwegian Grammar. A Manual for Students of Danish based on the Ollendorffian System. Third Edition. Crown 8vo, 7s. 6d. Key to above. Crown 8vo, 3s.
PONSARD, F.—Charlotte Corday. A Tragedy. Edited, with English Notes and Notice on Ponsard, by Professor C. CASSAL, LL.D. Third Edition. 12mo, 2s. 6d.
  L'Honneur et l'Argent. A Comedy. Edited, with English Notes and Memoir of Ponsard, by Professor C. CASSAL, LL.D. Second Edition. 12mo, 3s. 6d.
RASK, Erasmus.—Grammar of the Anglo-Saxon Tongue. from the Danish of ERASMUS RASK. By BENJAMIN THORPE. Third Edition. Post 8vo, 5s. 6d.

RIOLA, *Henry.*—How to Learn Russian. A Manual for Students, based upon the Ollendorffian System. With Preface by W. R. S. RALSTON. Fourth Edition. Crown 8vo, 12s.

Key to the above. Crown 8vo, 5s.

A Graduated Russian Reader. With a Vocabulary. Crown 8vo, 10s. 6d.

ROCHE, *A.*—A French Grammar. Adopted for the Public Schools by the Imperial Council of Public Instruction. Crown 8vo, 3s.

Prose and Poetry. Select Pieces from the best English Authors, for Reading, Composition, and Translation. Second Edition. Fcap. 8vo, 2s. 6d.

ROSING, *S.*—English-Danish Dictionary. Crown 8vo, 8s. 6d.

SAYCE, *A. H.*—An Assyrian Grammar for Comparative Purposes. Crown 8vo, 7s. 6d.

The Principles of Comparative Philology. Third Edition. Crown 8vo, 10s. 6d.

SINCLAIR, *F.*—A German Vocabulary. Crown 8vo, 2s.

SMITH, *M.*, *and* HORNEMAN, *H.*—Norwegian Grammar. With a Glossary for Tourists. Post 8vo, 2s.

THOMPSON, *A. R.*—Dialogues, Russian and English. Crown 8vo, 5s.

TOSCANI, *Giovanni.*—Italian Conversational Course. Fourth Edition. 12mo, 5s.

Italian Reading Course. Fcap. 8vo, 4s. 6d.

Trübner's Catalogue of Dictionaries and Grammars of the Principal Languages and Dialects of the World. Second Edition. 8vo, 5s.

Trübner's Collection of Simplified Grammars of the Principal Asiatic and European Languages. Edited by REINHOLD ROST, LL.D. Crown 8vo.

 I. Hindustani, Persian, and Arabic. By E. H. PALMER. Second Edition. 5s.

 II. Hungarian. By I. SINGER. 4s. 6d.

 III. Basque. By W. VAN EYS. 3s. 6d.

 IV. Malagasy. By G. W. PARKER. 5s.

 V. Modern Greek. By E. M. GELDART. 2s. 6d.

 VI. Roumanian. By R. TORCEANU. 5s.

 VII. Tibetan Grammar. By H. A. JASCHKE. 5s.

 VIII. Danish. By E. C. OTTÉ. 2s. 6d.

 IX. Turkish. By J. W. REDHOUSE. 10s. 6d.

Trübner's Collection of Simplified Grammars of the Principal Asiatic and European Languages—*continued.*

    X. Swedish. By E. C. Otté. 2*s.* 6*d.*
    XI. Polish. By W. R. Morfill. 3*s.* 6*d.*
    XII. Pali. By E. Müller. 7*s.* 6*d.*
    XIII. Sanskrit. By H. Edgren. 10*s.* 6*d.*
    XIV. Grammaire Albanaise. Par P. W. 7*s.* 6*d.*
    XV. Japanese. By B. H. Chamberlain. 5*s.*
    XVI. Serbian. By W. R. Morfill. 4*s.* 6*d.*
    XVII. Cuneiform Inscriptions. By George Bertin, 5*s.*
    XVIII. Panjābī Language. By the Rev. W. St. Clair Tisdall. 7*s.* 6*d.*
    XIX. Spanish. By W. F. Harvey. 3*s.* 6*d.*

VAN LAUN.—**Grammar of the French Language.** Crown 8vo. Parts I. and II. Accidence and Syntax. 4*s.* Part III. Exercises. 3*s.* 6*d.*

VELASQUEZ, M., de la Cadena.—**A Dictionary of the Spanish and English Languages.** For the Use of Young Learners and Travellers. In 2 parts. I. Spanish-English. II. English-Spanish. Crown 8vo, 6*s.*

A Pronouncing Dictionary of the Spanish and English Languages. 2 parts in one volume. Royal 8vo, £1 4*s.*

New Spanish Reader. Passages from the most approved Authors, in Prose and Verse. With Vocabulary. Post 8vo, 6*s.*

An Easy Introduction to Spanish Conversation. 12mo, 2*s.* 6*d.*

VELASQUEZ and SIMONNÉ.—**New Method to Read, Write, and Speak the Spanish Language.** Adapted to Ollendorff's System. Post 8vo, 6*s.* Key. Post 8vo, 4*s.*

VIEYRA.—**A New Pocket Dictionary of the Portuguese and English Languages.** In 2 parts. Portuguese-English and English-Portuguese. 2 vols. Post 8vo, 10*s.*

WELLER, E.—**An Improved Dictionary.** English and French, and French and English. Royal 8vo, 7*s.* 6*d.*

WHITNEY, W. D.—**Language and the Study of Language.** Twelve Lectures on the Principles of Linguistic Science. Fourth Edition. Crown 8vo, 10*s.* 6*d.*

Language and its Study, with especial reference to the Indo-European Family of Languages. Lectures. Edited by the Rev. R. Morris, LL.D. Second Edition. Crown 8vo, 5*s.*

WHITNEY, *Prof. William Dwight.*—Essentials of English Grammar, for the Use of Schools. Second Edition. Crown 8vo, 3s. 6d.

YOUMANS, *Eliza A.*—First Book of Botany. Designed to cultivate the Observing Powers of Children. With 300 Engravings. New and Cheaper Edition. Crown 8vo, 2s. 6d.

POETRY.

ADAMS, *Estelle Davenport.*—Sea Song and River Rhyme, from Chaucer to Tennyson. With 12 Etchings. Large crown 8vo, 10s. 6d.

ALEXANDER, *William, D.D., Bishop of Derry.*—St. Augustine's Holiday, and other Poems. Crown 8vo, 6s.

ARNOLD, *Sir Edwin, C.S.I.*—In my Lady's Praise. Being Poems Old and New, written to the Honour of Fanny, Lady Arnold. Imperial 16mo, parchment, 3s. 6d.

Poems: National and Non-Oriental. With some New Pieces. Selected from the Works of Sir EDWIN ARNOLD, C.S.I. Crown 8vo, 7s. 6d.

*** See also under ORIENTAL.

BADDELEY, *St. Clair.*—Lotus Leaves. Fcap. folio, boards, 8s. 6d.

BARNES, *William.*—Poems of Rural Life, in the Dorset Dialect. New Edition, complete in one vol. Crown 8vo, 6s.

BLUNT, *Wilfrid Scawen.*—The Wind and the Whirlwind. Demy 8vo, 1s. 6d.

The Love Sonnets of Proteus. Fifth Edition. Elzevir 8vo, 5s.

In Vinculis. With Portrait. Elzevir 8vo, 5s.

A New Pilgrimage, and other Poems. Elzevir 8vo, 5s.

BRYANT, *W. C.*—Poems. Cheap Edition, with Frontispiece. Small crown 8vo, 3s. 6d.

CODD, *John.*—A Legend of the Middle Ages, and other Songs of the Past and Present. Crown 8vo, 4s.

DASH, *Blancor.*—Tales of a Tennis Party. Small crown 8vo, 5s.

DAWE, *William.*—Sketches in Verse. Small crown 8vo, 3s. 6d.

DAWSON, *C. A.*—Sappho. Small crown 8vo, 5s.

DE VERE, *Aubrey.*—Poetical Works.
> I. THE SEARCH AFTER PROSERPINE, etc. 3s. 6d.
> II. THE LEGENDS OF ST. PATRICK, etc. 3s. 6d.
> III. ALEXANDER THE GREAT, etc. 3s. 6d.
>
> The Foray of Queen Meave, and other Legends of Ireland's Heroic Age. Small crown 8vo, 3s. 6d.
>
> Legends of the Saxon Saints. Small crown 8vo, 3s. 6d.
>
> Legends and Records of the Church and the Empire. Small crown 8vo, 3s. 6d.

DOBSON, *Austin.*—Old World Idylls, and other Verses. Elzevir 8vo, gilt top, 6s.
> At the Sign of the Lyre. Elzevir 8vo, gilt top, 6s.

DOYLE, *J.*—Cause. Small crown 8vo, 6s.

DURANT, *Héloïse.*—Dante. A Dramatic Poem. Small crown 8vo, 5s.

DUTT, *Toru.*—A Sheaf Gleaned in French Fields. Demy 8vo, 10s. 6d.
> Ancient Ballads and Legends of Hindustan. With an Introductory Memoir by EDMUND GOSSE. 18mo. Cloth extra, gilt top, 5s.

Elegies and Memorials. By A. and L. Fcap. 8vo, 2s. 6d.

ELLIOTT, *Ebenezer, The Corn Law Rhymer.*—Poems. Edited by his son, the Rev. EDWIN ELLIOTT, of St. John's, Antigua. 2 vols. Crown 8vo, 18s.

English Verse. Edited by W. J. LINTON and R. H. STODDARD. 5 vols. Crown 8vo, cloth, 5s. each.
> I. CHAUCER TO BURNS.
> II. TRANSLATIONS.
> III. LYRICS OF THE NINETEENTH CENTURY.
> IV. DRAMATIC SCENES AND CHARACTERS.
> V. BALLADS AND ROMANCES.

FIFE-COOKSON, *Lieut.-Col.*—The Empire of Man. Small crown 8vo, 2s. 6d.

GARRICK, *H. B. W.*—India. A Descriptive Poem. Crown 8vo, 7s. 6d.

GOSSE, *Edmund.*—New Poems. Crown 8vo, 7s. 6d.
> Firdausi in Exile, and other Poems. Second Edition. Elzevir 8vo, gilt top, 6s.
>
> On Viol and Flute: Lyrical Poems. With Frontispiece by L. ALMA TADEMA, R.A., and Tailpiece by HAMO THORNYCROFT, R.A. Elzevir 8vo, 6s.

G

GRAY, Maxwell.—**Westminster Chimes,** and other Poems. Small crown 8vo, 5*s.*

GURNEY, Rev. Alfred.—**The Vision of the Eucharist,** and other Poems. Crown 8vo, 5*s.*

   A Christmas Faggot. Small crown 8vo, 5*s.*

   Voices from the Holy Sepulchre. Crown 8vo, 5*s.*

HARRISON, Clifford.—**In Hours of Leisure.** Second Edition. Crown 8vo, 5*s.*

HEINE, Heinrich.—**The Love-Songs of.** Englished by H. B. BRIGGS. Post 8vo, parchment, 3*s.* 6*d.*

HUES, Ivan.—**Heart to Heart.** Small crown 8vo, 5*s.*

INGLEBY, Holcombe.—**Echoes from Naples, and Other Poems.** With Illustrations by his Wife. Crown 8vo, 3*s.* 6*d.*

KEATS, John.—**Poetical Works.** Edited by W. T. ARNOLD. Large crown 8vo, choicely printed on hand-made paper, with Portrait in *eau-forte.* Parchment or cloth, 12*s.* ; vellum, 15*s.* New Edition. Crown 8vo, cloth, 3*s.* 6*d.*

KING, Mrs. Hamilton.—**The Disciples.** Tenth Edition. Small crown 8vo, 5*s.* Elzevir Edition. Cloth extra, 6*s.*

   A Book of Dreams. Third Edition. Crown 8vo, 3*s.* 6*d.*

   The Sermon in the Hospital (from " The Disciples "). Fcap. 8vo, 1*s.* Cheap Edition for distribution 3*d.*, or 20*s.* per 100.

   Ballads of the North, and other Poems. Crown 8vo, 5*s.*

LANG, A.—**XXXII. Ballades in Blue China.** Elzevir 8vo, 5*s.*

   Rhymes à la Mode. With Frontispiece by E. A. ABBEY. Second Edition. Elzevir 8vo, cloth extra, gilt top, 5*s.*

Living English Poets MDCCCLXXXII. With Frontispiece by WALTER CRANE. Second Edition. Large crown 8vo. Printed on hand-made paper. Parchment or cloth, 12*s.* ; vellum, 15*s.*

LOCKER, F.—**London Lyrics.** Tenth Edition. With Portrait, Elzevir 8vo, cloth extra, gilt top, 5*s.*

LULWORTH, Eric.—**Sunshine and Shower, and other Poems.** Small crown 8vo, 5*s.*

LYALL, Sir Alfred.—**Verses written in India.** Elzevir 8vo, gilt top, 5*s.*

MASSEY, Gerald.—**My Lyrical Life.** Poems Old and New. Two Series. Fcap. 8vo, 5*s.* each.

MEREDITH, Owen [The Earl of Lytton].—**Lucile.** New Edition. With 32 Illustrations. 16mo, 3*s.* 6*d.* Cloth extra, gilt edges, 4*s.* 6*d.*

MORRIS, *Lewis*.—Poetical Works of. New and Cheaper Editions. In 5 vols., 5*s*. each.
 Vol. I. contains "Songs of Two Worlds." Thirteenth Edition.
 Vol. II. contains "The Epic of Hades." Twenty-third Edition.
 Vol. III. contains "Gwen" and "The Ode of Life." Seventh Edition.
 Vol. IV. contains "Songs Unsung" and "Gycia." Fifth Edition.
 Vol. V. contains "Songs of Britain." Third Edition. Fcap. 8vo, 5*s*.
 Poetical Works. Complete in 1 vol. Crown 8vo, 6*s*.
 The Epic of Hades. With 16 Autotype Illustrations, after the Drawings of the late George R. Chapman. 4to, cloth extra, gilt leaves, 21*s*.
 The Epic of Hades. Presentation Edition. 4to, cloth extra, gilt leaves, 10*s*. 6*d*.
 The Lewis Morris Birthday Book. Edited by S. S. COPE-MAN, with Frontispiece after a Design by the late George R. Chapman. 32mo, cloth extra, gilt edges, 2*s*.; cloth limp, 1*s*. 6*d*.

OWEN, *John*.—Verse Musings on Nature. Faith and Freedom. Crown 8vo, 7*s*. 6*d*.

PFEIFFER, *Emily*.—Flowers of the Night. Crown 8vo, 6*s*.

PIERCE, *J.*—In Cloud and Sunshine. A Volume of Poems. Fcap. 8vo, 5*s*.

POE, *Edgar Allan*.—The Raven. With Commentary by JOHN H. INGRAM. Crown 8vo, parchment, 6*s*.

Rare Poems of the 16th and 17th Centuries. Edited by W. J. LINTON. Crown 8vo, 5*s*.

ROWBOTHAM, *J. F.*—The Human Epic. Canto i. Crown 8vo, 1*s*. 6*d*.

RUNEBERG, *Johan Ludvig*.—Nadeschda. A Romantic Poem in Nine Cantos. Translated from the Swedish by Miss MARIE A. BROWN (Mrs. JOHN B. SHIPLEY). With Illustrations. 8vo.
             [*In preparation.*

SCOTT, *G. F. E.*—Sursum Corda; or, Songs and Service. Small crown 8vo, 5*s*.

SEARELLE, *Luscombe*.—The Dawn of Death. Crown 8vo, 4*s*. 6*d*.

SYMONDS, *John Addington*.—Vagabunduli Libellus. Crown 8vo, 6*s*.

TAYLOR, *Sir H.*—Works. Complete in Five Volumes. Crown 8vo, 30*s*.
 Philip Van Artevelde. Fcap. 8vo, 3*s*. 6*d*.
 The Virgin Widow, etc. Fcap. 8vo, 3*s*. 6*d*.

TRENCH, Archbishop.—Poems. Collected and Arranged anew. **Tenth Edition.** Fcap. 8vo, 7s. 6d.

    Poems. Library Edition. 2 vols. Small crown 8vo, 10s.

    Sacred Latin Poetry. Chiefly Lyrical, Selected and Arranged for Use. Third Edition, Corrected and Improved. Fcap. 8vo, 7s.

Twilight and Candleshades. By EXUL. With 15 Vignettes. Small crown 8vo, 5s.

TYNAN, Katherine.—Louise de la Valliere, and other Poems. Small crown 8vo, 3s. 6d.

    Shamrocks. Small crown 8vo, 5s.

WADDIE, John.—Divine Philosophy. Small crown 8vo, 5s.

WILSON, Crawford.—Pastorals and Poems. Crown 8vo, 7s. 6d.

Wordsworth Birthday Book (The). Edited by ADELAIDE and VIOLET WORDSWORTH. 32mo, limp cloth, 1s. 6d.; cloth extra, 2s.

Wordsworth, Selections from. By WM. KNIGHT and other members of the Wordsworth Society. Large crown 8vo. Printed on hand-made paper. With Portrait. Parchment, 12s.; vellum, 15s.

YEATS, W. B.—The Wanderings of Oisin, and other Poems. Small crown 8vo, 5s.

NOVELS AND TALES.

BANKS, Mrs. G. L.—God's Providence House. Crown 8vo, 6s.

BILLER, Emma.—Ulli. The Story of a Neglected Girl. Translated from the German by A. B. DAISY ROST. Crown 8vo, 6s.

CABLE, G. W.—Strange True Stories of Louisiana. 8vo, 7s. 6d.

CAIRD, Mona.—The Wing of Azrael. Crown 8vo, 6s.

COLERIDGE, Hon. Stephen.—The Sanctity of Confession. A Romance. Crown 8vo, 5s.

CRAWFURD, Oswald.—Sylvia Arden. With Frontispiece. Crown 8vo, 1s.

DERING, Ross George.—Giraldi; or, The Curse of Love. A Tale of the Sects. 2 vols. Crown 8vo, 12s.

EBERS, Georg.—Margery. A Tale of Old Nuremberg. Translated from the German by CLARA BELL. 2 vols. 8s.; paper, 5s.

ECKSTEIN, *Ernst.*—Nero. A Romance. Translated from the German by CLARA BELL and MARY J. SAFFORD. 2 vols. Paper, 5*s.*

FLETCHER, *J. S.*—Andrewlina. Crown 8vo, cloth, 1*s.* 6*d.* ; paper covers, 1*s.*

The Winding Way. Crown 8vo.

FRANCIS, *Frances.*—Mosquito. A Tale of the Mexican Frontier. Crown 8vo, 3*s.* 6*d.*

GALDOS, *B. Perez.*—Leon Roche. A Romance. From the Spanish by CLARA BELL. 2 vols. 16mo, cloth, 8*s.* ; paper, 5*s.*

GARDINER, *Linda.*—His Heritage. With Frontispiece. Crown 8vo, 6*s.*

GRAY, *Maxwell.*—The Reproach of Annesley. With Frontispiece. Crown 8vo, 6*s.*

Silence of Dean Maitland. With Frontispiece. Crown 8vo, 6*s.*

GREY, *Rowland.*—In Sunny Switzerland. A Tale of Six Weeks. Second Edition. Small crown 8vo, 5*s.*

Lindenblumen and other Stories. Small crown 8vo, 5*s.*

By Virtue of his Office. Crown 8vo, 6*s.*

Jacob's Letter, and other Stories. Crown 8vo, 6*s.*

HARRIS, *Emily Marion.*—Lady Dobbs. A Novel. In 2 vols. 21*s.*

HUNTER, *Hay, and* **WHYTE**, *Walter.*—My Ducats and My Daughter. With Frontispiece. Crown 8vo, 6*s.*

INGELOW, *Jean.*—Off the Skelligs. A Novel. With Frontispiece. Crown 8vo, 6*s.*

LANG, *Andrew.*—In the Wrong Paradise, and other Stories. Crown 8vo, 6*s.*

MACDONALD, *G.*—Donal Grant. A Novel. With Frontispiece. Crown 8vo, 6*s.*

Home Again. With Frontispiece. Crown 8vo, 6*s.*

Castle Warlock. A Novel. With Frontispiece. Crown 8vo, 6*s.*

Malcolm. With Portrait of the Author engraved on Steel. Crown 8vo, 6*s.*

The Marquis of Lossie. With Frontispiece. Crown 8vo, 6*s.*

St. George and St. Michael. With Frontispiece. Crown 8vo, 6*s.*

What's Mine's Mine. With Frontispiece. Crown 8vo, 6*s.*

Annals of a Quiet Neighbourhood. With Frontispiece. Crown 8vo, 6*s.*

The Seaboard Parish : a Sequel to "Annals of a Quiet Neighbourhood." With Frontispiece. Crown 8vo, 6*s.*

MACDONALD, G.—continued.

    Wilfred Cumbermede. An Autobiographical Story. With Frontispiece. Crown 8vo, 6s.

    Thomas Wingfold, Curate. With Frontispiece. Crown 8vo, 6s.

    Paul Faber, Surgeon. With Frontispiece. Crown 8vo, 6s.

    The Elect Lady. With Frontispiece. Crown 8vo, 6s.

MALET, Lucas.—**Colonel Enderby's Wife.** A Novel. With Frontispiece. Crown 8vo, 6s.

    A Counsel of Perfection. With Frontispiece. Crown 8vo, 6s.

MULHOLLAND, Rosa.—**Marcella Grace.** An Irish Novel. Crown 8vo, 6s.

    A Fair Emigrant. With Frontispiece. Crown 8vo, 6s.

OGLE, Anna C.—**A Lost Love.** Small crown 8vo, 2s. 6d.

PONTOPIDDAN, Henrik.— **The Apothecary's Daughters.** Translated from the Danish by GORDIUS NIELSEN. Crown 8vo, 3s. 6d.

ROBINSON, Sir J. C.—**The Dead Sailor,** and other Stories. Crown 8vo, 5s.

SAVILE, Ames.—**A Match Pair.** 2 vols. 21s.

SEVERNE, Florence.—**The Pillar House.** With Frontispiece. Crown 8vo, 6s.

SHAW, Flora L.—**Castle Blair:** a Story of Youthful Days. Crown 8vo, 3s. 6d.

STRETTON, Hesba.—**Through a Needle's Eye.** A Story. With Frontispiece. Crown 8vo, 6s.

TASMA.—**A Sydney Sovereign,** and other Tales. Crown 8vo, cloth, 6s.

    Uncle Piper of Piper's Hill. An Australian Novel. Third Edition. Crown 8vo, 6s.

    In her Earliest Youth. 3 vols. Crown 8vo, 31s. 6d.

TAYLOR, Col. Meadows, C.S.I., M.R.I.A.—**Seeta.** A Novel. With Frontispiece. Crown 8vo, 6s.

    Tippoo Sultaun: a Tale of the Mysore War. With Frontispiece. Crown 8vo, 6s.

    Ralph Darnell. With Frontispiece. Crown 8vo, 6s.

    A Noble Queen. With Frontispiece. Crown 8vo, 6s.

    The Confessions of a Thug. With Frontispiece. Crown 8vo, 6s.

    Tara: a Mahratta Tale. With Frontispiece. Crown 8vo, 6s.

TOORGEYNIEFF, Ivan.—**The Unfortunate One.** A Novel. Translated from the Russian by A. R. THOMPSON. Crown 8vo, 3s. 6d.

TREHERNE, Mrs.—**A Summer in a Dutch Country House.** Crown 8vo, 6s.

Within Sound of the Sea. With Frontispiece. Crown 8vo, 6s.

BOOKS FOR THE YOUNG.

Brave Men's Footsteps. A Book of Example and Anecdote for Young People. By the Editor of "Men who have Risen." With 4 Illustrations by C. DOYLE. Ninth Edition. Crown 8vo, 2s. 6d.

COXHEAD, Ethel.—**Birds and Babies.** With 33 Illustrations. Second Edition. Imp. 16mo, cloth, 1s.

DAVIES, G. Christopher.—**Rambles and Adventures of our School Field Club.** With 4 Illustrations. New and Cheaper Edition. Crown 8vo, 3s. 6d.

EDMONDS, Herbert.—**Well-Spent Lives:** a Series of Modern Biographies. New and Cheaper Edition. Crown 8vo, 3s. 6d.

MACKENNA, S. J.—**Plucky Fellows.** A Book for Boys. With 6 Illustrations. Fifth Edition. Crown 8vo, 3s. 6d.

MALET, Lucas.—**Little Peter.** A Christmas Morality for Children of any Age. With numerous Illustrations. Fourth Thousand. 5s.

REANEY, Mrs. G. S.—**Waking and Working;** or, From Girlhood to Womanhood. New and Cheaper Edition. With a Frontispiece. Crown 8vo, 3s. 6d.

Blessing and Blessed: a Sketch of Girl Life. New and Cheaper Edition. Crown 8vo, 3s. 6d.

Rose Gurney's Discovery. A Story for Girls. Dedicated to their Mothers. Crown 8vo, 3s. 6d.

English Girls: their Place and Power. With Preface by the Rev. R. W. Dale. Fifth Edition. Fcap. 8vo, 2s. 6d.

Just Anyone, and other Stories. Three Illustrations. Royal 16mo, 1s. 6d.

Sunbeam Willie, and other Stories. Three Illustrations. Royal 16mo, 1s. 6d.

Sunshine Jenny, and other Stories. Three Illustrations. Royal 16mo, 1s. 6d.

STORR, Francis, and TURNER, Hawes.—**Canterbury Chimes;** or, Chaucer Tales re-told to Children. With 6 Illustrations from the Ellesmere Manuscript. Third Edition. Fcap. 8vo, 3s. 6d.

STRETTON, *Hesba.*—**David Lloyd's Last Will.** With 4 Illustrations. New Edition. Royal 16mo, 2*s.* 6*d.*

WHITAKER, Florence.—**Christy's Inheritance.** A London Story. Illustrated. Royal 16mo, 1*s.* 6*d.*

PERIODICALS.

Amateur Mechanical Society's Journal.—Irregular.

Anthropological Institute of Great Britain and Ireland (Journal of).—Quarterly, 5*s.*

Architect (American) and Building News.—Contains General Architectural News, Articles on Interior Decoration, Sanitary Engineering, Construction, Building Materials, etc. 4 full-page Illustrations accompany each Number. Weekly. Annual Subscription, 38*s.* Post free.

Bibliotheca Sacra.—Quarterly, 3*s.* 6*d.* Annual Subscription, 14*s.* Post free.

British Archæological Association (Journal of).—Quarterly, 8*s.*

British Chess Magazine.—Monthly, 8*d.*

British Homœopathic Society (Annals of).—Half-yearly, 2*s.* 6*d.*

Browning Society's Papers.—Irregular.

Calcutta Review.—Quarterly, 6*s.* Annual Subscription, 24*s.* Post free.

Cambridge Philological Society (Proceedings of).—Irregular.

Englishwoman's Review. — Social and Industrial Questions. Monthly, 6*d.*

Geological Magazine, or Monthly Journal of Geology, 1*s.* 6*d.* Annual Subscription, 18*s.* Post free.

Index Medicus.—A Monthly Classified Record of the Current Medical Literature of the World. Annual Subscription, 50*s.* Post free.

Indian Antiquary.—A Journal of Oriental Research in Archæology, History, Literature, Languages, Philosophy, Religion, Folk-Lore, etc. Annual Subscription, £2. Post free.

Indian Evangelical Review.—Annual Subscription, 10*s.*

Indian Magazine. Monthly, 6*d.*

Library Journal.—Official Organ of the Library Associations of America and of the United Kingdom. Monthly, 2*s.* 6*d.* Annual Subscription, 20*s.*, or with Co-operative Index, 25*s.* Post free.

Kegan Paul, Trench, Trübner & Co.'s Publications. 89

Mathematics (American Journal of).—Quarterly, 7s. 6d. Annual Subscription, 24s. Post free.
Meister (The).—Journal of the Wagner Society. 4to, 1s.
Nineteenth Century.—Monthly, 2s. 6d.
Orientalist (The).—Monthly. Annual Subscription, 12s.
Orthodox Catholic Review.—Irregular.
Philological Society (Transactions and Proceedings of).—Irregular.
Psychical Research (Society of), Proceedings of.
Publishers' Weekly: The American Book-Trade Journal.—Annual Subscription, 18s. Post free.
Punjab Notes and Queries.—Monthly. Annual Subscription, 10s.
Revue Internationale.—Issued on the 10th and 25th of each Month. Annual Subscription, including postage, 36s.
Scientific American.—Weekly. Annual Subscription, 18s. Post free.
Supplement to ditto.—Weekly. Annual Subscription, 25s. Post free.
Science and Arts (Americal Journal of).—Monthly, 2s. 6d. Annual Subscription, 30s.
Speculative Philosophy (Journal of).—Quarterly, 4s. Annual Subscription, 16s. Post free, 17s.
Sun Artists.—Quarterly, 5s.
Sunday Review.—Organ of the Sunday Society for Opening Museums and Art Galleries on Sunday. Quarterly, 1s. Annual Subscription, 4s. 6d. Post free.
Theosophist (The).—Magazine of Oriental Philosophy, Art, Literature, and Occultism. Monthly, 2s.
Trübner's Record.—A Journal devoted to the Literature of the East, with Notes and Lists of Current American, European, and Colonial Publications. Small 4to, 2s. per number. Annual Subscription, 10s. Post free.

MESSRS.

KEGAN PAUL, TRENCH, TRÜBNER & CO.'S
(LIMITED)

EDITIONS OF

SHAKSPERE'S WORKS.

THE PARCHMENT LIBRARY EDITION.

THE AVON EDITION.

The Text of these Editions is mainly that of Delius. Wherever a variant reading is adopted, some good and recognized Shaksperian Critic has been followed. In no case is a new rendering of the text proposed; nor has it been thought necessary to distract the reader's attention by notes or comments

[P. T. O.

SHAKSPERE'S WORKS.

THE AVON EDITION.

Printed on thin opaque paper, and forming 12 handy volumes, cloth, 18s., or bound in 6 volumes, 15s.

The set of 12 volumes may also be had in a cloth box, price 21s., or bound in Roan, Persian, Crushed Persian Levant, Calf, or Morocco, and enclosed in an attractive leather box at prices from 31s. 6d. upwards.

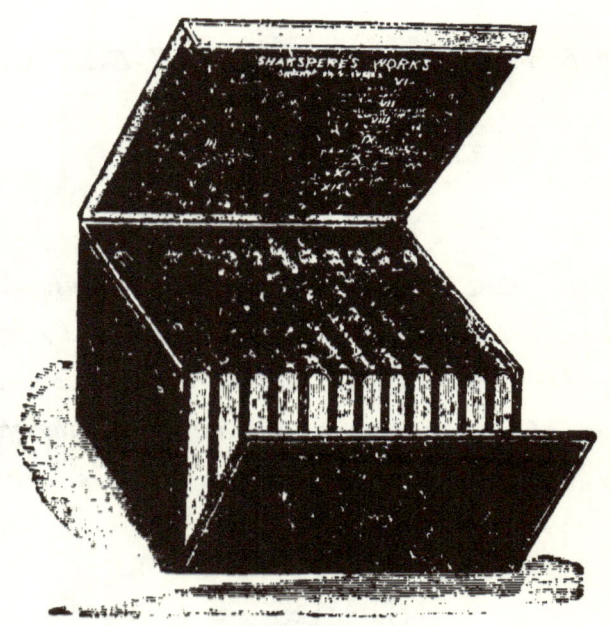

SOME PRESS NOTICES.

"This edition will be useful to those who want a good text, well and clearly printed, in convenient little volumes that will slip easily into an overcoat pocket or a travelling-bag."—*St. James's Gazette.*

"We know no prettier edition of Shakspere for the price."—*Academy.*

"It is refreshing to meet with an edition of Shakspere of convenient size and low price, without either notes or introductions of any sort to distract the attention of the reader."—*Saturday Review.*

"It is exquisite. Each volume is handy, is beautifully printed, and in every way lends itself to the taste of the cultivated student of Shakspere."—*Scotsman.*

LONDON: KEGAN PAUL, TRENCH, TRÜBNER & CO., LTD.

SHAKSPERE'S WORKS.

THE PARCHMENT LIBRARY EDITION.

In 12 volumes Elzevir 8vo., choicely printed on hand-made paper, and bound in parchment or cloth, price £3 12s., or in vellum, price £4 10s.

The set of 12 volumes may also be had in a strong cloth box, price £3 17s., or with an oak hanging shelf, £3 18s.

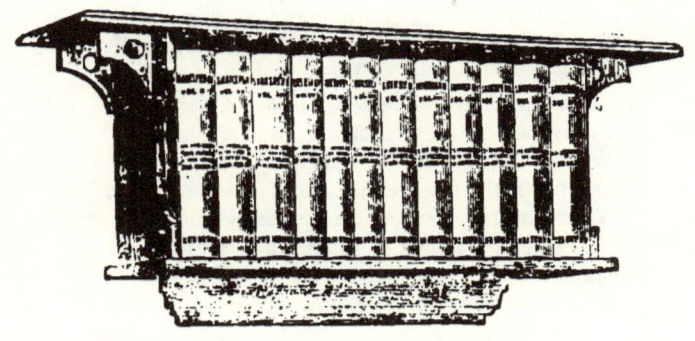

SOME PRESS NOTICES.

"... There is, perhaps, no edition in which the works of Shakspere can be read in such luxury of type and quiet distinction of form as this, and we warmly recommend it."—*Pall Mall Gazette.*

"For elegance of form and beauty of typography, no edition of Shakspere hitherto published has excelled the 'Parchment Library Edition.' ... They are in the strictest sense pocket volumes, yet the type is bold, and, being on fine white hand-made paper, can hardly tax the weakest of sight. The print is judiciously confined to the text, notes being more appropriate to library editions. The whole will be comprised in the cream-coloured parchment which gives the name to the series."—*Daily News.*

"The Parchment Library Edition of Shakspere needs no further praise."—*Saturday Review.*

Just published. Price 5s.

AN INDEX TO THE WORKS OF SHAKSPERE.

Applicable to all editions of Shakspere, and giving reference, by topics, to notable passages and significant expressions; brief histories of the plays; geographical names and historic incidents; mention of all characters and sketches of important ones; together with explanations of allusions and obscure and obsolete words and phrases.

By EVANGELINE M. O'CONNOR.

London: Kegan Paul, Trench, Trübner & Co., Ltᴅ.

SHAKSPERE'S WORKS.

SPECIMEN OF TYPE.

THE MERCHANT OF VENICE   Act 1

  Salar.   My wind, cooling my broth,
Would blow me to an ague, when I thought
What harm a wind too great might do at sea.
I should not see the sandy hour-glass run
But I should think of shallows and of flats,
And see my wealthy Andrew, dock'd in sand,
Vailing her high-top lower than her ribs
To kiss her burial. Should I go to church
And see the holy edifice of stone,
And not bethink me straight of dangerous rocks,
Which touching but my gentle vessel's side,
Would scatter all her spices on the stream,
Enrobe the roaring waters with my silks,
And, in a word, but even now worth this,
And now worth nothing? Shall I have the thought
To think on this, and shall I lack the thought
That such a thing bechanc'd would make me sad?
But tell not me: I know Antonio
Is sad to think upon his merchandise.
  Ant. Believe me, no: I thank my fortune for it,
My ventures are not in one bottom trusted,
Nor to one place; nor is my whole estate
Upon the fortune of this present year:
Therefore my merchandise makes me not sad.
  Salar. Why, then you are in love.
  Ant.   Fie, fie!
  Salar. Not in love neither? Then let us say you
      are sad,
Because you are not merry; and 'twere as easy
For you to laugh, and leap, and say you are merry,
Because you are not sad. Now, by two-headed
      Janus,
Nature hath fram'd strange fellows in her time:
Some that will evermore peep through their eyes
And laugh like parrots at a bag-piper;
And other of such vinegar aspect

LONDON: KEGAN PAUL, TRENCH, TRÜBNER & CO., LTD.

PRINTED BY WILLIAM CLOWES AND SONS, LIMITED,
LONDON AND BECCLES.

www.ingramcontent.com/pod-product-compliance
Lightning Source LLC
Chambersburg PA
CBHW021939240426
43669CB00047B/548